True Christianity:

The Five Essential Questions of the Faith

True Christianity: The Five Essential Questions of the Faith

Charles R. Kessler, DMin

ISBN: 978-0-578-60421-3 (Paperback)

Library of Congress Control Number: 2019918119

Front cover design by Canva.

Back cover photo taken by Christine Cannon and used by permission from the Hilton Head Monthly magazine

Printed in the United States of America.
First Printing: 2019

Publisher's Address: P. O. Box 3003
                      Bluffton, SC 29910

Dedicated to the three
most endearing entities in my life:
my dear mother, Dora;
my wonderful wife, Pat;
and the ever-present care of Almighty God

ACKNOWLEDGEMENTS

As with any project, its success is never the effort of just one person, even if his name is the only one that appears on the cover. Such is the case with the publication of this book. I should start by acknowledging my appreciation to the various libraries that allowed me access. Specifically, I need to thank the University of South Carolina library system; which, although I was never a student at the university, they allowed me access to their library and the resource materials available there. In addition, I need to thank two schools in my home state of Kentucky. The first is Centre College (Danville), where I earned a BA in Religion. The second is the Southern Baptist Theological Seminary (Louisville), where I received my Masters and Doctoral degrees. Even though my last appearance on campus as a student at those institutions was back in 1973 and 1985, respectively, they both graciously allowed me access to their online library which provided me with a wealth of resource material for this book. Without their support, the securing of the scholastic resources necessary for the completion of this project would have been significantly more difficult, if not impossible.

Beyond the institutional support, several individuals need to be recognized as integral elements in the process of bringing this work to fruition. The first word of appreciation goes to my brother, Reif Kessler, who provided some valuable proof-reading support as well as offering critical suggestions on what constituted the most effective "readability" of the narrative. Without his keen eyes painstakingly perusing the text, it is possible that a couple of problems may have gone unnoticed until publication.

In addition to the family acknowledgement, another valuable asset was Dr. David Ulbrich. Dr. Ulbrich serves as the Program Director for the Master of History degree programs at Norwich University in Northfield, VT. He was my professor for an "Amphibious Warfare" class and served as my faculty advisor for the Capstone project of my Masters in Military History degree from Norwich. I remember him as a remarkable professor and compassionate advisor. His personal encouragement helped propel the idea behind this book from that of a hobby to a conviction that getting it published might even become a reality. His advice and feedback became invaluable as I moved forward and I will always consider him a true friend and an amazing mentor.

The final scholastic recognition goes to Dr. John Broom. He serves as the Associate Program Director of Academics at Norwich. It was through his personal sacrifice that I was able to enroll and complete my degree at Norwich within the limited time period that was available to me. In that capacity, I found him to be an incredibly gifted scholar and a dedicated Christian who is an inspiration to all his students. During this endeavor, I collaborated with him on a variety of issues. However, his major contribution was to bring a clearly Eastern Orthodox perspective into view. Throughout the process, he provided wise counsel and brought into focus a Christian perspective that was dramatically different from my own. As such, he became a valuable asset for the direction of this project and remains a faithful friend.

Three other individuals need to be properly acknowledged. The first person that necessitates some special recognition is my mother, Dora Kessler. My mother and I always had a special relationship, especially as it related to biblical truth and theological issues. A dedicated and devout Christian woman, we often had lengthy theological discussions. For years she tried to encourage me to write a book to explain in simple terms the nature of faith and what it means to be a Christian. I finally decided to take her advice and now I realize how important it always is to follow the wise counsel of your mother.

Obviously, any project of this nature requires a great deal of time and commitment. The repercussion of that reality is less time with your family. Although both of our children are grown and have their own families, the amount of time away from my wife, Pat, was significant. An old adage states that behind every great man there is a great woman. That might not be a politically correct statement these days and may not apply to me (or this book) as being anything "great." Regardless, none of this was possible without the loving support of my wife. We were high school sweethearts and have been married for nearly fifty years. Through all those years, she remains a constant source of personal support and encouragement. It is important that I take this opportunity to acknowledge that reality.

Finally, as I try to do in all things, I want to thank God! My spiritual pilgrimage and ministry represent a unique and varied trajectory. As I acknowledge in the introduction, my life traces through a couple of denominational experiences and my family illustrates even more of an ecumenical perspective. However, through it all, I relied on God's direction and Will for my life.   I began this book as a "something to keep me busy in my retirement" project, but still understood the idea that God provided it as a personal pilgrimage.   Let it be noted that whatever success this book might achieve, it is ultimately for His benefit and for the further establishment of His kingdom in the lives of His people.

TABLE OF CONTENTS

INTRODUCTION

It might seem odd to begin a book committed to answering the right questions with a question, but it is often a viable tool for addressing a specific issue. So, here goes. The question is: Does Christianity only profess five tenets that constitute the essence of the Christian Faith? The easy answer would be "Yes" and the presentation of the five questions highlighted in this book represent the basic tenets of the Christian Faith. On the other hand, a more difficult answer is "No" since many people would proclaim (even as a criticism of the book) that the complexity and scope of the Christian Faith far exceeds five simple questions or five basic tenets.

I would have to agree, at least in part, with this second response. It is easy to assign more than simply the five tenets expressed in this book as essential to Christianity. For instance, readers who give a cursory examination of the book might raise questions like "Where is the trinitarian doctrine, a concept of salvation by grace, the reality of heaven and hell, or justification by faith?" And I would agree that all of those doctrines constitute vital elements of the Christian Faith. However, in response to those concerns I would submit that a close examination of the answers offered to the five questions address a wide range of additional elements essential to Christianity. The Trinity is discussed in the first section on "Who Is God" (see Chapter 4), with other elements addressed in the sections on Jesus and the Bible as the Word of God. On the other hand, the basic premise of this book is to lead the reader to understand the dynamic Truth of the Christian Faith without having to attend a seminary course on Systematic Theology.

Therefore, I developed the five questions addressed in this book after following a long, personal pilgrimage through my own Christian journey. My grandfather was a Roman Catholic and my mother was raised as a Methodist. My parents united the family and we became Presbyterians (PUSA). To add to my ecumenical spirit, I am currently ordained as a Southern Baptist minister and have a daughter who serves as an Anglican priest. In addition to those realities, I served for twenty-eight years as a chaplain in the United States Navy, facilitating services for every imaginable Faith Group. In that capacity I also tried to provide a general Protestant Christian service that could meet the needs of all denominations represented in the unit or chapel where I served. It opened my eyes to a great deal more than the average denominationally centered minister ever experienced in a parish ministry and provided to me what I believe to be a unique perspective and insight in which I developed the ability to write this book.

So, my life experience represents a unique and clearly ecumenical mindset regarding the Christian Faith and a genuine appreciation for those who practice other faiths. As a result, the book is not aimed at leading non-Christians to accept the Christian Faith or reject their chosen faith. It is also not an attempt to direct individuals to question or renounce their denominational practices. I spent my naval career championing the "practices of faith" of the various Protestant denominations and appreciate their unique contribution to the Christian Faith as a whole. I also staunchly defend the right for individuals to worship in any manner they wish.

That leads to the main challenge I faced in attempting to write a book that unifies the Christian Faith around five tenets that often bring Christians to a debate within the community of faith. The main issue here lies in the difference between the East and West elements of Christianity—the Western denominations that most believers in the United States would recognize and the Eastern Orthodox arm that might be foreign to many of those believers. For instances, the doctrinal concept of Man as a sinner and the theology of the Atonement are two elements that present major challenges. For instance, the West proclaims that Man is a sinner as a result of his "nature." In other words, Man is a sinner by virtue of his disposition and for which his actions deserve punishment. Of course, even in the area of Man as a sinner, the Western denominations proclaim different beliefs as represented in the concept of "original sin." The Eastern view holds a slightly different take on the subject. Orthodoxy believes that sin represents a "condition" of Man (i.e., an affliction of Man) from which he needs to be cured, vice punished.

That concept also becomes evident in the two positions on atonement. The West looks to the Cross as the atoning power provided by God through the sacrifice of Christ. Again, for the West, the nature of Man's sinfulness demands punishment and the crucifixion pays that price. However, the Eastern Church notes that the word "atonement" originated in Europe during the Post-Middle Ages (circa mid-Sixteenth Century). As

2

such, the East's concept of atonement is coupled with the "healing need" of Man's sinfulness to the point that the resurrection becomes the focal point. A more detailed discussion of this topic appears in the chapter, "Jesus and Atonement."

That problem also exists within the Western scope of the Christian faith. The various denominations within the Western orthodoxy express conflicting views on the concept of original sin, the idea of predestination and the dispensation of grace, just to highlight a few of the more obvious differences. It is in that vein that I faced the challenge to present a middle ground that all Christians can acknowledge as Truth. Then, as a means of unifying us on that middle ground, address the general concepts (basic tenets) of the Christian faith on which we can all agree.

With that basis, the attempt is to present a position that can unite us in our faith. So, in reference to Man as a sinner, the conclusion is simply that Man *is* a sinner and as a result needs forgiveness. Additionally, as it pertains to Atonement, Chapter 11 highlights the reality of the atoning power of Christ's sacrifice. Whether that power brings Man into a oneness with Christ (a "theosis," as expressed in the Eastern Orthodox community) or as a oneness with God through faith in Christ, the result is the same.

Through all the struggles to present a unifying Christian apologetic, the title of this book identifies my attempt to provide a truthful (i.e., biblical) presentation to the faith-based questions important to all Christians. If, in that process, it helps non-Christians to understand the tenets of the Christian Faith more clearly that would achieve an additional benefit. Regardless, my real motivation for writing this book was to highlight that which unites us as Christians, not what separates us denominationally. The initial question I asked was: What are the basic tenets of the Christian Faith? My desire is to discover that which unites us in the *Truth*, even if we tend to be denominationally segregated on Sunday morning by how we practice our faith.

In that regard, we must posit that the spirituality and application of the Christian Faith in the United States and around the world evolved dramatically over the past two thousand years. Some would say that such an evolution is for the best, as the Faith developed in such a way as to become more palatable and acceptable for a wider range of believers. However, as wonderful and as agreeable as that might sound in some corners of our churches, should we accept the premise that making Christianity more palatable to the masses is a biblically based goal for the Faith, any Faith? Certainly, most adherents would agree that the purpose and goal of any religion is to share their faith and increase the number of those who can be brought into the fold. That is certainly true for Christianity as Christians accept the directive of the Great Commission to "make disciples" throughout the world.

With that directive in mind, do we really believe that the Christian Faith should "evolve" into that which alters the Truth or attempts to rewrite Scripture simply to add numbers to our church roles? We certainly should not do it to appease some type of political correctness or try to make Christianity more acceptable to a larger percentage of people that, as a result, rejects the basic Truths that Scripture reveals to us. Truths that are the tenets of our Faith and the foundation on which countless martyrs sacrificed their lives. As such, the Church must stand against that which attempts to manipulate, dilute, or rewrite the true Word of almighty God.

I believe most would agree that the acceptance of a faith that is not the true expression of that Faith is not a good theological position to profess. And even though we might acknowledge that point, we routinely identify large Christian churches with the concept that "They must be doing something right" or "Isn't it wonderful that the Faith is reaching so many" as a sign that the specific church is proclaiming the Truth. Unfortunately, such is not necessarily the case. Just because a charismatic minister or evangelist can draw thousands, even tens of thousands, of people to a church service on a given Sunday morning does not mean that the Truth of the Christian Faith is being proclaimed. It is quite possible that the opposite is true. Established Church leaders, evangelists, preachers and certainly the "false teachers" of Matthew 7 and the "false prophets" of 2 Peter 2 have the ability to proclaim a watered-down, palatable version of the Truth. One they claim is True, but one they manipulated into a truth that they believe is more acceptable to a larger number of people. They can boast the regular addition of new "converts" and acknowledge ever-increasing numbers, but are they actively proclaiming the Truth? Chances are . . . they are not! A case in point is the documented presentation by a well-known evangelist's wife who was speaking on the concept of worship and stated that when we worship we are not doing it for God, but for ourselves.

Really? I'm still trying to find the biblical passage that will support that theological perspective.

That concern can also be raised regarding various religious groups in America that proclaim themselves to be Christian. Adherents to these groups can sound and appear, at least at face value, to be Christian. Unfortunately, the adage "If it looks like a duck, walks like a duck, and quacks like a duck; then it must be a duck" does not work in this situation. Simply because it looks and sounds Christian doesn't mean that it is Christian. These religious groups may use a certain "Christianese" language, but they clearly do not accept the tenets of faith that distinguish a believer as a true, theologically orthodox, Christian.

As a result, and after dealing with this issue through nearly fifty years as an ordained minister and twenty-eight years as a Navy chaplain, this book is written to help all Christians and non-Christians understand the theological concepts that should unite us within the Christian Faith. It is not drawn exclusively from my Presbyterian roots or from my years as an ordained Baptist minister, but from the universally accepted source for Christian perspective . . . the Bible! In that respect, it is an attempt to answer the ultimate question: "What makes us Christian?" The church and Christian scholars addressed that very point through the centuries. The early Church Fathers developed faith statements (i.e., creeds) which proclaimed what they believed and accepted as the expression of the Christian Faith.

Two of the most widely used statements throughout Eastern and
Western orthodoxy are the Apostles' Creed and the Nicene Creed. Of course, I understand the immediate push-back from my fellow Baptists and perhaps from other Congregationalists. The point is that Baptist Churches represent a "non-creedal" denomination. That is, they do not practice the inclusion of creedal statements in their worship services. However, even with that "practice of faith" issue, the question becomes "What is it in the Creeds that is untrue (i.e., that expresses a belief that is not a basic Truth of the Christian faith)?" Read and examine the creeds for yourself. The 1988 version of the Apostles' Creed (with added emphasis) states:

> *I believe in* <u>*God, the Father almighty,*</u>
> <u>*creator*</u> *of heaven and earth. I*
> *believe in* <u>*Jesus Christ, God's only*</u>

Son, our Lord, who was conceived by the Holy Spirit, born of the Virgin Mary, suffered under Pontius Pilate, was <u>crucified, died, and was buried</u>; he descended to the dead. <u>On the third day he rose again</u>; he ascended into heaven, he is seated at the right hand of the Father, and he will come to judge the living and the dead. I believe in the Holy Spirit, the holy catholic Church, the communion of saints, the forgiveness of sins, the <u>resurrection of the body, and the life everlasting</u>. Amen.

The Nicene Creed (with added emphasis) states:

We believe in <u>one God, the Father Almighty</u>, the maker of heaven and earth, of things visible and invisible. And in <u>one Lord Jesus Christ, the Son of God</u>, the begotten of God the Father, the Only-begotten, that is of the essence of the Father. God of God, Light of Light, true God of true God, begotten and not made; of the very same nature of the Father, by Whom all things came into being, in heaven and on earth, visible and invisible. Who for us humanity and for our salvation came down from heaven, was <u>incarnate</u>, was made human, was born perfectly of the holy virgin Mary by the Holy Spirit. By whom He took body, soul, and mind, and everything that is in man, truly and not in semblance. He suffered, <u>was crucified, was buried, rose again</u> on the third day, ascended into heaven with the same body, [and] sat at the right hand of the Father. He is to come with the same body and with the glory of the Father, to judge the living and the dead; of His kingdom

6

> *there is no end. We believe in the*
> *Holy Spirit, in the uncreated and the*
> *perfect; Who spoke through the Law,*
> *prophets, and Gospels; Who came down*
> *upon the Jordan, preached through the*
> *apostles, and lived in the saints. We*
> *believe also in only One, Universal,*
> *Apostolic, and Holy Church; in one*
> *baptism in repentance, for the*
> *remission, and forgiveness of sins;*
> *and in the <u>resurrection of the dead</u>,*
> *in the everlasting judgement of souls*
> *and bodies, and the Kingdom of Heaven*
> *and in the everlasting life.*

The underlined portions in both creeds highlight four of the five tenets addressed in this book. They are: God, as the one true God and Almighty; Jesus as the Son of God and incarnate; the sacrifice of Christ on the Cross; and His resurrection from the dead. The only tenet that is missing from the creed is the Bible as the True Word of God.

Of course, it is not perfect. The Apostles' Creed does not, specifically, address the divinity of Jesus and other specifics that are more clearly depicted in the Nicene Creed. Also, there is one line in both creeds that creates some anxiety for the hard-shell Baptists, as well as for other denominations. It is the statement regarding belief in the "Holy catholic church" (Apostles' Creed) and in the "Universal, Apostolic, and Holy Church" of the Nicene Creed. The angst comes from the autonomous (i.e., the authority of the local church) perspective that Baptists accept. Pledging faith in what appears to be a church hierarchy understandably creates some problems. However, the phrase is not one that expresses any denominational loyalty; but, ironically, is a statement that establishes the basic premise of this book: establishing the very construct that unifies us as "one universal (small "u") Church."

To that end, and apart from the denominationalism that separates us in a "practice of faith" application, we need to accept that true Christianity espouses five "tenets of faith." These are doctrines that I believe Scripture dictates every person must accept in order to be a Christian. It is clearly understandable that some may disagree with that premise. On the other hand, a person cannot believe anything they want to

7

believe and then label it as Christian. That simply is theologically and biblically implausible.

In that respect perhaps it is important to reiterate one important clarification. Specifically, the aim of this book is not to prompt readers to question their Christian faith. To the contrary, my hope is that it will help all of us understand the true nature of our Christian Faith more clearly. And, in that Truth, we might be better equipped to articulate to a changing world and a changing Church exactly what makes us Christian.

This book is the outcome of a long walk through a personal faith. I documented my Christian pilgrimage and family heritage within Christianity earlier in this Introduction. With an understanding of that pilgrimage, this project was not possible twenty years ago. It is not that the Truth changed; but that the clarity of that Truth became more of a reality to me as a Christian and as a minister. It is as C. S. Lewis noted in his classic work, *Mere Christianity*, "There are a great many things (about the Christian faith) that cannot be understood until you have gone a certain distance along the Christian road."[1] I have gone that certain distance and this book is the outcome of that trek. I trust that it will enhance your Christian journey and prepare you for whatever "trek" you might face.

---

[1] C. S. Lewis, *Mere Christianity* (New York: MacMillan, 1952), 126.

Question #1

Who Is God?

CHAPTER 1

THE EXISTENCE OF GOD

"For I know the plans that I have for you," declares the Lord, "plans for welfare and not for calamity to give you a future and a hope. Then you will call upon Me and come and pray to Me, and I will listen to you. You will seek Me and find Me when you search for Me with all your heart. I will be found by you," declares the Lord. (Jeremiah 29:11-14)

W here does one start to try and answer the question "Who is God?" It is both the easiest of the five questions in this book to answer and, in some respects, the hardest. Regardless of whether we take the easy road or the more difficult one, it is important to understand that it is the first, and arguably the most important, question to answer. The reality is that, even from a simple approach to faith, the true Christian must grasp the concept of the reality of God, since everything else in the Christian Faith is contingent on the Believer accepting the premise that God does, indeed, exist.

As one contemplates that concept, two obvious and opposing sides must be addressed. They are, quite simply, either God does exist or God doesn't exist. The Christian stands on the one side and represents the Believers who clearly accept and acknowledge the existence of God. They worship Him in their churches, they read about Him in the Scriptures, and they speak (pray) to Him. Many believers will acknowledge personal encounters with God and testify to divine or miraculous events in their lives as proof of the existence of God. The bottom line here is that the existence of God is a vital element of the Christian faith.

Unfortunately, although the United States still maintains a high percentage of citizens who accept the existence of God, our society seems to be moving in a more skeptical direction. Space does not allow for a complete examination of this evolution but suffice it to say that our nation is in a cultural shift in reference to religion and the overt practice of one's faith. Stephen L. Carter, a law professor at Yale University, wrote that "our culture teaches that religion is not to be taken seriously."[2] Carter provided numerous illustrations supporting his point noting a wife wearing a cross during her husband's inauguration to a Supreme Court decision striking down a Connecticut law requiring employers to allow employees to observe a sabbath.[3] Carter's observations are disturbing, but even more problematic when you understand that he published his conclusions over two decades ago! It seems this nation is progressing in a direction that questions the existence of God and biblical history portrays a numbing account of what happens to nations that forsake their faith in God.

Continuing down that same path, the other side of this debate is represented by those who identify themselves as "Atheists." An atheist is a person who does not believe in, nor accepts the existence of, God . . . any god. The argument that has been repeatedly put forward by contemporary atheists appeals to the inability to put faith in something that cannot be proven to exist. The irony of such a position is that not believing in something is as much a demonstration of faith as accepting it. To make the argument as a "faith" statement, an Atheist might say, "I have faith that God does not exist." It would be like a parent that takes a position not to take their children to church because they do not want to "force"

---

[2] Stephen Carter, *The Culture of Disbelief: How American Law and Politics Trivialized Religious Devotion* (New York: HarperCollins, 1993), 7.
[3] Ibid, 4-5.

religion on them. Again, the irony of such a decision is that by not exposing them to the concept of God you impose (indeed, "force") the opposing viewpoint on them that God does not exist.

Of course, this is not meant to be a seminar on the debate between believers and atheist; but simply a presentation of the two sides to the question about the existence of God. However, a third position does exist and that is represented by those who call themselves "agnostic." It is often difficult to get a definitive understanding of what an agnostic believes, since the term is often applied to represent numerous different opinions and beliefs about the existence of God. A strict dictionary definition would be "a person who holds the view that any ultimate reality (such as God) is unknown and probably unknowable."[4] Broadly applied, many agnostics would simply state that they are not committed to believing in either the existence or the nonexistence of God, or any god. Succinctly put, agnostics do not take an affirming or non-affirming stand on the existence of God.

An additional manifestation of the agnostic "belief" would be the concept that although God might exist, the actual being (character) of God cannot be known. Interestingly, all of the points within the agnostic construct actually reach the same conclusion and that is one of being non-committal to the existence of God. To the agnostic, God might exist. In fact, some agnostics might even grant the Christian the benefit of the doubt and acknowledge that God does, indeed, exist. However, the agnostic would also provide a caveat to that admission by stating that even if God does exist, His character (being) cannot be known. Therefore, operationally speaking, in terms of the practical life of the agnostic, the being of God cannot be known. This presents an interesting conundrum for the agnostic. Look again at their position. The agnostic proclaims that the character of God cannot be known, but the argument defeats itself. The concept that the nature of God cannot be known is a demonstration of a specific nature of God. In other words, the agnostic is arguing that the character of God cannot be known by using a character of God (His hidden nature) as the basis of their conclusion. It is a completely illogical argument and falls completely under the weight of its own testimony.

---

[4] Webster's New Riverside University Dictionary, s.v. "Agnostic."

13

Now, some agnostics may disagree with the conclusions proclaimed to this point and may even acknowledge that they consider themselves "Christian." In fact, "Agnostic Christian" churches have been established across the country. Adherents will identify themselves as being "Christian" and "Agnostic" at the same time. The word to describe that claim is "Impossible!" The idea of an Agnostic Christian church is a clear illustration of what is called, linguistically, an oxymoron—a combination of contradictory or incongruous words, such as "unsuccessful rescue." You could have an unsuccessful rescue *attempt*, but the definition of "rescue" identifies an event that was successful. Therefore, we can understand that the term "unsuccessful rescue" represents an oxymoron. In reference to Agnostic Christianity, it also represents a contradiction in terms between "agnostic," which entails that the character of God cannot be known, and "Christianity," a faith that clearly proclaims belief in God and certain basic divine attributes. So, it seems incoherent to claim the unknowability of God on the one hand while also proclaiming oneself to be a Christian (a particular type of God-believer) on the other.

A clear illustration of this contradiction is found in what could be called a "Progressive Christian" theology. It is hard to grasp a universal definition for "progressive Christianity" as a denomination; but it does represent and express an "alternative" Christian theology. One Progressive Christianity website specifically proclaims a viewpoint that questions the "beliefs and dogmas" of Christianity and asks, "Are you repelled by claims that Christianity is the 'only way'?"[5] Those two points alone, regardless of the agnostic premise expressed by many accepting a progressive theology, should be enough to question their concept of Christianity. While it may be true, as Shakespeare had Juliet lament that "A rose by any other name would smell as sweet" (*Romeo and Juliet*, Act II, Scene II); simply because it smells as sweet, doesn't make it a rose. Call it what you will, the theology expressed as "progressive" is not consistent with Christianity, since it rejects a basic tenet of the Faith: that the nature of God cannot be known.

Again, some Progressive Christians may want to provide a rebuttal to such a statement. Many claim to believe in Jesus

---

[5] The question was found on a Progressive Christianity website
(www.progressivechristianity.org).

as a teacher and even read the Bible (especially Jesus' teachings) to discover a proper direction for their life. Therefore, since they follow Jesus' teachings, they believe they are correct in identifying themselves as Christians. That conclusion has two fatal flaws. First, it denies the substance on which all of the Christian faith has been established . . . the existence of God. Without the presence of God and the work of God to restore Man's broken relationship with Him through Jesus (more on this point in the next section), the nature of Christianity falls apart.

The second flaw is in the label "Christian" as "a follower of Christ." The concept of Jesus as "the Christ" identifies Him as "God incarnate" which is a distinction of who He was, not a name given to him. If the agnostic does not believe in the existence of God, cannot be sure if God exists, or that the character of God cannot be known; then it seems impossible for the agnostic to accept Jesus as "the Christ" (God incarnate). It is therefore theologically incorrect for the individuals holding that belief to identify themselves as Christians. Obviously, if the Progressive sees Jesus as simply a teacher, rejecting His incarnation as the Christ, they cannot be described as a follower of "the Christ" (a "Christ"-ian).

It should be acknowledged at this point that throughout history mainline Christian denominations have continually gone through periods of revival and periods of doubt regarding the question concerning the existence of God. Most notably, in the mid-1960s the Christian church battled what was labeled "The Death of God" theology. Finding its primary impetus from a growing Secularism in America during that time, it was certainly fueled throughout the decade by social upheaval, including the assassinations of John F. Kennedy, Robert Kennedy, and Martin Luther King, Jr.; as well as experiencing the escalation of the war in Vietnam, with casualties in the tens of thousands. One can understand the theological turmoil that was felt within the Christian Church regarding the existence of God during what may have felt like an age of the absence of God.

The presence of evil in the world has long been a favorite mantra of those who wish to question the existence of God. They would posit, "If God is all-powerful and so loving, why does He allow so much suffering in the world, and specifically the suffering of those who truly believe?" Obviously, the full answer to this question would necessitate another book;

but here the simple answer is that the true Believer understands that evil is in the world, not as the result of God's inaction; but His justice in the face of Man's sin. As a result of Man's original sin, evil found a place in the world. From that moment on, evil has had a place in the world and living in the world results in evil, in some capacity, touching the lives of Believer and Unbeliever alike. As Jesus Himself acknowledged, "It rains on the just and the unjust" (Matthew 5:45).

The 2014 film, *God is Not Dead*, addressed this difficult question. In the film a young Christian student debates his atheistic professor regarding the existence of God. The Christian student makes strong arguments for God's existence and even uses the professor's own words against him to prove his point. As the student and professor make their final arguments, the student asks the professor why he hates God so much. The professor finally answers "Because He took everything away from me (an obvious reference to some tragedy or evil which happened in his life). Yes, I hate God." The student then calmly asks the professor, "How can you hate something that doesn't exist?" He made his point and any further statements to prove God's existence became unnecessary.

Granted, the illustration is simplistic and perhaps even a feeble attempt to address the formidable objection to the problem of evil in the world articulated by acknowledged scholars like J. L. Mackie, William Rowe, and Paul Draper. In that light, theologians commit entire books trying to explain the obvious question: Does the presence of evil in the world reject the existence of God? The basic response can be that the very concept of evil (as the absence or contradiction of goodness) presupposes a standard for goodness (i.e., God). In other words, the concept of evil is indirectly parasitic upon the concept of God. The bottom line here is that the presence of evil fails to render theism illogical. Rather, one can begin to understand that in a certain view it is the presence of evil that substantiates the existence of God (as evil's antithesis).

On the other hand, those who believe in the existence of God cite references to miraculous events; either within their own lives or citing historical situations. For instance, many reference historical accounts, such as the "miraculous" victory the American Colonists achieved against what was arguably the greatest fighting force on the planet at the time. Continuing on the same trek, many note the "miracle" that saved the nation during the Constitutional Convention. After months of debate and the potential for the Convention being dissolved, Benjamin Franklin made a motion that the Convention should call a chaplain to open the next day's session with prayer.[6] They did. The next day a chaplain offered an invocation and, as they say, the rest is history.

However, from a more academic approach, Craig S. Keener, a professor of New Testament at Asbury Theological Seminary, offers a record of contemporary miracles that he compiled in his book, *Miracles: The Credibility of the New Testament Accounts*. Keener noted that the main focus of the book is to "persuade readers skeptical of NT miracle accounts" and present those contemporary miracle accounts that "stem from eyewitnesses."[7] He goes on to note that "some superhuman being, such as God, sometimes causes some such phenomena."[8] For Keener, God is still in the miracle-making business and that reality substantiates the presence of God in the world through His interaction with Man and, therefore, establishes the reality of His existence.

Certainly, cynics will criticize the premise that such events constitute the existence of God and dismiss the conclusion drawn above as being nothing more than a coincidence. Perhaps that is true. Perhaps all of the events that have some miraculous quality to them all lined up and the dots all were perfectly connected. Perhaps it was all a coincidence. However, the final question is, "How many coincidences does it take until one can begin to realize that something else was at work?"

At this point, it is important to clearly delineate the importance, as a Christian, for accepting the existence of God. It may be preaching to the choir, but all Christians must accept the reality for the existence of God. That fact is the basis of every other tenet of our faith. God must exist in order to establish a relationship with humans following the Creation. God must exist in order to restore the broken relationship with humans as a result of sin. God must exist in order to become incarnate in Jesus. God must exist in order to offer salvation through His sacrifice. God

---

[6] Carol Berkin, *A Brilliant Solution* (Boston: Haughton Mifflin Harcourt Publishing, 2002), 107.
[7] Craig Keener, *Miracles: The Credibility of the New Testament Accounts* (Grand Rapids, Baker Academic: 2011), 16.
[8] Ibid.

must exist in order to inspire and preserve His Holy Word as a guide for all who believe. Reject the existence of God and the foundation on which the entirety of the Christian Faith is set no longer exists.

Still, questions can be raised as to how anyone can emphatically claim the existence of God. The opponents for the existence of God would simply ask, "Where is the proof?" It is a legitimate question, since God is not something that you can take into a lab, place under a microscope and declare, "Aha, there He is!" Although, certainly one answer to the question of trying to prove the existence of God *is* a sort of "Aha" moment. For many Christians the very presence of the universe and the Earth's place in it is proof enough. In Plato's *Phaedo*, Socrates said that "if you could see the Earth from space, you would recognize a concept of the real heaven and the real light." Granted, Socrates considered reason to be a trump to faith and so one might argue that he was not speaking of God, per se; but that is a discussion for the philosophers. Socrates did believe in a higher power and as such one could then easily conclude that his statement was a reasonable conclusion that he had reached to support the existence of God.

Staying within the discipline of philosophy we can find three presentations for the existence of God. They are the cosmological argument, the ontological argument, and the teleological argument. Granted, the arguments are not based on biblical references and many Christians would reject the concept of using philosophy to explain or support their faith. However, the Christian would be wise to understand their merit as a valuable asset for our interaction with those who reject God's place in the world.

In a section of his *Summa Theologia*, Thomas Aquinas argued a cosmological position for the existence of God. His primary focus was on the physical evidence that points to the reality that all things in existence had some beginning, a creation (and as such, a Creator). Perhaps that explanation is simplistic enough, but to be clear the Cosmological Argument has three main points. Basically, the three points are: 1) Everything in the world has being (it exists); 2) everything that exists had a cause (a point of creation); therefore 3) there is a cause for the world (which we may call God).

It is a succinct and compelling argument. It is brilliant in its simplicity (everything must have a beginning) and reaches a conclusion that is hard, if not impossible, to refute. The basic premise is that everything has a beginning (a point of creation) and therefore must have a Creator. In fact, unbelievers have a hard time successfully arguing against the Cosmological Argument for the existence of God. Lee Strobel, a journalist who sought to investigate the scientific evidence for the existence of God, wrote that "atheists are finding it hard to deny that the universe had a beginning."[9] He continued that line of thinking by stating the essence of the argument that "whatever begins to exist has a cause" and that cause is God.[10]

Anselm, the Archbishop of Canterbury (1093-1109), set in motion the formulation of the ontological argument for the existence of God. The argument rests on a foundation of reason, without any presentation of empirical evidence or proof, for God's existence. Anselm posited several points, such as Man, by his very nature, understands the presence of God. In other words, for Anselm, God exists in our minds. He presented a very intricate argument regarding the relationship between mental understanding and reality. However, in a nutshell Anselm's argument stated the following: Man has the concept of God and understands that such a being would be most perfect. But God cannot be a mere idea or concept, because it would not be most perfect if it was only an idea. Therefore, God exists in reality as well as in our understanding.

The final approach is the teleological argument, which is often referred to as "the argument from design." It may help to understand the root word here. The main Greek word for "teleological" is "telos," which means "purpose" or "design." As such, the argument states that the universe provides evidence of a great complexity or design. As a result, it must have been designed by a great Designer, or God. This brings to mind the typical story that demonstrates the nature of the teleological argument.

The story is about two men who were in a debate about the creation of the world. One was a renowned scientist and the other a noted theologian. The scientist made the point that the world is far older than the Bible attests and provided some convincing arguments for a "natural process" for the creation of the world. He seemed to be making good points and perhaps even winning the debate with a sort of "Big Bang" and

---

[9] Lee Strobel, *The Case for a Creator: A Journalist Investigates Scientific Evidence that Points toward God* (Grand Rapids: Zondervan, 2004), 98.
[10] Ibid.

Evolutionary Theory approach combined. During the recess, the theologian walked outside the auditorium and found a watch lying on the ground. It gave him an idea of how to win his argument. When the debate resumed, he brought out the watch and indicated that he found the watch on the ground outside the building. He also acknowledged the thunderstorm that everyone heard during the earlier portion of the debate and as a result concluded the watch fell out of one of the clouds during the storm. The scientist, although being courteous through most of the debate, now burst out in laughter and even insinuated that the theologian had lost his mind. "How can you possibly believe that something so intricate as a watch could simply fall out of the sky?" the scientist bellowed. "Its very existence is evidence that some master craftsman put it all together." "I suppose you are right", admitted the theologian. "However, I do have one final question for you", he continued. "How can you possibly believe that something so intricate as this world could simply fall out of the sky?"

The conclusion to the argument is that the universe expresses too much complexity to be the product of a random chance event. All one needs to do is watch the heavens and chart the perfectly accurate movement of the celestial bodies. Additionally, our own bodies and the delicate balance of nature are further evidences of an incredible complexity that give testimony to the existence of a Supreme Creator, a testimony to the existence of God.

Many early philosophers used the teleological argument to support the existence of God. They argued that the empirical design and order of the universe proved God's existence and offered that humans have the ability to grasp intellectually the intricate design and order of things to conclude the imperative that such design required the acceptance of a "Creator" (the power that established the design). As a result, the order of the universe could not be understood as a random event; but must be explained in terms of design and purpose ordained by God.

Moving ahead a few centuries, William Paley, an Eighteenth-Century English clergyman and Christian apologist, championed a more modern application of the teleological argument. Paley relied heavily on the teleological concepts and arguments. His conclusion regarding the question of God as the Creator was that the design of the world was so perfect it must have a "Designer," the "Designer" had to be a being and that being was God.

One final note before we leave the philosophical arguments for the existence of God and that is that each of the three concepts end in the word "logical." The point here is that the arguments are logical, leading to a logical position of faith that proclaims the true existence of a Creator, of God.

Another response to the question regarding proof for the existence of God is simply to acknowledge that no proof exists. Now, that may seem like a defeatist statement; but it leads to a significant point for the true Christian and that is the idea of faith. The Bible defines faith as "the assurance of things hoped for, the conviction of things not seen" (Hebrews 11:1). The word that has been interpreted as "assurance" is rendered "confidence" in some ancient manuscripts and relates to unseen elements of the future. As one commentator put it, "What is meant is that faith is that which gives assurance or certainty . . . it is by faith that they (the unseen things) are realized."[11] Therefore, the Christian is assured and certain of the existence of God as the result of faith. Since faith, by its very (i.e., biblical) definition, grants that assurance as a reality. God does, indeed, exist.

Once we establish the fact that God does exist, we need to move forward into three additional concepts that are integral to the Christian's faith in the existence of God. The first step is examining more closely the idea of God as Creator. Part of this first chapter highlighted that truth as a part of the argument for the existence of God—He exists as Creator. However, a more specific and detailed approach would help to solidify that Truth. The second concept presents the point that the Christian Faith professes a belief in the "One, True and Living God." Other world religions may worship a god, but Christianity proclaims the Judeo-Christian God as the one and only God. The final step examines the Christian principle of the Trinitarian nature of God.

"Who Is God?" From a Christian perspective, the three answers to that question are: 1) He exists as the Creator; 2) He exists as the "One and Only" God; and 3) He has a trinitarian nature as God the Father, God the Son, and God the Holy Spirit. The next three chapters will address each of those points.

---

[11] J. R. Drummelow, *A Commentary on the Holy Bible* (New York: The MacMillan Company, 1973), 1026.

21

CHAPTER 2

GOD AS CREATOR

In the beginning God created the heavens and the earth. The earth was formless and void, and darkness was over the surface of the deep, and the Spirit of God was moving over the surface of the waters. Then God said, "Let there be light"; and there was light. God saw that the light was good; and God separated the light from the darkness. God called the light day, and the darkness He called night. And there was evening and there was morning, one day. (Genesis 1:1-5)

We all understand that Christian denominations differ on some concepts that relate to what we call "Practices of Faith." For instance, some liturgical denominations practice a belief of transubstantiation in the observance of the Lord's Supper. Transubstantiation is the belief that the elements of the Supper become the actual body and blood of Christ. Others practice a consubstantiation, a belief in the "essence" of Christ being present in the elements. Still others practice an acceptance of a "symbolic presence" of Christ in the elements. As stated, those are practices of faith and those practices do separate us denominationally. However, they are not "Tenets of Faith."

The tenets of faith acknowledge those elements of faith essential within the doctrinal structure of all Christian denominations. One of those tenets is the reality of God and specifically the reality of God as Creator. With that perspective, and apart from the initial chapter's inclusion of God as Creator within its presentation of the Truth for the existence of God, a more in-depth examination of that Truth is important. As such, it is the focus of this chapter. So, let us take a closer look at "God as Creator."

The first part of this discussion comes from what we were taught "in the beginning" from our early days in Sunday School. In fact, that is exactly the point . . . God "in the beginning." Genesis 1:1 states, "In the beginning God created the heavens and the earth." So, the obvious answer to a creation of the world question is that God was the Creator. The Bible provides no ambiguity on this issue and that is the answer most of us remember from our Sunday School classes as children—God is the Creator.

Beyond that one verse, the biblical evidence for God as Creator is overwhelming. As one might imagine, most of the passages that refer to God as Creator are found in the Old Testament. The notable passages are:

> *And God saw all that He had made and behold, it was very good.* (Genesis 1:31)

> *For thus says the Lord, who created the heavens, He is the God who formed the earth and made it, He established it and did not create it a waste place but formed it to be inhabited.* (Isaiah 45:18)

> *"For My hand made all these things, thus all these things came into being,"* declares the Lord. (Isaiah 66:2)

> *It is He who made the earth by His power, Who established the world by His wisdom; and by His understanding He has stretched out the heavens. When He utters His voice, there is a*

> *tumult of waters in the heavens, and*
> *He causes the clouds to ascend from*
> *the end of the earth; He makes*
> *lightning for the rain and brings out*
> *the wind from His storehouses.*
> (Jeremiah 10:12-13)

Even though the Old Testament may be the major source of the biblical passages acknowledging God as Creator, New Testament passages also proclaim that Truth. Such as:

> *All things came into being through*
> *Him, and apart from Him nothing came*
> *into being that has come into being.*
> (John 1:3)

> *For by Him all things were created,*
> *both in the heavens and on earth,*
> *visible and invisible, whether*
> *thrones or dominions or rulers or*
> *authorities; all things have been*
> *created through Him and for Him.*
> (Colossians 1:16)

> *Worthy are You, our Lord and our God,*
> *to receive glory and honor and power;*
> *for You created all things, and*
> *because of Your will they existed,*
> *and were created.* (Revelation 4:11)

The biblical Truth is clear and although the answer is easy to state it is harder for some Christians to understand and accept. That is especially true considering the "scientific" data that is expressed in some circles. Evolution, the Big Bang Theory, and other concepts all attempt to challenge the irrefutable truth presented in Scripture that God, and God alone, served as the Creator.

For the most part, this is an elementary discussion because all the various Christian denominations accept the answer and proclaim the Truth that God is the Creator. We can examine some of the denominations' doctrinal statements to get a sense of the universal acceptance of this Truth throughout Christianity. A look at the Shorter Catechism will reveal the answer to the question "What is the work of creation?" It states:

> *The work of creation is God's making all things of nothing by the word of His power in the space of six days and all very good.*[12]

Additionally, the official Methodist concept of God is expressed in their Articles of Faith that God is "the Maker (Creator) and preserver of all things."[13] Moving to another denomination, the Southern Baptist reference to God as Creator is contained in the *Baptist Faith and Message* which proclaims (emphasis added):

> *There is one and only one living and true God. He is an intelligent, spiritual, and personal Being, the <u>Creator</u>, Redeemer, Preserver, and Ruler of the universe.*[14]

The examples continue with denomination after denomination; each one expressing, in some official proclamation, the concept of God as Creator.

Now, before we continue this discussion any further, we may need to clear the air a little. This book is not attempting to be a theological treatise on creation. I am not attempting to answer the question "Do you believe God actually created the world in six days?" Although I do believe that Biblical Truth, that is not the question before us. The question asks, "Who is God?" and the short answer is "He is the Creator." How that creation happened or the details surrounding the event is not pertinent to the original question presented here, nor to the current discussion regarding the basic tenet of faith regarding the nature of God as Creator.

I am also not going to try and answer the typical "gotcha" questions naysayers like to ask ministers about creation. The questions like, "If, according to Scripture, Adam and Eve were

---

[12] The quote is taken directly from the Shorter Catechism (Question 9) as provided by the Orthodox Presbyterian Church.

[13] The statement is from The United Methodist Church's "Articles of Faith" as expressed at www.umc.org.

[14] *The Baptist Faith and Message*, Article II

the only people created by God, then where did Cain get his wife?" and "Where do the dinosaurs fit into the creation story?" and, of course, the "Can a Christian believe in evolution as God's method of Creation?" all have no real importance in this particular presentation. This chapter is simply attempting to answer the question at hand by establishing that the Christian tenant regarding the being of God is as the Creator.

In that vein, let's attempt to answer the question from a more difficult position. The Holy Scriptures state the being of God as Creator and denominations universally accept that answer as a tenet of faith. Even though those elements should be adequate for the Christian to accept God as the Creator, perhaps a more "logical" approach to the question could prove beneficial. That would mean returning to the philosophical arguments provided in Chapter 1. As a short review, the first was the cosmological argument: "Cosmological," from the Greek root word "kosmos," meaning "world." The cosmological argument for God as Creator stated that the world (the cosmos) could not exist by itself. Something created whatever exists and that creative force was God. Basically, the cosmological argument is often noted as the "First Cause" argument, noting that which is the first cause of all that exists is God. The ontological argument referenced Reason as a means of believing in the existence of God and God as Creator. It piggybacked on the cosmological argument and presented the "Prime Mover" concept as reasonable for accepting a Creator and accepting God as that Creator. Finally, "the argument from design" was the teleological argument and presented a position that complexity of the world dictates the presence of a "master clock maker," a Creator. Remember the earlier illustration (Chapter 1) about the two men debating creation and the presence of a watch after a thunderstorm?

Continuing that discussion, Wayne Oates, a renowned scholar in the area of psychology of religion and pastoral care, noted in one of his many books that religion demands the presence of a Creator. He noted that "religious concerns must also include an agonizing appraisal of the meaning of creation."[15] Although presented from a psychological standpoint, Oates highlighted the necessity of religious Man to understand his relationship to his world and to the Creator. In other words, Oates made the psychological point that religion, every

---

[15] Wayne Oates, *The Psychology of Religion* (Waco: Word Books, 1973), 136.

religion (which would, of course, include the Christian Faith) has a tenet of faith that accepts the reality of a Creator, accepts the reality of God as Creator.

So, as we acknowledge the Truth that God exists as the Creator, we need to move to answer the question posed at the beginning of this section: "Who is God?" For the Christian, one clear answer to that question is that God is the Creator. The Christian accepts that reality from the biblical passages that express the Truth, substantiated in denominational Statements of Faith and acknowledged as a logical conclusion of the many philosophical arguments. All proclaim that God is the Creator. A Truth that all Christians accept.

In addition to that Truth, the Christian acknowledges God as the "One and Only God." That perspective becomes the discussion point for the next chapter.

CHAPTER 3

GOD AS THE "ONE AND ONLY"

To you it was shown that you might know that the Lord, He is God; there is no other besides Him. He personally brought you from Egypt by His great power, driving out from before you nations greater and mightier than you, to bring you in and to give you their land for an inheritance, as it is today. Know therefore today, and take it to your heart, that the Lord, He is God in heaven above and on the earth below; there is no other.
(Deuteronomy 4:35-39)

Now that we established the imperative of the Christian's acceptance for the existence of God and acknowledge Him as the Creator, the next step is to understand the point that the God we worship as Christians is the "One and Only" God. Of course, the many doubters and detractors will immediately raise their typical question. They invariably ask, "Does that mean that the gods of other world religions are not 'true' gods?" As noted in the Introduction, the debate concerning the gods of other religions is not the focus of this discussion. Similarly, the relationship of the Christian Faith to other world religions is also not the focus of this book. And, the Christian's proclamation of faith about God is not meant to be some sort

True Christianity

of arrogant pronouncement that Christianity is the only true Faith. Rather, it is a simple presentation of the basis of the Christian Faith and the tenets of that faith that serve as its foundation

The issue at hand is the Christian's answer to the present question, "Who is God?" and a clear part of the answer is the acceptance of our God as being the "One and Only" God. That Christian perspective, as with the very existence of God, is a matter of faith ("the assurance of things hoped for and the conviction of things not seen," Hebrews 11:1). Christians accept by faith a reality that the God the Christian worships is the "One and Only" God.

As one examines this Truth from a faith perspective (as a Christian must), the Bible becomes the obvious starting point. Even with a cursory examination of the Scriptures, it is easy to discover that the Bible is filled with passages that clearly declare God as "One" and no other gods exist apart from Him. It is not a question of other religions and other "gods" that different religions accept. Instead, it is a matter of what Christianity proclaims; and therefore, what the Believer (who claims to be a Christian) must accept. With that concept in place, we can turn first to the Old Testament where we can read several passages like the ones below.

> To you it was shown that you might know that the LORD he is God; there is no other besides Him. Know therefore today and take it to your heart, that the LORD He is God in heaven above, and on the earth below: there is no other. (Deuteronomy 4:35, 39)

> O Lord, there is none like You, nor is there any God besides You, according to all that we have heard with our ears. (I Chronicles 17:20)

> For I am God, and there is none else; I am God, and there is none like me. (Isaiah 46:9)

And, from the New Testament, we can find the following passages:

30

This is life eternal, that they may know You, the only true God, and Jesus Christ, whom You have sent. (John 17:3)

For there is one God, and one mediator also between God and men, the man Christ Jesus. (I Timothy 2:5)

You believe that God is one, you do well; the demons also believe, and shudder. (James 2:19)

Of course, many other passages substantiate the point. However, the six noted above are enough to express an obvious biblical Truth. They each represent a clear acknowledgement for the Christian that there is but One, True God. G. Ernest Wright, a leading Old Testament scholar and archeologist in the mid-1900s, noted that the passage in Deuteronomy provides the belief that "There is no other Lord, no other power or authority in the universe."[16] To put it as succinctly as possible, the Judeo-Christian God has no equal.

Beyond the biblical proclamation, the Law that God provided to the people of Israel offers a clear picture of the "One God" concept. The people of Israel are in bondage in Egypt and God sends Moses to be His instrument by which Pharaoh agrees to let the people go. God leads Moses to bring the people to Mount Sinai. Moses then proceeds to climb the mountain and receive from God His "Ten Commandments" as a guide for the people in establishing them in the Promised Land. The very first Commandment provided to the people was, "You shall have no other God's before me" (Exodus 20:3).

Certainly, many scholars might raise some significant debate regarding the interpretation and application at this point. However, in the listing of the first four Commandments (all dealing with our relationship to God), God states "for I, the Lord your God, am a jealous God" (Exodus 20:5). Obviously, if God could be jealous, something must exist in the world about which He could become jealous. The Old Testament acknowledges that people worshiped "other gods" as even the Hebrew people at Mount Sinai worshiped a golden calf when Moses came down

---

[16] G. Ernest Wright, "Exegesis on Deuteronomy," *The Interpreter's Bible*, Vol 2 (New York: Abingdon Press, 1953), 360.

with the Ten Commandments. Regardless of the debate that scholars raise, the existence of the people worshipping a golden calf as representative of some type of "god" does not establish the reality of that the "whatever" is a true god. God simply acknowledged that people have the capacity to worship all sorts of things (i.e., a golden calf) and He, being the only True God, understandably expected total acceptance and belief in Him.

As evidence of what is an obvious biblical Truth, the Christian Church proclaims God as the "One and Only" God. As such, Christian churches universally teach it and include it in their doctrinal statements. Again, we can turn to the Westminster Shorter Catechism as a model of the doctrinal Truth taught to new members and communicants. Question Five of the Catechism asks a very direct and simple question by asking, "Are there more Gods than one?" It then provides the doctrinal response which states, "There is but one only, the living and true God."[17] Other denominations have similar proclamations. The Southern Baptist Convention has accepted a document entitled *The Baptist Faith and Message* as their doctrinal Statement of Faith. The document states unequivocally that "There is one and only one living and true God."[18]

The biblical proclamation of God as the "One and only" God is true for all Christians and has been incorporated into their doctrinal Statements of Faith. Unfortunately, regardless of the Truth the Christian Church expresses, the criticism proclaiming Christianity as an arrogant attitude of faith will, undoubtedly, continue. However, Christians should not faint in the face of such criticism or be unduly concerned about how it is perceived by others. The Bible presents the Truth (see Section V, "Is the Bible the True Word of God?"). So, it is incredible that some people, those who have a belief that is not scripturally sound, could be so convicted and so critical of God's Truth. It is the Truth of Scripture that the God Christians worship is "The One and Only God." That proclamation is found throughout the Old and the New Testaments and, as a result, all Christians should accept that Truth as a basic tenet of the Christian Faith.

---

[17] From the Shorter Catechism (Question 5) as provided by the Orthodox Presbyterian Church.
[18] *The Baptist Faith and Message*, Article II.

Additionally, church history adds a measure of support to the "One and Only" God perspective. As noted in the Introduction, many liturgical churches utilize creedal statements as part of their worship service. During the service, the minister will lead the congregation in a reciting of a creed as a statement of their faith. The Nicene Creed was adopted at the First Council of Nicaea in 325. Although it was changed slightly by the First Council of Constantinople in 381, the first words of the Creed remained the same. They state simply, "We believe in one God." The early church fathers established a creedal statement for the Church that specifically acknowledged God as "One."

The basic point here is that the Truth has always been the Truth. That Truth is that the Christian accepts God as the "One and only" God. The Bible has proclaimed it. God, Himself, acknowledged it. The early Church instituted it as a Statement of Faith. It is a Truth that has been a Truth from the beginning and a Truth that all Christians must accept until the end.

Even as we acknowledge God as "One," Christianity does proclaim a trinitarian doctrine regarding the nature of God. He is the One and Only God; but he exists in three presentations. The next chapter examines the trinitarian doctrine of the Christian Faith.

CHAPTER 4

THE TRINITARIAN NATURE OF GOD

And Jesus came up and spoke to them, saying, "All authority has been given to Me in heaven and on earth. Go therefore and make disciples of all the nations, baptizing them in the name of the Father and the Son and the Holy Spirit. (Matthew 28:17-19)

At this point some readers may believe that I missed a point regarding the being of God; that is, God as spirit. It is not that I missed that point, it is simply that the point should be an obvious one to all Christians and, as a tenet of faith, is best explained in a separate concept. That concept is the trinitarian nature of God: God the Father, God the Son, and God the Holy Spirit.

Perhaps the best place to start this discussion is at the beginning with "God the Father." The first possible step in understanding God as "Father" is that father, in one respect, means "beginning." A good illustration for this first point is George Washington. Washington is the "father" of our country. That moniker was given to him through the years as the one who served as Commander-in-Chief of the Continental Army that secured our independence at the battle of Yorktown,

35

who served as the President of the Constitutional Convention that drafted the document that is the basis of our rights and freedoms as citizens of the United States, and who served as the nation's first President. Washington was the leader from the beginning, helped create the nation, and as a result has been identified as the "father" of our country. In a similar manner, and not meaning to be in any manner irreverent, we can identify God as "Father" because He was from the beginning and he was responsible for the founding of the world in which we live. This point goes back to the identification of God as Creator, noting that God has been in the world from the beginning, creating it out of nothing.

The second illustration of "father" can sometimes be hard for many people to accept or even comprehend. After graduating from seminary, I served as the Associate Pastor of a county-seat church in central Georgia. During that time the church had a ministry to a local children's home. The children were not orphans but were court-directed to the facility based on an abusive environment that existed in their home. As a result of the abuse many of the children had experienced from their father, they had a difficult time understanding and accepting the concept that God was also their "father." Their negative reaction to God, as "father," was understandable; but the concept was still a Truth for them then, as it is for Christians today.

Apart from the experience at the children's home, we know that the true idea of a father is one that through his love has a desire to facilitate a care for his children. That is exactly the nature we profess when we, as Christians, proclaim God as "Father." He is the true loving Father that provides a care for His children. The love a true father has for his children is undeniable. Carrying out that important point to a specific application, we can certainly understand that a father's love is demonstrated in the care and protection he provides to his children. The father has the desire to provide for the needs of his children. No father, possessing that true love, wants to watch his children suffer and struggle through life without the necessities that he can provide. Note, I didn't say "wants" (which is more of a parenting issues and perhaps fodder for a different book). And finally, we can understand that a father seeks to protect his children.

All those points are clearly delineated for the Christian when we accept God as our Father. However, certainly the best acknowledgement of God as father is found in the Bible. And, the Bible is quite clear on this point. From the Old Testament we can read the following:

> *Do you thus repay the Lord, O foolish and unwise people? Is not He your Father who has bought you? He has made you and established you.* (Deuteronomy 32:6)

> *A Father of the fatherless and a judge for the widows, is God in His holy habitation.* (Psalm 68:5)

> *For You are our Father . . . You, O Lord, are our Father, our Redeemer from of old is your name.* (Isaiah 63:16)

And from the New Testament, we find the following:

> *Do not call anyone on earth your father; for One is your Father, He who is in heaven.* (Matthew 23:9)

> *Yet, for us there is but one God, the Father, from whom are all things and we exist through Him.* (I Corinthians 8:6)

> *And One God and Father of all who is over all and through all and in all.* (Ephesians 4:6)

If we, as Christians, are going to accept the Bible as the True Word of God then the clear acknowledgement of Scripture is that God is Father.

The second element of the Trinitarian nature of God is God, the Son. This aspect of the Trinity will be discussed at length is Section 2, "Is Jesus God?" So, let's delay that discussion for later.

The third, and final, person of the Trinity is God, the Holy Spirit. As we try to get a handle on this final point, we can attempt to take it from the easiest aspect to grasp: a purely

"Being of God" standpoint that God is, by nature, spirit. The Bible specifically states that Truth, as recorded for us in the Gospel of John. In chapter 4, we can read about the encounter that Jesus had with the Samaritan woman at a well. The exegesis of that encounter is not relevant to this discussion, but his comment to the woman is. As they discussed the perspective of worship, Jesus spoke to the woman and said, "God is spirit and those who worship Him must worship in spirit and truth" (John 4:28).

That is a definitive statement. It is also a statement made by Jesus, Himself. Jesus also made other statements regarding the spiritual nature of God as it applies to the Holy Spirit, referencing God's continual, omnipresent availability to all Believers. Specifically, those passages are also recorded in John and are found in John 14-16, a section of Scripture identified as the "Paraclete Passages." In those chapters, John recorded five statements of Jesus concerning the ministry of the Holy Spirit, or Paraclete. Note that the word "paraclete" is a transliteration of a Greek word meaning "to be called to one's side" as an aide or an assistant. The point Jesus made in the statements was to acknowledge that even though He was "going away" (i.e., would die) the presence of God, through the ministry of the Holy Spirit, would continue to provide care, comfort and direction for the disciples and all other Believers.

Each of the passages in John 14-16 presents a clear picture of the direct ministry of God through His Holy Spirit. For instance, two of the statements appear in John 14.

> *And I will ask the Father, and He will give you another Helper, that He may be with you forever; that is the Spirit of truth, whom the world cannot receive, because it does not behold Him or know Him, but you know Him because He abides with you, and will be in you.* (14:16-17)

> *These things I have spoken to you while abiding with you. But the Helper, the Holy Spirit, whom the Father will send in My name, He will teach you all things, and bring to*

> *your remembrance all that I said to you.* (14:25-26)

The initial statement (John 14:16-17) simply expresses the main purpose for the Holy Spirit as a "Helper" and One that will "be with you forever." Jesus continued by adding that this "Helper," the Holy Spirit of God, will "abide with you and will be in you." The passage expressed as a guarantee that the presence of God, through the Holy Spirit, would be forever linked to all Believers. Jesus provided those words as a comfort for the disciples' concern as to what would happen after He died. Where could they continue to receive the support and direction of faith that they received from Jesus while he was with them? Obviously, Jesus would eventually die; but He noted that God would "fill the gap" for them by providing a personal, eternal relationship with Him through the ministry of His Holy Spirit.

The second passage gives a more definitive idea of the actual ministry of what, specifically, the Holy Spirit would be able to accomplish. Jesus gave the disciples a clear function of the Holy Spirit as being able to "teach you all things" and "bring to your remembrance all that I have said to you." In this passage Jesus was making a definitive statement supporting the inspiration role of the Holy Spirit. In other words, Jesus proclaimed a basic ministry of the Holy Spirit as providing an inspiration for Truth, the absolute Truth that is represented in His words and recorded for us in Scripture.

The next three statements reflect and expound on that idea, elaborating on the point that the Holy Spirit will represent all Truth.

> *When the Helper comes, whom I will send to you from the Father, that is the Spirit of truth who proceeds from the Father, He will testify about Me, and you will testify also, because you have been with Me from the beginning.* (15:26-27)

> *But I tell you the truth, it is to your advantage that I go away; for if I do not go away, the Helper will not come to you; but if I go, I will send Him to you. And He, when He comes,*

> *will convict the world concerning sin
> and righteousness and judgment.*
> (16:7-8)

> *I have many more things to say to
> you, but you cannot bear them now.
> But when He, the Spirit of truth,
> comes, He will guide you into all the
> truth; for He will not speak on His
> own initiative, but whatever He
> hears, He will speak; and He will
> disclose to you what is to come.*
> (16:12-13)

The passage in John 15 makes two very important points. First, the Holy Spirit will "proceed from the Father." Just as Jesus was "from the father," so the Holy Spirit will be sent from God to all believers. In Jesus God took on a fleshly manifestation (again, more on this point in Chapter 8). Through the ministry of the Holy Spirit, believers become aware of God's omnipresence (i.e., that He possesses the ability to be present everywhere and at every time). The second point encompasses the concept of faith and believing that Jesus is the Christ, the Messiah. In Jesus' own words, the Holy Spirit will come in order to "testify about Me." The Holy Spirit of God will have the established purpose of acknowledging the Truth that Jesus was the physical manifestation of God, God incarnate.

That concept is a direct link to the first passage in John 16. In that statement, Jesus acknowledged that the Holy Spirit would come to "convict the world concerning sin, righteousness and judgment." Of course, "conviction" in a legal sense is not the same as Jesus stated it here. In our current legal system, it is certainly possible for an innocent person to have a "conviction" on their record, a label regarding something that is not true. However, in this theological and scriptural sense, it is quite a different word. The Greek word is "plerophoria" and means "to bring to full measure of certainty." So, when Jesus spoke those words to His disciples that the Holy Spirit would "convict the world," He meant that the ministry of God's Spirit would bring Truth to the world. And, it would not be *a* truth; but *the* Truth.

The final passage is a culmination of this idea of Truth. First, Jesus identifies the "Helper" as the "spirit of truth," identifying Truth as being the very nature of the Holy Spirit. Second, He reiterates a previous point that the Holy Spirit's ministry will be to "guide you into all truth." This is a link back to the previous passage noting that the Spirit will "teach you all things" (14:26). And, Jesus claimed that the Spirit will only speak of what He hears. The reference to Jesus' own claim of authority is unmistakable. In another Johannine passage, Jesus stated that "I have many things to speak and to judge concerning you, but He who sent Me is true; and the things which I heard from Him, these I speak to the world" (8:26). In the same manner, the Holy Spirit is receiving from God the Truth to proclaim to His people. In the most simplistic of terms, the Holy Spirit will be the voice, serving as the inspiration, the conviction, even the conscience for the Believer.

Now, armed with a full proclamation regarding the reality and the specific ministry of the Holy Spirit, we can more directly tackle the question of the Trinitarian nature of God. Granted, it is a difficult concept to grasp; but perhaps we can begin with the basics. God has existed, in some form, from the beginning. Christians acknowledge Him as Creator and believe that He exists. Jesus represents the incarnation of God and as such can be described as God in fleshly form. Indeed, John 1:14 states that "the Word became flash and dwelt among us." Add to those two points the reality of the Holy Spirit as described above and you have the theological construct of the Trinity: God the Father (as Creator); God the Son (as Jesus); and God the Holy Spirit (as His omnipresent nature).

Obviously, that presents a very simplistic presentation of the Trinity. It is certainly true that God is proclaimed as "the Father" in the Scriptures and identified as the Creator. On the other hand, that statement is not meant to limit the character of God beyond that which we can possibly comprehend. Similarly, to equate the phrase "God the Son" to Jesus as the physical manifestation of God misses other physical events of God's presence in the world (see Gen. 3:8, Gen. 18, Gen. 32, Dan. 3:25, et.al.). Finally, it is problematic to note the Holy Spirit as only an attribute of God's character (omnipresence) when the Holy Spirit represents a distinct entity within itself.

I can already see the hands going up anxiously wanting to proclaim what they believe to be the negating point for not accepting a trinitarian nature of God. These folks are quick to point out that the word 'trinity' never appears in the Bible. And to concede a point, that is a true statement; but it is not Truth! Some people, in order to try and support their non-Christian view of the Trinity, have confused "word" with "concept" and that results in a misrepresented Truth. A clear rebuttal to their point is the fact that "transubstantiation" does not appear in the Bible; but, as noted earlier, many Christian churches follow that application for their observance of the Lord's Supper. The reason they use that theological concept is because they believe it is clearly delineated in the Scriptures, although the word does not actually appear in a specific passage.

In the same manner, the word "trinity" may not appear in the Bible; but certainly the trinitarian concept of God (the Father), Jesus (the Son), and the presence of God as the Holy Spirit is proclaimed throughout and, as such, is an essential element of the Christian Faith. As the noted Scottish theologian, D. M. Baillie acknowledged in his book, *God Was in Christ: An Essay on Incarnation and Atonement*, the trinitarian concept marked "the true basis for sound Christian living."[19] Certainly, other scholars note that same point regarding the association of the trinitarian doctrine to the basic belief within the Faith. So, as we consider the nature of God as a tenet of Christianity, we must include, as a theological principle of that tenet, a belief in the doctrine of the Trinity.

It would be beneficial to stop the discussion at this point; but unfortunately the debate must continue into a more theologically based presentation. This is not meant to be a seminary-level examination; but an important question regarding the Trinity has, so far, not been addressed. The issue at hand is whether the elements of the Trinity (Father, Son and Spirit) are of the same substance (homousian), are they of similar, but not exactly the same, substance (homoiousian), or are they distinct entities, with no substantive relationship at all (heteroousian).

One might ask at this point, "Does all of that really make any difference?" The answer to that question needs to be

---

[19] D. M. Baillie, *God Was in Christ: An Essay on Incarnation and Atonement* (New York: Charles Scribner's Sons, 1948), 159.

"Yes." Yes, it does make a difference for the obvious reason that if the persons of the Trinity do not possess the true, same, actual essence of God, then they are not God. And, if they are not God, then the entirety of the trinitarian doctrine of the Christian Faith, as well as the Truth of Scripture, is lost.

Now, many people will vehemently disagree. Those who practice a faith that rejects the divinity of Jesus or the Holy Spirit as the real presence of God in our midst certainly will be among those who disagree with the conclusion expressed above. However, it must be understood that to accept Jesus as "just a man," that He was an actual, literal flesh and blood, biological son of God person, negates the basic premise of the entire New Testament; as well as calling into question the prophetic sections of the Old Testament. That being the case, the Christian trinitarian doctrine requires an acceptance that the three entities of the Trinity have the same, exact substance. It is scripturally proclaimed as a Truth and accepted as a tenet of the Christian Faith that God the Father, God the Son, and God the Holy Spirit are, by nature, identically the same—they are God!.

This point must not be summarily dismissed as insignificant or unnecessary. It represents a foundational Truth of the Christian Faith and a vital part of the answer to the second "Essential Question of the Faith"—Who Is Jesus?

43

Question #2

Who Is Jesus?

CHAPTER 5

THE HISTORICAL JESUS

The angel said to her, "Do not be afraid, Mary; for you have found favor with God. And behold, you will conceive in your womb and bear a son, and you shall name Him Jesus. He will be great and will be called the Son of the Most High; and the Lord God will give Him the throne of His father David; and He will reign over the house of Jacob forever, and His kingdom will have no end." (Luke 1:30-33)

The preceding chapters made the case for the acceptance of a "One True and Living God" as the foundation of the Christian Faith. As noted earlier, without the acceptance of the reality that God is a real entity, everything else within Christianity ceases to exist.

That point also holds true as we begin to examine the next three questions that relate to the tenets of Christianity—the life of Jesus. Being the center of the Christian Faith, it is an imperative that we accept Jesus as a real person; much as it is for other world religions and the acceptance of their main historic figure.

Without a firm conviction in the historical reality of Mohammed, Islam would not exist. Without the firm conviction by millions of Buddhists in the real life and events of Siddhartha Gautama, Buddhism would not be a world religion. And so it is also true with Christianity and the life of Jesus. Christians must accept Jesus as a real person who lived and experienced a real life, as depicted in the Holy Scripture, or the foundation on which the Christian Faith exists will crumble.

The question is: "How do we find the historical proof for Jesus' life?" In other words, is it possible to present a historical proof for the existence of Jesus beyond the aspect of personal faith? At face value that seems like an impossible task and one that the historiography of that question creates more than a little consternation, with a significant amount of debate, among scholars as they attempt to provide a legitimate answer.

As one tries to address this question head-on, the individual is immediately overwhelmed with the vast number of monographs dedicated to this topic. Through the years, scholars attempted to answer the question regarding the historicity of Jesus from several different angles. Some examined the life of Jesus from the perspective of the Judaism professed during the New Testament period. Others looked to a specific examination, such as Jesus being "Christ." Their obvious point being that the establishment of the one (i.e., His Christology) would automatically acknowledge the other (Jesus as a man, historically). Scholars also attempted to try and discover a legitimate association between Jesus and His death in order to align a soteriology with a historical reference to Jesus' life.

At this point, Albert Schweitzer's work, *The Quest for the Historical Jesus*, emerges as the definitive work in the search for an answer to the historicity of Jesus as a person. Even though Schweitzer would acknowledge that the life of Jesus is a mystery, it does not mean that it is not a historical reality. In his over four hundred pages of argument, Schweitzer provided an examination of

48

numerous scholars from several different fields of study. He referenced philosophers, theologians, historians, along with other scholars, in order to give the reader the broadest explanation possible for a historical reference to the life of Jesus as a real person.

Unfortunately, space does not allow for a complete analysis of the presentations provided by the various scholars through the ages that addressed the question of the historicity of Jesus as a man. For the Christians, Jesus was a man who lived on the Earth, taught God's Truth, performed miracles, and suffered on a cross for the sins of the world. In that light, the magnitude of the problem the serious historian faces at this point is readily evident in a modern volume on the subject. That book is *Jesus Remembered*, by James D. G. Dunn. Dunn is a renowned British New Testament scholar, theologian, and professor. His attempt to answer the question concerning the historicity of Jesus was published in the early Twenty-First Century and took nearly one thousand pages (including the notes) to establish a conclusion. Granted, his brilliant work examined a vast number of historians and various historical perspectives which resulted in the tome that he published. However, one conclusion that he professed following his research was that faith played a vital role in proclaiming the historical reality of Jesus. He stated that "without taking account of their (the Believers') faith and the faith dimension integral to the Jewish tradition it will not be possible to provide a responsible historical account of the Jesus tradition."[20]

In a similar fashion, many other historians proclaimed a comparable truth. Schweitzer concluded his classic presentation on the subject with the following: "They (His followers) shall pass through in His fellowship, and, as an ineffable mystery, they shall learn in their own experiences Who He is."[21] In a more contemporary,

---

[20] James D. G. Dunn, *Jesus Remembered* (Grand Rapids: Eerdmans, 2001), 327.
[21] Albert Schweitzer, *The Quest for the Historical Jesus: A Critical Study of Its Progress from Reimarus to Wrede* (New York: MacMillan, 1910), 403.

but an equally definitive contribution of four volumes and well over three thousand pages, Tom Holmén and Stanley Porter provide a work with the thesis that the "Jesus of faith cannot be detached from history."[22]

Indeed, one cannot separate the concept of faith from the acceptance of the historic reality of Jesus' life on Earth. Obviously, many historians and theologians who address the historicity of Jesus reach, in part, a similar conclusion. Some speak of an "implied Christology" to indicate the reality of a historical Jesus. Others simply believe that the validity of Jesus as a historic figure cannot be conclusively acknowledged apart from the Scriptural references provided in the Gospel accounts and the Believer's faith in the proclamation of their Truth.

In other words, many proclaim faith as the essential element in the historicity of Jesus which is a point that the scientific scope of history cannot prove. Even though one might be inclined to accept the premise of no historical proof beyond faith, faith still stands as a strong voice for the Christian's acceptance of Jesus as a person of history. However, let's not throw up our hands and surrender to the idea that the only way to support a historic conclusion for the life of Jesus is through faith. As noted above, many scholars (Schweizer, Dunn, et. al.) give a significant amount of credibility to the Gospel accounts. With that perspective, it is important to examine the incredible amount of resources available during the First Century that support Jesus as a historic figure.

As stated previously, it is not my intention for this book to bring the reader into a seminary classroom and get bogged down in a lot of theology and hypotheses regarding the Christian Faith. Nevertheless, some hermeneutic examination regarding the Gospel accounts and their presentation is important at this point. So,

---

[22] Tom Holmén and Stanley Porter (ed.), *Handbook for the Study of the Historical Jesus* (Boston: Brill, 2011), 886.

without delving too far into the Gospel hypotheses that are available, let's examine a couple of possibilities.

First, and foremost, the four Gospels that the Holy Bible presents as the first four books of the New Testament are not the only Gospels written following the death of Christ. Most notably for many historians is the Gospel of Thomas. But, the Gospel of Mary, the Gospel of Peter, the Gospel of Philip, and the Gospel of James are also available, just to name a few. This becomes a significant point since all those authors are eyewitnesses of Jesus. Although the debate continues as to which "Mary" wrote the Gospel bearing her name, she was undoubtedly one that knew Christ directly. The others (Peter, Philip and James) were each a disciple of Jesus. As such, they each represent a "Primary Source" document for establishing the historicity of Jesus.

The second point that needs to be made is that the Gospels in the New Testament differ in their presentation. The first three are identified as the "Synoptic" (meaning "common, or similar view") Gospels. It is clear, even to the casual reader, that Matthew, Mark, and Luke are similar in their presentation and include most of the teaching (parabolic) ministry of Jesus. John, on the other hand, focused his writings towards the Gentiles and highlighted the divinity of Jesus as God.

The accepted conclusion by all biblical scholars is that the Gospel of John is distinctly different from the other three. That point is obvious from the very beginning of his Gospel. John completely omits any aspect of the birth narrative of Jesus, including the concept of the Virgin Birth. Instead, he begins immediately with a proclamation of Jesus being God. Note the opening lines of the Gospel of John. It states: "In the beginning was the Word, and the Word was with God, and the Word was God . . . And the Word became flesh and dwelt among us" (1:1, 14). We will come back to this passage and the idea of Jesus as God in Chapter 8, but the point to be made here is that an eye-witness to the life of Jesus (John, "the disciple whom Jesus loved") provided a testimony that the historicity of Jesus as a person who lived on this Earth is a reality that the reader can accept as authentic.

But, let's get back to the Synoptics, because they can provide an additional level of conviction regarding Jesus as a real person of history. As noted, the word "synoptic" means similar or common and the first three Gospels clearly represent that idea. The nature of their compilation is also a vital element in accepting the Gospels as a legitimate account of the life of Jesus. One of the interesting things about the Synoptics is that they are not only "synoptic" (i.e., similar), they are, in many respects, identical. It is true. Many of the accounts in the Synoptic Gospels, especially the parabolic material, provide an almost verbatim account from one Gospel to the next. An example is seen in Matthew 9:2-8, Mark 2:3-12, and Luke 5:18-26.

All three accounts reference Jesus' healing the paralytic and have clear similarities. Obviously, a few minor differences appear in the text; but even in this "similar" passage, some of the material is remarkably the same. For instance, look at a section from each of those passages.

> *Which is easier, to say, 'Your sins are forgiven,' or to say, 'Get up, and walk'? But so that you may know that the Son of Man has authority on earth to forgive sins"—then He said to the paralytic, "Get up, pick up your bed and go home."* (Matthew 9:5-6)

> *Which is easier, to say to the paralytic, 'Your sins are forgiven'; or to say, 'Get up, and pick up your pallet and walk'? But so that you may know that the Son of Man has*

> *authority on earth to forgive*
> *sins"—He said to the paralytic,*
> *"I say to you, get up, pick up*
> *your pallet and go home."* (Mark
> 2:9-11)

> *Which is easier, to say, 'Your*
> *sins have been forgiven you,' or*
> *to say, 'Get up and walk'? But,*
> *so that you may know that the*
> *Son of Man has authority on*
> *earth to forgive sins,"—He said*
> *to the paralytic—"I say to you,*
> *get up, and pick up your*
> *stretcher and go home."* (Luke
> 5:23-24)

While the entire passage on the healing of the paralytic is similar, this section in the three Gospels is nearly identical. On the other hand, some passages are, specifically, verbatim. A good example is Matthew 10:22, Mark 13:13, and Luke 21:17. In each of those passages, Jesus is recorded as stating to His Disciples "and you will be hated by all because of My name." While that is not a lengthy text, it is still a verbatim passage that is recorded directly in each of the Synoptic Gospels.

That being the case, one must now ask how that is possible. How can three different authors, who are writing the accounts from a different perspective and separated by several years, produce the exact same text? The answer to that question gets into the hypotheses about the origin of the Gospels and a discussion on how they were produced. Although I promised not to get into the weeds or make the discussion too laborious, it is an important concept to understand.

The obvious answer is that the authors copied their text from a single source. It is simply impossible for two people, using a loose oral tradition and without the intervention of God's inspiration (see Chapter 16), to produce the exact same passage. As an instructor for two college-level courses, I always get a little concerned when two students give identical answers to a subjective question. The immediate conclusion is that they copied the answer from each other or from a "cheat sheet" they both possessed. The consensus among the faculty is that it is impossible for two students to produce identical answers without one of them copying the information from the other, or at least from a common source.

Therefore, the question now becomes how did the Gospel writers get the original source document? To keep it simple, let's just examine two possible answers to that question. The first possibility is a general idea that an additional, lost to antiquity, document existed and all three of the Synoptic authors copied from it to produce their Gospels. This is called the "Q-document Hypothesis." "Q" is used for the German word "Quelle" meaning "source" and stipulates that a source document, primarily the teachings of Jesus, existed prior to the writing of any of the Synoptic Gospels. That is certainly plausible, given the number of Gospels written during the First Century. With the "Q" document readily available, the Synoptic authors simply copied the stories.

The second is referred to as the "Markan Hypothesis" and states that Mark was the first Synoptic Gospel written and that the other synoptic authors copied from that one source. Mark was the original text, with Matthew and Luke copying from his manuscript which resulted in all three Synoptic Gospels being verbatim at various points. Since the Q-document no longer exists, historians and scholars find themselves ascribing to the Markan Hypothesis as the most logical conclusion for the synoptic nature of the first three Gospels of the New Testament.

But we would do a disservice to the argument if we failed to include John's Gospel in the discussion. As noted earlier, John was writing to proclaim the person of Jesus as being God. Granted, that is a discussion for Chapter 8; however, John still had a need to proclaim Jesus as a real person. John was writing to Gentiles, not the Jewish community that understood the prophecy concerning the Messiah. Therefore, John's proclamation that the miracle-worker named Jesus was God incarnate would be a moot point if he could not convince the Gentile people that the man, Jesus, did live as a real person.

John succeeded in making that case in the fifth chapter of his Gospel. In that chapter, he recorded the words of Jesus speaking to the people. According to John, Jesus made four proclamations as a witness to His life: 1) "You have sent to John, and he has testified to the truth" (5:33); 2) "The works which the Father has given Me to accomplish—the very works that I do—testify about Me" (5:36); 3) "The Father who sent Me, He has testified of Me" (5:37); and 4) "You search the Scriptures because you think that in them you have eternal life; but it is these that testify about Me" (5:39).

The four "proofs" that Jesus gave that day included the witness of John the Baptist, the witness of the works that Jesus performed during his ministry, the testimony of God, and the Truth found within the Scriptures. Obviously, some will claim that the proof being offered by John involves some aspect of personal faith (i.e., faith in God and faith in an inspired Scripture that profess Truth). Regardless, the testimony from John represents a proclamation by an eyewitness to the reality of Jesus as a historic figure.

Now, the non-Christian community will cast stones at the above conclusions on the basis that it is all part of the Bible. As such, accepting the Gospel accounts as factual presentations of the truth regarding Jesus' life requires a personal faith in the Bible as being "inspired" by God. The argument does have a certain validity to it since Christians do believe the Bible to be inspired by God. However, the argument misses the more significant point that the Gospels do represent a first-hand, eyewitness account of Jesus' life as a historic figure. As stated, Christians do believe the biblical accounts in the Gospels are inspired. It is a matter of personal faith that the Believer might accept the Truth of Christ's teachings and accept the other elements of His life, to include the Virgin Birth, the Incarnation, His death and resurrection, etc. In other words, Christians do possess a faith in the Scriptures as inspired. However, apart from an inspiration issue, the Gospel of John is a historic document that professes a testimony from an eyewitness that a man named Jesus lived on the Earth. So, one could argue those elements from the perspective of faith but that does not negate the fact that the Gospel accounts were written by individuals who were personal associates of Jesus and wrote what they saw and experienced. The Gospels, those that became part of the Canon and the others, are quite clearly historical documents that give a legitimate testimony to the reality of the historic Jesus.

That is all very compelling data for concluding that Jesus was, indeed, a historic figure. However, the evidence does not stop there. Beyond the Gospel accounts, we can read from the Early Church historians that give us their unbiased perspective on the life of the one called Jesus of Nazareth. One of the main historians in question was a Roman-Jewish scholar named Flavius Josephus. Born after the death of Jesus, he was not an eyewitness to Jesus' life. He did, undoubtedly, know of Jesus and wrote extensively of His life and the conditions of the First Century Church and Christianity. The other point to note is that Josephus, the name by which he is most widely known, was not a supporter of Jesus, specifically, or even of Christianity, in general. He was, in fact, a Roman and a Jew. Those two points would not place him as one dedicated to the Christian cause nor possessing a commitment to validate the life of Jesus as a historical figure. Regardless, Josephus provided a wealth of information on both concepts and therefore becomes an accepted and legitimate source for the historicity of Jesus.

His main work in relationship to the question at hand was entitled *The Antiquities of the Jews* and was an attempt to chronicle the history of his race. In a

56

familiar, often cited, portion of one of the books in his *Antiquities*, Josephus noted,

> *Now, there was about this time Jesus, a wise man, if it be lawful to call him a man, for he was a doer of wonderful works; a teacher of such men as receive the truth with pleasure. He drew over to him both many of the Jews, and many of the Gentiles. He was [the] Christ; and when Pilate, at the suggestion of the principal men amongst us, had condemned him to the cross, those that loved him at the first did not forsake him; for he appeared to them alive again the third day, as the divine prophets had foretold these and ten thousand other wonderful things concerning him; and the tribe of Christians, so named from him, are not extinct at this day.* (Book XVIII, Chap. III, sec. 3)

It is clear in the passage that he claimed Jesus to be, not only a man who lived during the First Century, but also as the Christ, who died on a cross and was resurrected from the grave. That is more information than we need for the discussion before us in this chapter; but the point of the historicity of Jesus is made, nonetheless.

Of course, the other side of this argument is that Josephus was a Jew and a Roman. Living in the period that immediately followed the death of Jesus, he was aware of the growing "Church" associated with Christ's ministry. As a Roman and as a Jew, it seems logical that Josephus would want to stop the spread of Christianity, not give credence to its foundation. So, why did he write so much in support of Jesus as a historic figure?

He did it as a dedicated historian who must put their own prejudice aside in order to find and explain the facts. For Josephus, the obvious fact was that the person Jesus was a real man who lived in the First Century AD. As one might ask in reference to Josephus' *Antiquities*, "If Jesus wasn't a real person, why didn't Josephus say that?"

All that leads us to a point where we might consider a non-historic illustration for concluding Jesus as a true man of history. That illustration comes from an account of one man who tried to discredit the existence of Jesus as a reality. The man was Lee Strobel. In 1980, Strobel worked as an investigative journalist with the *Chicago Tribune*. As a non-believer, he set out on a quest to determine the historical reality of Jesus, with a personal bias that rejected Him as a real person. He interviewed numerous Christian scholars who acknowledged a belief in the historicity of Jesus. Strobel was a professional investigative reporter. His was on a determined effort to find the truth and not allow himself to be swayed by any personal feelings, emotions, and certainly not by simple faith. Strobel chronicled his experience in a book, *The Case for Christ*, where he proclaimed his conclusion that Jesus was a real person and that He lived a real life on this Earth. Of course, many will reject Strobel's experience as not constituting true historical research. After all, his primary source material came from people of faith, not the empirical data that true historians are trained to utilize. However, one cannot dismiss the data he collected and the conclusion that he reached: Jesus as a true, historic figure.

All things considered, a compelling case can be made for the reality that the man Jesus did live and His life is a historic fact. Although examining the Gospels requires a demonstration of faith on the part of the Believer, it is faith that accepts their presentation as being inspired by God and as a result can be accepted as expressing His Truth. On the other hand, even if you take away the inspiration of Scripture, the Gospels still stand as First Century resources for examining and understanding the life of Jesus. In that respect, they each represent a Primary Source document that concludes Jesus was a living figure of history. And, as noted, in addition to the Gospel accounts, we have Josephus' *Antiquities* to provide additional credibility to the claim that Jesus was, indeed, a man who lived during the First Century AD.

The summation of the material referenced above leads many scholars to acknowledge the historicity of Jesus. In an article for *National Geographic*, Kristen Romey quoted Eric Meyers, a professor at Duke University, as follows:

> I don't know any mainstream scholar who doubts the historicity of Jesus. The details have been debated for centuries, but no one who is serious doubts that he's a historical figure.[23]

However, that is simply the first hurdle that needs to be successfully crossed. As important as it may be, establishing Jesus as a real person still does not answer the question asked as the topic of this section: "Who Is Jesus?" The point here is that if Jesus is just a man, just a teacher, a rabbi, or miracle worker, then what difference does it make? Surely, the entire world would not alter its calendar into "BC" (Before Christ) and "AD" (Anno Domini, "Year of God") distinctions because of one man, even if it was a righteous man who was crucified for sedition. No, Jesus must be something more than a man. He must be something more than a great teacher or even a great miracle worker. He must be something else entirely!

The next three chapters will answer the question more fully. They will explore the biblical Truth that Jesus was the Christ, the Messiah . . . that He was God!

---

[23] Kristen Romey, "The Search for the Real Jesus," *National Geographic* (Dec 2017): 42.

CHAPTER 6

JESUS AS GOD'S SON

And Jesus uttered a loud cry and breathed His last. And the veil of the temple was torn in two from top to bottom. When the centurion, who was standing right in front of Him, saw the way He breathed His last, he said, "Truly this man was the Son of God!" (Mark 15:37-39)

Now that we established the historicity of Jesus as a man who lived during the First Century AD, let us move to what many would consider the "weightier matters of the faith." The point here, as expressed for the earlier points, is that without belief in the Truth proclaimed in the next three chapters, Christianity does not exist as a religion. Such is the nature of the "tenets of faith." They represent the very foundation on which the Christian Faith rests. Indeed, a major aspect of Christianity is based on these three concepts: that Jesus lived as God's Son, that He is the true Messiah, and that He is God. A person who rejects any part of those three points cannot, in a biblical sense, be considered a Christian.

That may sound rather harsh and judgmental. It may raise the ire of some readers with a "Who does the author think he is?" Or, more directly, "What makes him think he has all the right answers?" Of course, such angst is misguided, since many scholars hold the exact same view. James Carroll is a respected and award-winning author and scholar. In his book, *Christ Actually: The Son of God for the Secular Age*, he made the following statement:

> *If the faith in Jesus as Son of God . . . does not survive the critically minded, scientifically responsible, properly secular inquiry of the kind I am to undertake, however imperfectly, then Jesus will surely drop back into the crowd of history's heroes, ultimately to be forgotten.*"[24]

The fact that Jesus did not shrink back into history as a forgotten hero provides the proof for Carroll, even in his "critically minded and scientifically responsible" examination, that Jesus stands in history as the Son of God.

The reader should also note that the definitive statement regarding the requirement of accepting Jesus as the Son of God to be considered a Christian is not a personal proclamation, per se. Although I do stand behind the statement, I qualified it to be "in a biblical sense." So, the focus of any disagreement should be on the Bible, from which the Truth for these next three points comes, and not placed on the author, specifically. With that disclaimer in place, let us move into the first of the three concepts: Jesus as the "Son of God."

I suppose the first step in this process is to look at Jesus as the Son of God from a historic perspective. Granted, this endeavor can cause some difficulty. Dunn made that point as he examined First Century thought. He stated:

> *It is important to grasp at once that, in contrast to later Christian usage, "son of God" was not such an exclusive title or distinctive designation in the thinking of the time.*[25]

---

[24] James Carroll, *Christ Actually: The Son of God for the Secular Age* (New York: Viking, 2014), 12.
[25] Dunn, *Jesus Remembered*, 709.

He continued by noting that numerous civilizations adopted and applied the title in several different ways. He even made a point that in some circles of philosophy the popular culture considered Zeus the father of all mankind.[26]

Unfortunately, as a historian moves to examine the title within Judaism, the picture remains a little fuzzy. The point here is that the concept of "sons of God" within the Jewish Scriptures is a reference to the nation of Israel, the Jewish people, collectively. The following passages acknowledge that biblical truth.

> *Then you shall say to Pharaoh, "Thus says the Lord, 'Israel is My son, My firstborn. So, I said to you, Let My son go that he may serve Me.'"* (Exodus 4:22)

> *Do you thus repay the Lord, O foolish and unwise people? Is not He your Father who has bought you? He has made you and established you.* (Deuteronomy 32:6)

> *With weeping they will come, and by supplication I will lead them; I will make them walk by streams of waters, on a straight path in which they will not stumble; for I am a father to Israel, and Ephraim is My firstborn.* (Jeremiah 31:9)

> *When Israel was a youth I loved him, and out of Egypt I called My son.* (Hosea 11:1)

Each of those passages makes a significant case for the concept that the title "son of God" for the Jewish people referenced the nation of Israel as a whole. The Exodus passage identifies Israel as His (God's) son, His firstborn. Obviously, that is not a reference to Israel the person (i.e., Jacob) since he is long since deceased. The Deuteronomy verse is God speaking to the Hebrews who sinned against Him during

---

[26] Ibid.

the Exodus from Egypt and makes the declaration that God is their "Father" (i.e., they are His children/sons). Additionally, both Jeremiah and Hosea acknowledged God as the Father of Israel.

All of that seems a little problematic when one tries to align the title "Son of God" to Jesus; especially if we try to attach any specific Christian, vice a Jewish, connotation to it. If the title is a routine moniker attached to any number of recipients and is claimed universally by Judaism, it seems the whole argument in relationship to its application to Jesus seems to fall apart. However, perhaps we missed a salient point that may add more clarity and credibility to the importance of the title "Son of God" as it applies to Jesus and the Christian Faith.

The beginning of that process would be to establish the legitimate point of reference that recognized Jesus as the Son of God. One could accomplish that through an examination of the etymology of the term "son of" from the Hebrew tradition. Scholars widely accept that the phrase was a familiar one within the Jewish culture of Jesus' day. It is a fact that Jewish men were often identified by their given name then adding "son of" to differentiate that person from any other who might have the same name. Simon Peter is a perfect example of that reality. When Peter is brought to Jesus by his brother, Andrew, Jesus says to him "You are Simon, son of John" (John 1:42). Jesus identified Simon as the "son of" John. That statement proclaimed Simon to be the literal son of a man named John. In that respect, it could be argued that the "Son of God" title assigned to Jesus represented the same point—that just as Simon was the true and literal son of a man named John, Jesus was the true and literal Son of God (at least as considered conceived through the Holy Spirit of God).

However, the complete understanding of the etymology of the phrase often revealed a "likeness of" or "connection to" and not specifically, and certainly not always, as the literal son of someone. For instance, to stretch that point to an extreme, it would be conceivable to refer to a wealthy man as the "son of money," noting his connection and personal relationship to his money as a wealthy person. As one begins to apply that concept to Jesus, we develop a picture of Jesus having some "connection" to, or serving in the "likeness" of, God. While it would be easy to support the life of Jesus as being in the likeness of and having a connection to God, it is not quite the guiding Truth necessary to conclude that Jesus was, in fact, the Son of God.

Therefore, we need to move to a more reliable source for revealing that Truth—the Bible. Biblically, we can accomplish that goal through an examination of four presentations where the Bible acknowledges Jesus as the Son of God. The Bible presents the four parts as follows: the birth narrative; God's specific proclamations; Jesus' acknowledgment of God as His Father; and the testimonies of several biblical personalities. Since the question at hand relates to Jesus being the Son of God, it seems logical that one would start the examination of that Truth with the birth narrative. The narrative associated with Jesus' birth gives a clear and distinct picture of God being the Father of Jesus. Luke records an encounter between Mary and Gabriel, an angel and messenger from God. In the account of the meeting, Gabriel informs Mary that "the Holy Spirit will come upon you and the power of the Most High will overshadow you; and for that reason the holy Child shall be called the Son of God" (Luke 1:35). Notice, Gabriel proclaimed, as a messenger of God, that the child, Jesus, would be called the Son of God. Of course, the statement from Gabriel comes after Mary was perplexed because she was a virgin. Gabriel's statement confirmed that the conception of the child would be the result of the Holy Spirit and through the power of "the Most High" she would conceive. In other words, God, through his power, would be responsible for her conceiving of the child. In a very true sense, God would be the Father of the baby . . . the Father of Jesus.

The second point references God's specific proclamations of Jesus as His Son. During two separate events in Jesus' life, God declared that Jesus was His Son. The first was following His baptism when all three Synoptic Gospels record that a voice came out of Heaven. Matthew noted "the Spirit of God" descending on Jesus and a voice proclaimed, "This is my beloved Son, in whom I am well-pleased" (Matthew 3:17). Mark and Luke have slightly different statements, but both acknowledge that the voice came from heaven. It is not deniable that for all three of the Synoptic authors the voice came from heaven and, as such, from God. All three noted God stating that Jesus was, indeed, His Son. In other words, the Bible substantiates that Jesus is the Son of God through the revelation that God, Himself, proclaimed that point to be True.

And, as I noted earlier, that was not the only time that God made such a pronouncement. The second time was during what is called the Transfiguration of Christ. Again, this is an account that is supported by all three of the Synoptic authors (Matthew 17:1-8, Mark 9:2-8, Luke 9:28-36). The event took place on a mountain outside of Caesarea-Philippi in the northern Galilee area and witnessed by three of the disciples: Peter, James, and John. During the event, Jesus is transfigured and his face "shone like the sun." The disciples also saw Moses and Elijah standing with Jesus and communicating with Him. During that event, a cloud appears to cover them and a voice speaks from the midst of the cloud stating, "This is My beloved Son, with whom I am well-pleased; listen to Him!" This was not a casual event for the three disciples on the mountain that day. As they saw the images of the other two entities appear, they wanted to build a tabernacle for each of them: Moses, Elijah, and Jesus. They wanted to have a time of worship and praise to God for what they believed to be a truly spiritual event. In fact, it made such an impression on Peter that he made a reference to it in his second epistle (2 Peter 1:17).

For those present at Jesus' baptism and certainly for the three disciples on the mountain where Jesus was transfigured, God's proclamations presented a Truth that they could not deny. That Truth proclaimed that Jesus was the Son of God.

Although those first two points are convincing all by themselves, the last two are also vitally important to the presentation of the biblical Truth that Jesus lived on Earth as the Son of God. The first of these last two testimonies came from Jesus where He, personally, professed Himself to be the Son of God. Of course, the critics of the Christian Church will always try and make the case that Jesus never publicly professed Himself to be God, which they loosely tie to the Son of God title. We will address the "God" part in Chapter 8. At this point, we need to focus our attention on passages where Jesus proclaimed himself to be the Son of God, and not simply stating that God was His Father.

Although Jesus routinely referred to God as His Father, those passages do not represent the important theological point professed by Christians when they proclaim Jesus as the Son of God. The main problem being that all Christians profess God to be their Father. In that respect, most of the evidence we can glean from Jesus acknowledging His Sonship came at the end of his life, while he was on trial before the

Pharisees. According to the synoptic authors, when asked if He was the Son of God, he stated "I am" (Matthew 26:63-64, Mark 14:61-62, and Luke 22:70). Although it may be hard to pinpoint a specific "I am the Son of God" statement that Jesus made during His ministry, He did proclaim that Truth quite succinctly as He stood before the Pharisees facing His crucifixion.

In an interesting side-note, two of the Gospels record that the Jews understood that Jesus proclaimed Himself to be the Son of God. When Pilate tells the Jewish leadership that he finds no fault in Jesus, they answer him with "We have a law, and by that law He ought to die because He made Himself out to be the Son of God" (John 19:7). Obviously, the Jewish people (and especially the Pharisees) knew Jesus proclaimed Himself to be the Son of God. Additionally, Matthew recorded an interesting statement from the Pharisees witnessing the crucifixion. As Jesus hung on the Cross, they taunted Him with "He trusts in God; let God rescue Him now, if He delights in Him; for He said, 'I am the Son of God'" (Matthew 27:43). In both instances, the Pharisees knew that Jesus, by virtue of His own testimony, proclaimed that He was the Son of God.

The Gospel of John is even more definitive when it comes to reporting points where Jesus proclaimed Himself to be the Son of God. As noted earlier, John wrote his Gospel to the Gentiles to proclaim to them the reality that the man Jesus was, indeed, God. He personally acknowledged that Truth in His Gospel when he stated, "These (the words in the Gospel) have been written so that you may believe that Jesus is the Christ, the Son of God" (John 20:31). So, it is understandable that we would find passages that either specifically acknowledge that point, or at least imply that Truth within his writings. We can examine two such passages in the Gospel of John.

The first is found in John 10, with another one in John 11. The John 10 passage came at a time when the Pharisees questioned Jesus as to whether He was the Christ, the Messiah. They made that inquiry of Jesus by asking Him, "How long will You keep us in suspense? If You are the Christ, tell us plainly" (10:24). A debate ensued and Jesus confronted His accusers with "do you say of Him, whom the Father sanctified and sent into the world, 'You are blaspheming,' because I said, 'I am the Son of God'?" (10:36). Jesus acknowledged to the Pharisees that He was the Messiah, the Christ, God; and then substantiated the affirmative reply with the proclamation that he was the Son of God.

In the second passage, John 11, Jesus confronted the death of Lazarus and stated that "this sickness is not to end in death, but for the glory of God, so that the Son of God may be glorified by it" (11:4). Who is the "Son of God" that Jesus identified in this statement? Who knew that Lazarus would not remain dead; but be raised by the power of God? Who knew that the event would proclaim the "glory of God? The only plausible answer is Jesus! In that verse, in the previous passage noted above, and in passages throughout the Synoptic Gospels, Jesus clearly proclaimed Himself to be the Son of God. When He found Himself confronted by the Jews who wanted to know if He was the Son of God. His answer to them was "Yes, I am." Amen!

That brings us to the final reference point of biblical Truth regarding Jesus as the Son of God: the testimony of other people. Since a tenant of the Christian Faith is an acceptance of the Bible as the inspired Word of God, the Christian believes the testimony found within the Bible to be a revelation of the Truth. In that respect, several personal testimonies of Jesus as the Son of God are recorded in the Bible and accepted as Truth.

One of the first of those testimonies came from Nathaniel, a disciple of Jesus. Nathaniel is an interesting individual. He was a disciple of Jesus, being first introduced to Him by a friend, Philip, who was also a disciple. Nathaniel is not as well-known as some of the others. In fact, John is the only Gospel writer to mention Nathaniel as a disciple and his name only appears twice (John 1 and 21). That fact leads many to question the authenticity of a disciple named "Nathaniel." However, a close examination of the listing of the disciples in the Synoptics and John reveals that Bartholomew is not mentioned in John, just as Nathaniel is not mentioned in the Synoptics. Considering that point, biblical scholars believe that the two individuals were, in fact, the same person. Also, Bartholomew's name appears with Philip's in the Synoptic listing (Matthew 10:3, Mark 3:18, and Luke 6:14), just as the Gospel of John alludes to some relationship between Nathaniel and Philip (John 1:45). It seems to make since that the authors of the Gospels would link the two men together in the listing of the disciples. It also is conceivable that Jesus changed the name of Bartholomew (meaning "son of Tolmai") to Nathanael (meaning "gift of God") in order to indicate a new spiritual quality that Jesus recognized in Bartholomew, much like He did with Simon Peter (Matthew 16:17-18).

Regardless of Nathaniel's relative obscurity in the Gospel accounts, he does make a clear statement regarding Jesus as the Son of God. According to John, Philip introduced Nathaniel to Jesus and Nathaniel stated "Rabbi, You are the Son of God" (John 1:49). That is a definitive statement, but it is made even more significant when one reads the entire context of Philip's introduction of Nathaniel to Jesus (John 1:45-49). In that passage, Philip tells Nathaniel that they had found the Messiah and identified Him as "Jesus of Nazareth." Nathaniel was less than impressed and remarked "Can anything good come out of Nazareth?" In that one passage, Nathaniel scoffs at the premise that the Messiah could possibly come from Nazareth. Then, after only a moment with Jesus, he proclaimed Him as the Son of God! It represents an incredible testimony of faith and a personal revelation to Nathaniel from God.

A second testimony came from Martha, who was the sister of Mary. They lived in a city near Jerusalem called Bethany and were the sisters of Lazarus, the man Jesus raised from the dead (John 11:43-44). The death of Lazarus was not the only time that Jesu had any dealings with Mary and Martha. According to the Gospel of Luke (Luke 10:25-37), Martha welcomed Jesus into their home as He was traveling through the region. As Jesus began speaking, Mary sat at His feet while Martha was busily making the necessary preparations for the meal. Martha asked Jesus to tell her sister to help with the chores; but Jesus refused. He indicated to Martha that Mary's decision to listen to Him was a better choice. The point of His remarks seems to be that is was more important to listen to the teachings of Jesus and hear the words of Truth than to worry about the routine tasks of preparing food.

Although Lazarus is not mentioned by name in the Luke 10 account, it is unclear whether the account in John 11 came before or after Jesus' Luke 10 visit to Bethany. Regardless, the account sets the stage for another dramatic personal testimony that Jesus was the Son of God. The event, as noted, was the death of Lazarus. Jesus is told initially that Lazarus was ill but delayed His trip to Bethany. By the time he arrived in the city, Lazarus was dead. Martha and Jesus had a somewhat terse exchange of words concerning Jesus' delay and the fact that Lazarus died as a result. During the conversation, Jesus asked Martha if she believed in Him. She replied with, "Yes, Lord; I have believed that You are the Christ, the Son of God" (John 11:27)

I suppose one could argue that Martha was grief-stricken and would make any professional statement to try and save her brother, if possible. However, no clear indication exists in the passage that gives any credible evidence that Martha made the statement based on a belief that Jesus could (or would) raise her brother. In fact, when Jesus asked them to remove the stone from the entrance of the tomb, she complained that "there will be a stench, for he has been dead four days" (John 11:39). It was obvious that she considered her brother to be dead, that Jesus was not going to raise him from the dead; and yet, she still professed Him to be the Son of God.

It seems like that should be enough testimony to make an excellent case for understanding Jesus as the Son of God. Two legitimate and credible witnesses making a statement for Jesus being the true Son of God is significant all by themselves. It begs the question of how many testimonies are necessary before the Truth becomes obvious? If this was a court case, the evidence presented above would be sufficient. However, a good lawyer always looks for a knockout blow. A piece of evidence that is so incredible and one that is completely unexplainable that it makes the truth undeniable. In this case, Scripture presents two such "knockout" testimonies.

The testimonies come from two of Jesus' enemies. They come from entities that would not be willing to simply acknowledge a Truth that they would prefer to keep hidden, even if they thought or, as in the biblical passages, knew to be true. One of the testimonies came from a Roman officer, a sworn enemy of the Hebrew people and one commissioned to destroy (in this case, crucify) the leader of a growing messianic movement within the Hebrew populace. The other comes from demons, the followers of Satan and the spiritual enemies of God, after a failed coup in Heaven (see Revelation 12:7-12). These demons, being spiritual creatures and therefore having a direct relationship to the Truth, have a unique place in proclaiming Jesus as the True Son of God.

The first extra testimony noted in the previous paragraph is the proclamation by the unlikely source of a Roman Centurion. To understand this individual's place in the overall scheme of things, we need to understand the compilation of the Roman Army. The main battle group of the army was the Legion, a group of approximately six thousand soldiers. Each Legion consisted of ten "Cohorts" of roughly six hundred men each.

The typical Cohort had six "Centuria" units. Obviously, each Centuria (meaning "one hundred") had about one hundred combatants. A Centurion was an officer in the Roman army who served as the commander of the Centuria, the smallest of the Roman military units.

As we begin to examine the testimony from the Centurion, we need to understand that neither the Synoptics nor the Gospel of John cover the entirety of the Crucifixion. Trying to determine exactly what happened at the Cross can only be completely compiled by merging the four Gospel accounts together. For instance, what the Church notes as "The Seven Last Words of Christ" represent a compilation of all four Gospel accounts of the Crucifixion. In fact, only one of Jesus' seven "Last Words" appears in more than one Gospel. The "My God, My God, why have You forsaken me" saying is that statement and Matthew and Mark both recorded it (Matthew 27:46 and Mark 15:34). Much of the accounts and sayings that surround the event were only reported in a single Gospel.

That makes the confessional statement by the Centurion at the Cross even more legitimate, since both Matthew and Mark recorded what he said that day (see Matthew 27:54 and Mark 15:39). Add to that fact the point that a Centurion, a Roman officer, made the statement. Obviously, the significance of this soldier's confession cannot be understated. Although the Gospel writers did not provide any supporting statement, such as we find with Peter's confession that God revealed the Truth to him, (see Matthew 16:17), the Centurion does confess Jesus to be the Son of God. From the Gospel of Matthew, we can read the following:

> Now the centurion, and those who were with him keeping guard over Jesus, when they saw the earthquake and the things that were happening, became very frightened and said, "Truly this was the Son of God!" (Matthew 27:54)

The only difference between Matthew's account and the Markan passage is that Mark added the word "man" into the statement. For Mark, the Centurion stated, "Truly this man was the Son of God" (Mark 15:39). Either way, the confession of a hardened Roman officer, a commander of a combatant unit within the Roman occupational army, stands as a remarkable statement of faith. It acknowledged a pronouncement that by just looking at the source one must accept as a legitimate testimony of faith that "Truly this (Jesus) was the Son of God."

The second unlikely testimony came from the demons who also professed Jesus as the Son of God. In three separate (although somewhat connected) Synoptic passages, the demons professed Jesus to be the Son of God. Of the three Synoptics, the first appears in Matthew 8, when Jesus cast out the demons from the Gadarene. On that account, the demons recognized Jesus and asked Him, "What business do we have with each other, Son of God? Have You come here to torment us before the time?" (Matthew 8:29). Some critics will try and confuse the issue and the interpretation of this encounter by claiming the demon-possessed individual asked the question and not the demons themselves. However, that is an incorrect conclusion as the second half of the question referenced the torment that Jesus will bring to them at a prescribed time in the future. An apparent suggestion to the ultimate defeat of Satan and his demons when Christ returns at the end of time.

The next account comes from Luke's Gospel and represents a more generic reference, vice the specific account noted in the Matthew passage. In Luke 4:38-41 Jesus entered the home of Simon Peter's mother-in-law who was suffering with a fever. Jesus healed her and as evening came many sick arrived to receive healing for their specific afflictions. In the midst of that scene, Jesus cast out demons from those possessed. Luke noted the proclamation of the demons referencing the Truth of Jesus with the following: "Demons also were coming out of many, shouting, 'You are the Son of God!'" (Luke 4:41). Another clear testimony from an element opposed to the Truth that Jesus was, indeed, the Son of God.

The final Synoptic passage that acknowledges a demon's profession that Jesus was the Son of God, comes from Mark 3. In that chapter, Mark simply noted that "whenever the unclean spirits saw Him, they would fall down before Him and shout, 'You are the Son of God!'" (Mark 3:11). Some scholars will argue a connection between this passage and the Lukan account. Both took place in the area of Galilee, but Simon's mother-in-law lived north of the specific Sea of Galilee area where the Mark account took place. It seems Mark provided an entirely separate account of demons professing Jesus as the Son of God.

In fact, all three accounts depict a distinctly different reference point for demons professing Jesus' Sonship. The Matthew event took place in "the country of the Gadarenes." Gadara was an area around the southeast border of the Sea of

Galilee. As such, it was quite a distance from the location of Peter's mother-in-law in northern Galilee. Both of those first two events proclaim a different account than the one found in Mark, since Mark indicated the events took place around the Sea of Galilee. That is a legitimate point, as Mark noted that Jesus went down to the seashore as an obvious reference to the Sea of Galilee. In that geographic location, the proclamation made by the demons in the Markan account was not associated with either of the other two Synoptic events.

Unfortunately, it is possible for the casual reader to miss the significance represented in some of these testimonies. Looking at the Centurion and the demons, these were not disciples of Jesus who were enamored with His miracles and parables and began to see Him as something other than just a rabbi. Of course, Nathaniel made his professional testimony at his very first meeting with Jesus! And, they were not from a grieving sister who wanted to reach out to whatever hope was available to her. These final testimonies were quite the contrary. The Centurion and the demons represented devout and committed enemies of Jesus. They were the ones who dedicated themselves to hiding the Truth of who he was from the public. The Centurion wanted to preserve the viability of the Roman Empire and devoted himself as a military officer to squelching anything that might jeopardize that cause. By the same token, the demons certainly had no desire to acknowledge the fact that the Messiah, the Christ, the "Son of God" was now in the world. Both of those entities would be more inclined to lie to keep the Truth intact, rather than to acknowledge that the "Son of God" was a reality. As such, they represent a legitimate testimony to the Truth that Jesus was the Son of God.

Of course, the cynics do not give up so easily. They raise a final objection to the concept that Jesus was the Son of God, represented something supernatural or that He was, by virtue of the moniker, something other than just a man. Their argument centers on the biblical references that all Believers are "sons" of God. They point to numerous passages that clearly delineate the application of the title "Son of God" to all who believe in Jesus as the Christ (see John 1:12, Romans 8:16, Galatians 3:26, and I John 3:1). And, when Jesus preached His Sermon on the Mount, He began with what we call the Beatitudes. One of the Beatitudes stated, ""Blessed are the peacemakers, for they shall be called sons of God" (Matthew 5:9).

This treatise was not meant to be a complete hermeneutical examination of the Bible and therefore cannot adequately address each of the passages in question. In that light, perhaps it would suffice to make a few general statements as a means of addressing the critics. As noted earlier, the term "Son of" can mean "in the likeness of" and applied in different contexts. Even in the case of Jesus, the term can refer to His being "in the likeness of God." In that respect, it seems logical to accept that when the term is applied to Believers the idea would be that Believers are to live "in the likeness of" God. In other words, the Believer should act in a godliness through their relationship with the rest of the world.

That certainly makes sense. And, one can find numerous biblical passages acknowledging that point (see Psalm 1:1-3, Romans 12:1-2, II Corinthians 5:17, and I Timothy 6:11-12). Again, although it is impossible to examination all the passages noted in the previous paragraphs, let us look at one of them—the Beatitude. Some scholars believe that Jesus preached the Beatitudes as a Plan of Salvation—the necessary steps to becoming a Christian. That interpretation does make some sense, both in the content and context of the Beatitudes (Matthew 5:3-12). The content is a well-defined, step-by-step, development of a person's spiritual maturity. The Beatitudes begin with "Blessed are the poor in spirit," as identifying one who has no spiritual quality, one who is spiritually bankrupt. In that capacity, it identifies a person who lacks any concept of a spiritual relationship with God. The Beatitudes that follow identify steps of spiritual maturity. The second one is for the person who "mourns," perhaps as a realization of their spiritual separation from God. Then comes those who are "meek," to represent humbling oneself before God to acknowledge their sin and seek reconciliation. The next one is "hunger and thirst for righteousness" and could relate to Paul's criticism of the Corinthians for remaining "babes in Christ (see I Corinthians 3:1-2). Then, they move through other dynamics of the Christian Faith such as being "merciful," "pure in heart," and living as "peacemakers." In that respect, the Believer does become a "Son of" God, functioning in the likeness of God (i.e., exemplifying mercy, being pure in heart and as a peacemaker). Finally, the Believer becomes persecuted for the Faith, which represents a true spiritual maturity for the Christian.

However, let's not lose the focus here. The argument provided above supports the term "Son of God" as applied to the Believer. It does not concede that point to be the only application for Jesus. Jesus was called "Son of God" because He did live in the likeness of God, serving according to God's Will and direction for His life. He was also called the "Son of God" because He was the True "Son of God" (i.e., "the Christ"). The Bible provides that testimony from four distinct and reliable sources: the birth narrative, with a proclamation by a messenger of God; God's pronouncement directly to the people present at Christ's baptism and Transfiguration; Jesus' own personal statements; and the personal testimonies from his friends, as well as His enemies.

The point is that Jesus as the "Son of God" is something entirely different than his Believers being called "Sons of God." As such, it is a presentation of Him as the Christ, as God. This is a great introduction to the next chapter, Jesus as the Christ!

CHAPTER 7

JESUS AS THE CHRIST (MESSIAH)

He said to them, "But who do you say that I am?" Simon Peter answered, "You are the Christ, the Son of the living God." And Jesus said to him, "Blessed are you, Simon Barjona, because flesh and blood did not reveal this to you, but My Father who is in heaven. (Matthew 16:15-17)

The understanding of Jesus as the Son of God creates the perfect lead-in to the discussion of Jesus as the Christ, the Messiah, the Savior. In fact, a person could successfully argue that the two titles for Jesus are synonymous, at least from the perspective of Christianity. The point being that Jesus as the Son of God is representative of Jesus as the Christ, but the two terms are also distinctly different.

That difference is a matter of personal faith and it is what separates Christianity from Judaism. Jesus was born a Jew and lived as a Jew. He, undoubtedly, observed the Jewish Law and holidays. Although he had more than a few arguments with the Pharisees about the Law, Jesus proclaimed that He did not come to abolish the law, but to fulfill it (Matthew 5:17). In addition, His last act with His disciples was a Seder meal to

77

observe the Passover. It is conceivable that a devout Jew could accept the teachings of Jesus as being those from an inspired rabbi who brought a viable interpretation of the Law that the Pharisees (and, perhaps, time) misrepresented. The separation between Judaism and Christianity, as it pertains to Jesus, is found in the faith Christians profess in Jesus as the Christ, the Messiah. It is the nature of the Christology that removed the "Jewishness" of Jesus and established Him as the Messiah who came to save the people from their Sin.

Carroll made that point quite clear when he noted that through the years Jews and Christians forgot that Jesus "had ever been fully Jewish."[27] In other words, the idea seems to be that faith in Jesus went through a type of transformation as Christianity spread and became a major entity in the world. Acts 11 states that the followers of Jesus were first called "Christians" in Antioch (Acts 11:26). A label placed on them as followers of Christ. The label was not "Jesusians," identifying those who followed the teachings of the recent, miracle-working Jewish rabbi that Roman soldiers crucified a few years earlier. The First Century Christians accepted Jesus as the Christ and followed Him faithfully as the Messiah.

Paul made that statement, himself, when he visited the synagogue in Thessalonica. He spoke to the Jews who were there and told them plainly, "This Jesus whom I am proclaiming to you is the Christ" (Acts 17:3). Numerous other testimonies are found in the New Testament. Some of those are like the ones discussed earlier that acknowledged Jesus as the Son of God. For instance, the demons in the Luke 4 account proclaimed Jesus to be the Son of God. In response to that statement, Jesus rebukes them and Luke recorded that "He would not allow them to speak, because they knew Him to be the Christ" (Luke 4:41). Similarly, the passage in John noted earlier that depicts the discourse between Jesus and Martha after Lazarus' death included her statement that Jesus was the Son of God but also included a confession by Martha that he was the Christ (John 11:27). We can also note that all three Synoptic authors recorded Peter's confession when he stated that Jesus was "the Christ" (Matthew 16:16, Mark 8:29, and Luke 9:20). And, in John 1:41 we find Andrew speaking to his brother, Simon Peter, about his initial encounter with Jesus.

[27] Carroll, *Christ Actually*, 145.

He told him plainly, "'We have found the Messiah' (which means Christ)."

Beyond the obvious references that the people (and even the demons) recognized Jesus as the Christ, we need to look more specifically at the New Testament record. Jesus is often, if not routinely, identified as "Jesus Christ" or "Christ Jesus" in the Gospels and literally throughout the entirety of the New Testament. The point here goes back to John's editorial of the Andrew comment that they had found the Messiah. John added the parenthetical explanation, "which means Christ," to clarify Andrew's point. For John, as well as for the New Testament Christians and the whole of Christianity, the two titles were synonymous. The title of "Christ" and that of "Messiah" were inseparable. Being able to accept that conclusion as a Truth rests on two important supporting dynamics. The first comes from an examination of the Greek word "christos." The second concept is the point that the term "Christ" is not a name, but a title.

A full presentation of the origin and usage of the title "Christ" as a reference to who Jesus was takes some effort. First, we need to understand that the original language of the New Testament was Greek, while the original language of the Old Testament was Hebrew. Although Jesus probably spoke in a form of Hebrew called Aramaic, His words appear in the New Testament in Greek. To determine exactly what Jesus said in His original tongue, scholars use an ancient book called the Septuagint, which is a Greek translation of the Hebrew Scriptures. Finding the Greek word in the Septuagint and comparing it to the translated word in Hebrew gives scholars a clearer picture of what Jesus said and what His words meant.

Looking in the Septuagint, the Hebrew word associated with the Greek word "christos" is "masiah." The word literally means "anointed" but in English it is "Messiah." Therefore, the word "christos" in Greek is a translation from a Hebrew word for Messiah. Trying to translate the Greek into English presented another problem. Scholars translating the ancient manuscripts could not find a comparable word in English for "christos." The solution was a transliteration of the letters. In other words, scholars simply took the letters from the Greek and transposed them into English. The Greek "chi" became "ch," the "rho" was the "r," the "iota" became an "i," etc. The result was that the Greek "christos" became "Christ" in English. The bottom line is clear: Jesus as the

Christ is, according to the Old Testament, the Anointed One, the Chosen One, the Messiah.

That leads us to the next piece of the puzzle. Since the title "Christ" came from the Old Testament word for "Messiah" and the Christian's acceptance of Jesus as the Messiah, it then becomes an imperative to understand Jesus as the fulfillment of that Old Testament concept. For the Christian, that means an examination of the Old Testament prophecies concerning the coming of the Messiah.

Scholars vary on exactly how many prophecies exist that specifically reference the coming of the Messiah. For instance, the often-quoted prophecy that we typically hear during the Christmas season came from Isaiah's words to King Ahaz when he said, "Therefore, the Lord Himself will give you a sign: Behold, a virgin will be with child and bear a son, and she will call His name Immanuel" (Isaiah 7:14). The debate over the passage rests on the fact that Isaiah directed those words to the king regarding a war with the Assyrians. It was a prophecy for Ahaz's benefit to confirm to him that the Assyrians would not attack Judah. It was not, or so it seems by the context, meant to reference a birth that would take place several hundred years in the future. On the other hand, Matthew made a reference to the Isaiah prophecy in the proclamation of Jesus' birth as a fulfillment of Isaiah 7:14 by stating,

> *Now all this took place to fulfill what was spoken by the Lord through the prophet: "Behold, the virgin shall be with child and shall bear a Son, and they shall call His name Immanuel."* (Matthew 1:22-23)

Such is the dilemma, at least for some scholars, to accurately identify the context of a specific prophecy. That problem makes a direct link trying to relate them to Jesus' birth, life, and ministry as being the fulfillment of prophecies concerning the Messiah.

Even with that challenge in mind, most scholars acknowledge a collection of 40-50 Messianic prophecies in the Old Testament that point to Jesus as the Anointed One. Some relate to the birth of Jesus, while others highlight His ministry and even His death. A close examination of a few of those should be enough to establish the pertinent point for this discussion. Three of the most quoted and well-known of the prophecies (apart from Isaiah 7:14, as discussed above) are: Isaiah 40:3-5, Isaiah 53:4-5, and Zechariah 9:9). Of course, prophecy is one thing, but the fulfillment of that prophecy in Jesus is another. In respect to that point, this discussion provides a corresponding "fulfillment" text.

The first passage is from Isaiah 40 and reads:

> *A voice is calling, "Clear the way for the Lord in the wilderness; Make smooth in the desert a highway for our God. Let every valley be lifted up and every mountain and hill be made low; and let the rough ground become a plain, and the rugged terrain a broad valley; then the glory of the Lord will be revealed and all flesh will see it together."*
> (Isaiah 40:3-5)

Isaiah spoke of one that would come before the Messiah to proclaim His entrance into the world. The two points in that prophecy indicate that 1) God, the Messiah, is coming; and 2) Someone will acknowledge His arrival.

The key fulfillment here is the presence of John the Baptist. John not only pronounced the coming of Christ and directed the people to prepare themselves for His arrival (per the Isaiah prophecy), he used the exact rendering from Isaiah to make his proclamation. The Gospel of John presents an inquiry a few Levites brought to John the Baptist as to who he was. He replied, "I am a voice of one crying in the wilderness, 'Make straight the way of the Lord,' as Isaiah the prophet said" (John 1:23). The Baptist clearly believed himself to be "the voice crying in the wilderness," the fulfillment of Isaiah's prophecy. Now, match that with his declaration when he saw Jesus for the first time: "Behold, the Lamb of God who takes away the sin of the world" (John 1:29). John the Baptist fulfilled the prophecy of Isaiah 40 on both points noted by the prophet.

The second prophecy also comes from Isaiah and states:

> *Surely our griefs He Himself bore and our sorrows He carried; yet we*

> *ourselves esteemed Him stricken,*
> *smitten of God and afflicted. But*
> *He was pierced through for our*
> *transgressions. He was crushed*
> *for our iniquities. The chastening*
> *for our well-being fell upon Him*
> *and by His scourging we are*
> *healed.* (Isaiah 53:4-5)

The reference here is to establish the requirement that the Messiah would suffer and die for the sins of the world. The theology of this passage referencing the sacrifice of Jesus on the Cross is a discussion point for Section III. Here the focus is on the fact that Isaiah provided a prophecy that the Messiah would suffer "for our iniquities" and that through His suffering "we are healed."

The fulfillment of that prophecy rests on two points. The first is the scriptural support for Jesus' suffering and death. Exact passages are not necessary, as everyone can easily find accounts for the Passion of Christ in all four of the Gospels. The second point becomes strictly a matter of faith. Christians accept that Jesus died on a Cross and see the act as fulfillment of the prophecy that He bear "our sorrows" and "our iniquities." In other words, part of the context for the Christian's sense of fulfillment for this prophecy is a matter, at least on this side of Heaven, of faith.

Finally, a little less familiar passage and one often used on Palm Sunday comes from the prophet Zechariah. In that book we can read the following:

> *Rejoice greatly, O daughter of Zion!*
> *Shout in triumph, O daughter of*
> *Jerusalem! Behold, your king is*
> *coming to you. He is just and*
> *endowed with salvation, humble and*
> *mounted on a donkey, even on a colt,*
> *the foal of a donkey.* (Zechariah 9:9)

Now, the cynic will argue that this prophecy could apply to any "king" coming to rescue his people. After all, Zechariah wrote this book to the people of Judah following the Fall of Jerusalem to the Babylonians. After the fall of their capitol, the Jewish people found themselves in Babylon as an

exiled nation.   It was early Sixth Century BC and it made
sense that the people would look for "the Anointed One" who
would rescue them from exile and return them to their Promised
Land.

The key for this fulfillment also has two points.   First,
Zechariah identified the One coming as being "endowed with
Salvation."   The idea of being "endowed" is that it is
something bequeathed, granted, or bestowed upon someone.   It
is something the individual has by mandate or as part of their
personal character.   In other words, the king that is coming
will bring, as part of His very nature, salvation.   That can
only mean that this king is the Savior, the Messiah.   The
second point is that He comes to them seated on a donkey.
What image comes to mind when you read the passages in the
Gospel accounts that relate the Triumphant Entry of Jesus into
the city of Jerusalem?   It is the image Christians proclaim
and celebrate as the day Jesus entered Jerusalem on the first
"Palm Sunday" riding on a donkey.

As noted, these are only three of nearly fifty prophecies
that some scholars ascribe to being clearly proclaimed by
early prophets and fulfilled in the life of Jesus.   They
represent a reality for the Christian that substantiates the
man Jesus as the Christ, the Messiah.   Certainly, we accept
the translation, transliteration, and fulfillment of biblical
prophecy as compelling arguments.   However, they do not
present the entirety of the references to the witnesses that
acknowledged Jesus as the Messiah.   In his Gospel, John
provided four witness that proclaim Jesus as the Anointed One,
the Messiah, the Christ.   They are: the witness of John; the
witness of Jesus' works; the witness of the Father; and the
witness of the Scriptures.

We noted these testimonies as supporting documentation for
an earlier discussion.   However, there was no direct exegesis
of the passages.   Therefore, to address adequately the
important topic of Jesus as the Messiah and the testimony that
supports that position, a more in-depth examination of the
passages is in order.

The first of the four related to John the Baptist.   John
recorded that Jesus spoke of the Baptist when He stated the
following:

> *"There is another who testifies of Me*
> *and I know that the testimony which*
> *He gives about Me is true.   You have*

> sent to John, and he has testified to
> the truth." (5:32-33)

The immediate question is "Which John is mentioned here?" Is it John the Baptist or the author of the Gospel? Although John was sometimes cryptic in identifying himself in his Gospel, often using the "disciple whom Jesus loved" identifier, the consensus here is that the John in this passage is John the Baptist. That is obvious as one considers the "you sent to John" comment to the reference of the encounter John the Baptist had with the priests and Levites recorded earlier in John.

The second point is the witness of the works that Jesus performed during His ministry.

> But the testimony which I have is
> greater than the testimony of John;
> for the works which the Father has
> given Me to accomplish—the very works
> that I do—testify about Me, that the
> Father has sent Me. (5:36)

This passage has one minor problem. Jesus made this statement at a very early stage in His ministry. In other words, He did not have a great many "works" to display as "proof" of who He was. Of course, we understand that John was not concerned with a strict chronological rendering of Jesus' life. Still, John recorded some significant events in the first five chapters of his Gospel. Some of those were turning the water into wine at the marriage feast in Cana (John 2:1-11), cleansing the temple (John 2:13-22), the discussion with the Samaritan woman at the well (John 4:7-26), healing of the official's son (John 4:43-54), and healing at the Bethesda pool on the Sabbath (John 5:1-18). The healing on the Sabbath and cleansing of the temple certainly established His authority and gave a witness that He was more than just a rabbi, prophet, or teacher.

The third "witness" provided an appeal to the central element of the Christian's faith, God! Jesus said,

> And the Father who sent Me, He has
> testified of Me. You have neither
> heard His voice at any time nor seen
> His form. You do not have His word

abiding in you, for you do not
believe Him whom He sent. (5:37-38)

At first, Jesus made a basic statement. He told the people "The Father has testified of Me." Jesus probably thought that should settle it. The people of faith in the Father should accept the testimony of the Father, as provided by Him following the baptism of Jesus (see Matthew 3:17, Mark 1:11, Luke 3:22). What else needed to be said? But Jesus continued by indicating the problem. The people cannot accept the Truth about Jesus being the Messiah because the Truth is not in them. As the passage stated, "You do not have His word abiding in you." The testimony was True. The testimony came from God. According to Jesus, many of the hearers were not "of God" and, as a result, they missed the Truth.

Finally, Jesus proclaimed the witness of the Scriptures. The passage states,

> *You search the Scriptures because you*
> *think that in them you have eternal*
> *life; it is these that testify about*
> *Me; and you are unwilling to come to*
> *Me so that you may have life.* (5:39-
> 40)

It is important to grasp the meaning of this passage so that we can understand its relationship to the topic at hand. During His ministry Jesus criticized the Pharisees for their attempt to adhere to the Law (the Scriptures) as a concept that it was the path to a righteousness before God. Jesus stated in His Sermon on the Mount that our righteousness must surpass that of the Pharisees (Matthew 5:20). Paul reiterated that Truth when he stated,

> *By the works of the Law no flesh will*
> *be justified in His sight; for*
> *through the Law comes the knowledge*
> *of sin. But now apart from the Law*
> *the righteousness of God has been*
> *manifested.* (Romans 3:20-21)

He noted that no justification can come from the Law, since the Law simply exposes knowledge of our sins. He further noted that the True righteousness was manifested by God, apart

85

from the Law. So, "the Word became flesh and dwelt among us" (John 1:14). The Scriptures do not bring eternal life, but they do proclaim the Truth that Jesus was the Anointed One, the Messiah, the Christ. As such, the Scriptures do proclaim the truth regarding the availability of salvation.

The final piece of this puzzle does not lend itself to a type of empirical analysis. It is not a point that offers a plethora of primary source documentation. It is also one that is susceptible to credible criticism. The final point, as it is routinely, is individual faith. Perhaps scholars could argue about some items of empirical data, but not vey conclusively. Primary sources do reflect on it, talk about it, illustrate it; but neither can they disprove it. Of course, the cynics and critics are almost too numerous to mention. Unfortunately, no matter how skilled one is in the Apologetics for the Faith, the end of the debate with the cynics is often an acknowledgement that faith is the only answer available. On the other hand, it is a perfect piece to the puzzle that many cannot begin to see or ever truly appreciate.

The picture in the puzzle is finally in focus. Piece number one: The personal testimonies of Jesus' followers (Peter, Martha, Andrew, et.al.). Piece number two: The evidence found in the Septuagint which interpreted the Hebrew word for Messiah as "christos." Piece number three: The English word "Christ" came from the transliteration of the Greek word "christos." Piece number four: Jesus as the fulfillment of the Old Testament prophecy for the coming of the Messiah. Piece number five: The four witnesses ascribed by the Gospel of John as being John the Baptist; the works and ministry of Jesus; God, the Father; and the Scriptures. Piece number 6: Our personal Faith. All those pieces come together to acknowledge that Jesus was "the Christ," the Messiah.

The concluding point here is the understanding that the term "Christ" represents a title, not a name. Unfortunately, the common usage of "Jesus Christ" lends itself to the belief that Jesus is "Jesus Christ" like another person is "John Doe." It is as if Mary Christ and Joseph Christ had a son and named Him Jesus Christ. Obviously, that was not the case and per the previous points, the term "Christ" identifies Jesus as the Messiah. Perhaps an easier way to highlight this Truth is to understand the phrase with some proper punctuation and the use of an "implied 'the'" into the name of Jesus Christ. Inserting those two elements establishes the phrase, "Jesus, the Christ" or from the other perspective, "the Christ, Jesus." Both additions are completely legitimate. The most ancient Greek manuscripts available did not use punctuation marks of any kind. Where to insert the punctuation within a text is a major task of biblical literary scholars. Additionally, the insertion of an "implied 'the'" often allowed for a better understanding of the Greek text. So, with that perspective, we begin to acheive a clear picture of Jesus as not simply Jesus Christ, but as Jesus, the Christ (which means Messiah).

With that Truth intact, we can move to the definitive point of Jesus' nature: Jesus as God!

CHAPTER 8

JESUS AS GOD

In the beginning was the Word, and the Word was with God, and the Word was God. And the Word became flesh and dwelt among us and we saw His glory, glory as of the only begotten from the Father, full of grace and truth. (John 1:1, 14)

A reoccurring theme since the first chapter is that each new point becomes a new foundational basis for the whole of the Christian Faith. While it might seem a little laborious, it is indeed true. As noted earlier, if God is not God, the very foundation of Christianity crumbles. Along that same line, if we cannot acknowledge Jesus as a true figure in history then faith in Him becomes a moot issue and the basis of the Christian Faith ceases to exist. Obviously, accepting the historicity of Jesus represents an imperative for the Christian Faith. Beyond that Truth, the last two chapters examined the idea of Jesus as the "Son of God" and as "Christ," the Messiah. The final point to be made regarding the nature of Jesus is to note that the person identified as Jesus was not simply a man, but was the incarnation of God, Himself.

89

In that respect, one of the great criticisms against the Christian Faith is the position that no proof exists for the incarnation of Jesus, that proclaims Jesus as truly God. Trying to answer that criticism presents a significant problem for most Christians. After all, what kind of "proof" can one offer for Jesus being God? It is not the kind of thing that primary source documents can adequately support and the lack of what many consider to be acceptable empirical evidence simply compounds the problem even more.

Of course, that does not concede a complete lack of any empirical evidence. The Bible records several accounts of Jesus performing miracles such as walking on the water, healing the sick, and raising the dead. Each miracle demonstrated a power over Nature, over God's Creation, as a possible interpretation of Jesus being God. However, the critics fault that "proof" on two fronts. First, many do not accept the Bible as proof of anything, much less Jesus being God. They also are quick to point out that Peter walked on water (at least momentarily, Matt 14) and performed many other miracles. He healed a lame beggar, (Acts 3) and raised Dorcas from the dead (Acts 9). Certainly, the cynics will proclaim, those feats do not make Peter God. As such, they continue, one cannot use the same demonstration of those events in Jesus' life as an acknowledgment of Him being God.

Obviously, Peter was not God incarnate; but that is not the "empirical evidence" on which Christians should argue Jesus as the incarnation of God. The proof for that aspect of our faith comes from a clearly reliable source: The proclamation from God's Word.

Since Christians accept the Bible as the inspired Word of God, Christians accept on faith what the Bible proclaims as being True. That being said, the Bible makes a very clear statement regarding Jesus as God. The passage is the one stated at the beginning of this chapter (John 1:1, 14). In those verses, John identified Jesus as "the Word" and concluded that "the Word was God." After giving an accounting of "the Word" and Its characteristics, John then proclaimed, "and the Word became flesh and dwelt among us." Although John did not specifically identify Jesus as "the Word," what other conclusion is possible? What other manifestation of the Word into flesh can one proclaim? Jesus is the obvious "Word made flesh" as John dedicated his entire Gospel account to substantiating that Truth.

Jesus As God

Although John's proclamation represents a clear Truth for the Christian, and even in the face of mounting evidence, the naysayers maintain one final argument to try and negate Christianity's claim of Jesus as God. Their argument is that Jesus never, personally, acknowledged it. Certainly, they argue, if Jesus was the incarnation of the One, True and Living God, the Creator of the universe, it seems more than logical that He would take every opportunity to make His case for that Truth. The fact, in their estimation, that He did not make that claim is clear evidence to the contrary, that He was not God. They contend that he lived as a rabbi that God used to accomplish some divine purpose for those who willingly believe in Him and accept His teachings.

Their criticism, although misguided, is often successful in leading people to question their faith or to reject entirely this specific premise of Christianity. At the center of their success is the reality that many Christians are not biblical scholars nor are they trained in the discipline of Christian Apologetics (from the Greek, apologia, meaning "to speak in defense"). Unfortunately, some pastors and other Christian ministry leaders fall into the same trap set by those seeking to raise doubts regarding the Christian Faith. Therefore, it is important for all Christians to be armed with the full Truth regarding Jesus, the Christ, as God incarnate.

To start the discussion, let's clear the playing field of a basic misconception. The truth is, both Scriptural accounts and Jesus clearly profess Him to be God. That is not simply one man's personal faith making a bold profession, but the Truth that is found in biblical passages and what one Gospel author recorded as Jesus' own words.

Several passages allude to Jesus expressing the Truth that He was, indeed, God. During the questioning by the Pharisees and Pilate, Jesus was asked if He was the Christ, the Son of God and/or the King of the Jews. Jesus answered each of them in the affirmative (see Matthew 26:64; Mark 14:62, 15:2; Luke 23:3; and John 18:33-37). Beyond those passages, John recorded two accounts of Jesus answering the Pharisees' questions where He provided definitive statements that referenced His being God. In John 8, the main emphasis of the discussion centered on Abraham. Jesus noted His relationship to Abraham and then said, "Truly, truly, I say to you, before Abraham was born, I am" (8:58). The statement may not make good grammatical sense; but when read in the light of Exodus 3:14, it makes perfect theological sense. In Exodus 3, Moses is at the burning bush as God is commissioning him to go and lead the Hebrews out of their bondage in Egypt. Concerned about whether the people might question who sent him, Moses inquired as to God's name. In response to the question, God replied with the simple statement, "I am." Couple God's identification of Himself with Jesus' grammatically awkward identification to the Pharisees and we can see the theological reality: Jesus was not simply relating Himself to God and the idea of being one with God; but was expressing Himself to be God, specifically. In that passage, Jesus proclaimed His name to be the exact same name God provided to Moses.

That seems to be a definitive passage; but if it is not clear enough for you, in John 10 the Pharisees were again questioning Jesus about who He was and about His ministry. During the confrontation, they asked Jesus directly, "If you are the Christ, tell us plainly" (John 10:24). In response to that request, Jesus stated succinctly, "I and the Father are one" (John 10:30). However, even with that clear statement, the critics will continue to question the Truth that Jesus was God. They will try and deflect the interpretation of that statement with the idea that Jesus meant that He and God were "one in purpose" or "one in ministry." Their point being that Jesus was not saying He was God, but only that He was one with God as They try to accomplish God's purpose for the people.

Unfortunately for the critics, the context of the passage does not support their conclusion. As the Pharisees heard Jesus make the statement that He and the Father are one, John recorded that the Pharisees wanted to stone Him. When Jesus asked them why they were going to stone him, they replied that "You, being a man, make yourself out to be God" (John 10:33). No matter how one tries to parse this into something else, the Pharisees heard and responded to the statement from Jesus that, to them, was clear: This man, Jesus, claimed to be God!

In addition to that encounter, John recorded two similar incidents in his Gospel. In John 5:18 we can read,

> *"For this reason, therefore, the Jews were seeking all the more to kill Him, because He not only was breaking the Sabbath, but also was calling God His own Father, making Himself equal with God."*

Again, the Pharisees sought to kill Jesus because they believed that He proclaimed Himself to be God. They had the same response in the earlier "I am" passage (John 8). After Jesus' "I am" statement regarding Abraham, the passage indicates that "they picked up stones to throw at Him" (8:59). As with the previous incident, the Pharisees considered Jesus as a blasphemer. They clearly understood the "I am" statement as being a link to God as "Yahweh" and Jesus' proclamation that He was Him, that He was God.

All of that is interesting and compelling; but another dilemma for the Christian's acceptance of Jesus as God comes from the theological position that Jesus was totally God and totally Human at the same time. In a real and true sense, the incarnation directs that God became a Man and lived on Earth. While maintaining His full divinity, He lived a fully human life. As stated in earlier chapters, Jesus was a historic figure. So, the only possible conclusion becomes that Jesus was human; that He was a physical being who lived on this Earth. However, if we accept Jesus as God, then the picture changes a little. Now we see a historic figure that is not simply human but represents a "visitation" of a heavenly being. As such, Jesus experienced a normal life as a man including all its pains and struggles (see John 11:35, where Jesus wept in grief over the death of Lazarus). At the same time, He lived His life as the incarnation of God.

With that concept intact, the critics return to make a proclamation that while some may believe that Jesus was God, He could not be both God and man at the same time. They use both a logical, as well as a philosophical, argument to make their point. First, they posit that it is illogical for something to be 100% of two separate substances. The logic is clear: It only takes 100% of anything to represent a whole and 100% of two elements is 200%, which is impossible and thus illogical. The philosophical argument rests with a concession on the part of the critics. They may grant the Believer the faith-based position that Jesus was God, but they quickly counter with "being God discredits His humanity given that Jesus, as God, would have the power and authority to thwart any problem or difficulty that He might suffer as a physical man in this earthly life."[28]

---

[28] This argument is a staple of unbelievers presented in apologetic debates experienced through my nearly half-century of ordained ministry.

Both of those criticisms hold no basis in, well, logic! The fact that God is omnipotent means he can do anything necessary to accomplish His direct Will. Does that mean that God can function in a way the seams totally "illogical" to the world? Absolutely! As the Creator of everything, God controls the laws of nature. Does that mean that he can alter the dynamics of the physical realm in order to achieve His prescribed purpose in the world? Undoubtedly! So, the Christian Faith proclaims Jesus as both God and man; and God, being omnipotent, possesses the ability to accomplish that reality.

Now, to substantiate the human quality of Jesus, we need to return to the consideration of Jesus as a man. Several biblical accounts can help us appreciate the human struggles He endured during his relatively short life on Earth. We should see these struggles as an indication of Jesus' human characteristics and accept them as a testimony that He remained sinless throughout His life and willing to become the sacrificial "lamb without blemish" for the sins of the world (I Peter 1:19).

The first event that depicts the struggle Jesus endured as a man would be the temptations Satan offered Him while He was in the Wilderness following His baptism. Matthew recorded the account and excerpts from the passage read as follows:

> *After He had fasted forty days and forty nights, He then became hungry. And the tempter came and said to Him, "If You are the Son of God, command that these stones become bread." Then the devil took Him into the holy city and had Him stand on the pinnacle of the temple, and said to Him, "If You are the Son of God, throw Yourself down; for it is written, 'He will command His angels concerning You'; and 'On their hands they will bear You up, So that You will not strike Your foot against a stone.'" Again, the devil took Him to a very high mountain and showed Him all the kingdoms of the world and their glory; and he said to Him, "All these things I will give You, if You fall down and worship me." Then the devil*

*left Him; and behold, angels came and
began to minister to Him.* (Matthew
4:2-3, 5-6, 8-9, 11)

From a theology of sin standpoint, churches often place all sins into one of three specific categories: The Lust of the Flesh, the Lust of the Eyes, and the Pride of Life. It is conceivable, as we analyze the concept of sin, to consider the point that all sin falls into one of the three categories. In fact, when Eve experienced the first recorded temptation in the Garden of Eden, Satan provided all three to her. As a result of his temptation, Eve noticed that "the tree was good for food, and that it was a delight to the eyes, and that the tree was to be desired to make one wise" (Genesis 3:6). Eve experienced the temptation of the Lust of the Flesh (the tree was good for food), the Lust of the Eyes (the fruit was a delight to the eyes), and the Pride of Life (eating of the fruit would make her wise).

In the same way, Satan confronted Jesus with the same three types of sins. Following His baptism and prior to officially beginning His ministry, Jesus was led into the Wilderness where He fasted for forty days and forty nights. At the end of that experience, Satan came to Jesus and tempted Him with the option of sating his hunger by turning stones into bread (the Lust of the Flesh). Being unsuccessful, Satan offered Him the chance to make a big splash by throwing Himself off the pinnacle of the temple and allowing the angels to save Him (the Pride of Life). Unable to break Jesus, Satan had one more card up his sleeve, the Lust of the Eyes. He would offer Jesus everything in the world. Jesus would have everything he could see and be "King of the World" if He would simply worship Satan. Through the entire barrage that Satan threw at Him, Jesus remained steadfast and did not sin against God.

Beyond the direct confrontation with Satan, other human dynamics played a part in Jesus' earthly life. Jesus, as any man would, experienced the human emotions of anger, frustration, disappointment, and a desire to follow His own will, vice God's direction. It is conceivable that in each of those situations, Jesus faced the possibility to sin; but remained a "lamb without blemish" throughout His entire human manifestation in this world.

A closer look at a couple of the events in Jesus' life will help to clarify His humanity, while securing the sinless nature that allowed Him to be the "propitiation for our sins"

(I John 2:2). The first element would be a demonstration of His anger. The reality that Jesus expressed anger at the Pharisees does create something of a dilemma, since many people, Christian or not, might consider being angry as a sin and we acknowledged above that Jesus did not sin. The support for this position comes from the Sermon on the Mount when Jesus said, "Whoever says to his brother 'You fool' shall be guilty enough to go into the fiery Hell" (Matthew 5:22). Most latch onto that point as being a proclamation against an expression of anger towards others. Space does not allow for a full exegesis of that verse; but, thankfully, Paul clarified the situation when he expressed a directive to the Ephesians by writing, "Be angry but do not sin" (4:26). For Paul, and the Truth he expressed, the sin is not being angry. The sin is how the individual allows the anger to adversely direct their life.

Indeed, Jesus expressed an anger towards the Pharisees, but not in a sinful or evil manner. The situation was the event identified as the "Cleansing of the Temple." The account appears in each of the four Gospels (Matthew 21:12-17; Mark 11:15-19; Luke 19:45-48; and John 2:13-16). Taking the account in John, we can read:

> *The Passover of the Jews was near, and Jesus went up to Jerusalem. And He found in the temple those who were selling oxen and sheep and doves, and the money changers seated at their tables. And He made a scourge of cords, and drove them all out of the temple, with the sheep and the oxen; and He poured out the coins of the money changers and overturned their tables; and to those who were selling the doves He said, "Take these things away; stop making My Father's house a place of business."*

At face value, we can accept the fact that Jesus was angry. Look at some of the evidence. He made "a scourge of cords." A dictionary definition of "scourge" is "a means of inflicting harsh punishment or affliction."[29] The passage also states

---

[29] Webster II: New Riverside Dictionary, s.v. "scourge."

that He "drove them all out of the temple," "poured out the coins of the money changers," and "overturned their tables." No one can make a legitimate case that, according to the passage, Jesus was not angry.

However, righteous anger, even Jesus' anger that manifested itself in a demonstrative manner, is not sinful. God, Himself, expressed an anger towards the Hebrew people at Mount Sinai. In Exodus 32, God revealed the evil activities of the Hebrews as they waited for Moses to come down from the mountain. In that chapter God states, "Now then let Me alone, that My anger may burn against them and that I may destroy them" (Exodus 32:10). God possessed an anger towards the people as a result of their sinful activity. Certainly, we do not ascribe any sin to God for that anger. Nor, in a similar manner, should we assign any sin to Jesus for the anger he expressed during the cleansing of the temple.

Another human characteristic experienced by Jesus would be the frustration He suffered because of His disciples. Numerous accounts throughout Jesus' ministry indicate a disappointment with the disciples' lack of faith or understanding of the Truth He proclaimed to them. The Gospels highlight those incidents. Specifically, Matthew recorded several accounts where Jesus expressed His frustration. Listed below are four of those accounts.

> But if God so clothes the grass of the field, which is alive today and tomorrow is thrown into the furnace, will He not much more clothe you? You of little faith! (6:30)

> Why are you afraid, you men of little faith? (8:26)

> "You of little faith, why did you doubt?" (14:31)

> You men of little faith, why do you discuss among yourselves that you have no bread? Do you not yet understand or remember the five loaves of the five thousand, and how many baskets full you picked up? (16:8-9)

97

An additional account is found in John's Gospel which states, "Have I been so long with you, and yet you have not come to know Me, Philip?" (14:9). Each of the passages expresses a feeling of frustration and disappointment. They represent another clear aspect of Christ's humanity.

The final characteristic that revealed the human side of Jesus was a momentary desire to follow His own path, rather than submit to the direction God had for His life. The illustration comes from Jesus' prayer in the Garden of Gethsemane. Each of the Synoptic Gospels record a similar prayer from Jesus as He faced His crucifixion. They provide the following statements of Jesus: "My Father, if it is possible, let this cup pass from Me" (Matthew 26:39); "Abba! Father! All things are possible for You; remove this cup from Me" (Mark 14:36); and "Father, if You are willing, remove this cup from Me" (Luke 22:42). The passages acknowledge the desire of Jesus, however momentary that desire was, to avoid the Cross. In fact, we can further appreciate the anxiety Jesus felt as He realized His crucifixion was imminent when we read in Luke's account that "His sweat became like drops of blood, falling down upon the ground" (22:44).

Jesus possessed a specific human quality while on Earth. He became angry, experienced frustrations and disappointments, and sought a way to follow a path that was contrary to God's direct Will for His life. All of us can relate to those struggles, because we face them every day. The significant point for the Christian is that Jesus faced each of those issues and did not yield to the temptation to sin. Although the Bible clearly states that "all have sinned and fall short of the glory of God" (Romans 3:23), Jesus did not sin. That fact establishes two important points. First, that Jesus was God. The only possible answer for Jesus remaining sinless is His divinity. Which leads to the second point that by being sinless (being God) He became the perfect and only possible sacrifice for Man's sin.

Jesus was the physical manifestation of God; yet, He possessed a human quality that suffered through this physical life. As God, He remained sinless and willingly sacrificed Himself on the Cross for our sins. And with that Truth, we move to the next question: "Did Jesus Die on the Cross for My Sins?"

Question #3

Did Jesus Die for My Sins?

CHAPTER 9

MAN AS A SINNER

Now we know that whatever the Law says, it speaks to those who are under the Law, so that every mouth may be closed and all the world may become accountable to God; because by the works of the Law no flesh will be justified in His sight; for through the Law comes the knowledge of sin. But now apart from the Law the righteousness of God has been manifested, being witnessed by the Law and the Prophets, even the righteousness of God through faith in Jesus Christ for all those who believe; for all have sinned and fall short of the glory of God. (Romans 3:19-23)

As important as the question presented in this section is to the Christian Faith, it is impossible to begin an appropriate answer to the question without first establishing that Man is a sinner. That statement may seem to express a universally held Truth within the Christian Faith, since the question proclaims "my sins" as part of the issue being addressed. However, clear distinctions exist between the way the Eastern and Western arms of Christianity view the idea of Man's sinfulness.

101

The West, especially the fundamentalist denominations, view sin as a type of crime. The understanding is that Man's sin is an activity of defiance against the Will and/or Law of God. Indeed, as *The Baptist Faith and Message* of the Southern Baptist Convention states, "By his free choice man sinned against God and brought sin into the human race (and) through the temptation of Satan man transgressed the command of God."[30] The emphasis rests on the action of Man to commit an act which is identified as a sin. Man was free to make a choice and through the work of Satan in the world decided to commit a "crime" against God's commandment.

Moving to the East, one finds the concept of sin as being a condition of Man. The focus of sinful activity is not so much on the action of Man as much as it is the nature of the being of Man who commits sin. In Eastern Orthodoxy, for instance, one understands sin as being a "disease" that afflicts Man, causing him to sin. The Greek Orthodox Archdiocese of America website states in the "Fall and Regeneration of Man" section of their Statement of Faith that Man "fell into sin, through arrogance and disobedience."[31] Notice the concept that Man "fell into sin" vice committed an act of sin. It seems to express the idea that Man was predisposed to sin. In other words, he had a chronic disease for which there was no cure.

The distinction may be moot to the overall point that Man is a sinner. Both East and West acknowledge the variance, regardless how slight it might be. And, that is the beauty of this presentation. Even though we may note some differences between denominations on the theological application of the tenets of faith, they remain intact tenets for all of Christianity. That point is clearly delineated here in the concept of Man as a sinner. Two conspicuously different denominations in the practice of faith (the Orthodox Church even maintains a distinctly different church calendar) still agree on the same exact tenet of faith: that Man *is* a sinner.

Looking into the biblical account, Paul proclaimed in his letter to the Romans (highlighted as the introductory passage for this chapter) "all have sinned and fall short of the glory of God." Therefore, before we can address the question about the Cross directly, let's first establish the Truth that Man is a sinner. As such, we are each in need of forgiveness for

---

[30] *Baptist Faith and Message of the Southern Baptist Convention*, 2000 (Section III, Man).
[31] Taken from http://goarch.org/the-fundamental-teachings-of-the-eastern-orthodox-church 7 Dec 2018.

our sins and thus require some type of payment (or cure) for that sin. Hence the third question: "Did Jesus Die for My Sins?"

Unfortunately, the discussion of sin has two main pitfalls. First, regardless of the biblical evidence that acknowledges the presence of sin in all of us, it is not a subject that many people want to try to understand. For the most part, they wish to be removed from the debate, whether from friends, colleagues, or even from the pulpit. As one scholar noted simply, "Our culture avoids the issue of sin."[32] The other problem is the difficulty one has in trying to tackle the subject from a theological point of view. The concept is that different, and sometimes conflicting, positions regarding the theology of sin are prevalent within the structure of the Christian Faith.

Perhaps the main difference is what separates the different denominations on this point is the theological presentation of the concept of sin as presented in each person. The three basic presentations within the Christian denominations are "original," "ancestral," and "actual" sin. An in-depth explanation of each concept is not necessary to grasp the fundamental differences between various Christian Churches; however, perhaps a basic overview of the theology of sin is important to the discussion. The idea of original sin, derived by Augustine, is the belief that the "original sin" of Adam is passed on from generation to generation. Western Churches identified as traditionally liturgical accept that theological perspective and include it in their practice of faith. As a result, they baptize infants as a rite of the church that "covers" that original sin. Eastern Churches will also practice an infant baptism, but it serves as a covering for the consequences of that sin and begins the process of spiritual healing. On the other hand, non-liturgical churches believe in a personal "accountability" for sin, in that a Believer is only accountable for their own "actual" sins. Those churches traditionally practice a "believer's baptism" (typically by immersion) for those who confess their sinfulness and profess faith in Jesus as the Christ.

As stated in the Introduction, this book was not designed as an examination of the Practices of Faith between the various denominations of Christianity. Therefore, instead of entering

---

[32] Stuart C. Smith, *Dead to Sin, Alive to God: Discover the Power of Reckoning to Set You Free in Christ* (Eugene: Resource Publications, 2016), 1.

a lengthy theological debate on the pros and cons of "original" or "actual" sin, let it suffice to say that all Christian denominations acknowledge the absolute sinfulness of Man. That is the most pressing point for the current discussion and one upon which all Christian denominations can agree: that Man is a sinner and will commit sins.

With that hill successfully scaled, let's move on to an understanding of the concept of that sin. Perhaps the best avenue of approach is to examine the original wording for sin to see if we can gain an insight as to the meaning and application of Man being a sinner. Looking into the Old Testament, the Hebrew word often translated as "sin" is *chata*. The basic interpretation of "chata" is "miss," as in missing a target or a goal. In Exodus 20:20, we can read Moses' words to the people. He tells them: "God has come in order to test you, and in order that the fear of Him may remain with you, so that you may not sin (miss the target)." In Judges 20:16, the same Hebrew word is used to describe the accuracy of those with a slingshot, that they "could sling a stone at a hair and not miss."

In the New Testament, the Greek word translated as sin is *hamartia*. In a similar fashion with the Hebrew word chata, the Greek equivalent for sin references the idea of missing the mark. Paul used the word when he indicated in his letter to the Romans that "all have sinned (missed the mark) and fall short of the glory of God" (3:23). In both the Old and New Testaments, the translation of the original languages provides the concept that sin relates to "missing the target, the mark, the goal." Although scholars will continue to debate the theological concept of sin, let it suffice to say that for our need in this presentation sin is defined as a "missing of the mark." That is to say that it is a missing of God's expectation and direction for our life.

Now that we settled the debate between Original Sin versus Actual Sin and referenced the specific biblical application of sin per the ancient Hebrew and Greek languages, let us return to the Garden of Eden and to the familiar passage that highlights the commission of the first sin. Per the pronouncement provided in the Bible, the Garden offered Adam and Eve every possible need. In Genesis 1:29 we read, "Behold, I have given you every plant yielding seed that is on the surface of the earth, and every tree that has fruit yielding seed; it shall be food for you." Clearly, God provided in the Garden enough food for Adam and Eve to survive, indefinitely. They certainly had no need to seek food from any other place (i.e., the "forbidden tree," see Genesis 2:16-17).

As an interesting sidebar to their sin, one could argue that Adam and Eve had every possible food available on the earth, even fruit like, if not the same as, the fruit from the forbidden tree. What was the logical point in eating from that particular tree? In fact, to compound the discussion even further, did Adam and Eve have the ability not to sin? In other words, within the perfect world of the Garden of Eden, was the idea of disobeying God even remotely considered as a possibility? Two noted scholars teamed up to write a book that raised that exact question. In fact, their conclusion stated succinctly that "before the Fall the human being was capable of not sinning, but that capacity was totally lost thereafter."[33]

That whole argument makes a rational understanding of their committing a sin almost impossible to comprehend. If, indeed, the same fruit was available to them in the Garden and they were empowered with the knowledge of the perfect world in which they lived, what rationale would they have to eat from the Forbidden Tree? Of course, the concept of Man's sinful nature includes the presence of Satan that tempted Eve to commit her sin. In her defense Satan attacked her with all three weapons that he had in his arsenal: The Lust of the Eyes, the Lust of the Flesh, and the Pride of Life. Although Satan tempted Eve from all three directions, we all experience various temptations from at least one, if not all, of what Satan has at his disposal to throw at us. Adding to Satan's array of temptations he can use to lead us to sin, he seems to have the ability to tempt each of us at our weakest link. The result is that all of us yield to temptations and commit sins. We simply cannot escape the fact that we are, by nature or affliction, sinners.

The Bible is perfectly clear about that Truth. From the Old Testament, Solomon stated in the book of Ecclesiastes the following words: "Indeed, there is not a righteous man on earth who continually does good and who never sins" (7:20). It was a similar perspective that Solomon's father, David, recorded in the Book of Psalm. There, David wrote in Psalm 14:3 and 53:3 that "There is no one who does good, not even

---

[33] Lucinda Mosher and David Marshall, *Sin, Forgiveness, and Reconciliation: Christian and Muslim Perspectives* (Washington, DC: Georgetown University Press, 2016), 4.

one." For David, Solomon, and other Old testament writers, no Man is righteous as a result of his own efforts. No one is able to live a completely sin-free life.

In the New Testament, we can read similar words from Paul as he expressed that Truth in his letter to the Romans. In that letter he noted: "There is none righteous, not even one" (3:10). For Paul, no one can achieve justification by keeping the Law, since it is impossible for anyone to keep the entirety of the Law. Man simply does not have the ability to keep himself from disobedience, from sin.

Other passages make that Truth abundantly clear. They are:

> *For I know my transgressions, and my sin is ever before me. Against you, you alone, have I sinned and done what is evil in your sight,*
> *so that you are justified in your sentence and blameless when you pass judgment. Indeed, I was born guilty, a sinner when my mother conceived me.* (Psalm 51:3-5)

> *Therefore, just as through one man sin entered into the world, and death through sin, and so death spread to all men, because all sinned.* (Romans 5:12)

> *For since death came through a human being, the resurrection of the dead has also come through a human being; for as all die in Adam, so all will be made alive in Christ.* (I Corinthians 15:21-22)

Each passage gives a clear presentation of the fact that Man is a sinner and has been such from the beginning. That is true as it relates to the beginning of time with Adam and the First Corinthians passage. It is also true from Psalm 51 as it pertains to the beginning of each Man's own, personal, life as it relates to being born with a sinful affliction. It all recalls the illustration of a preacher asking his congregation a trick question: "Who in this church believes they can live without committing a sin?" Of course, if a person raises a

106

hand then they are, by that act, committing a sin since their belief that they do not commit sins is a "false witness."

As we delve more into this idea of Man as a sinner, one of the most dramatic passages in the Bible regarding our difficulty to avoid sinful behavior comes from Paul when he stated the following:

> *We know that the Law is spiritual, but I am of flesh, sold into bondage to sin. For what I am doing, I do not understand; for I am not practicing what I would like to do, but I am doing the very thing I hate.* (Romans 7:14-15).

Paul, the great apostle of Christ and a man of committed faith, recognized that his sinful nature would always yield to the temptations that he faced every day of his life. He even confessed to Timothy that he was the worst sinner of all (I Timothy 3:15). Now, it should be noted that many scholars believe that Paul was speaking rhetorically and not speaking specifically about himself. They point to the fact that his words of Romans 7 do not match his personal presentation found in the surrounding chapters. Smith is one of those scholars who stated emphatically that the proclamation Paul made in Romans 7 was "an example of Paul's sophisticated rhetoric" and that he is actually speaking figuratively of Man and not about himself.[34] Regardless, it represents a fascinating passage.

In that same light, Paul made a related comment in his letter to the Galatians when he noted that righteousness did not come from observance of the Law. The reason is because of the following two points: 1) We cannot keep the whole law, as Paul noted in respect to his own sinfulness; and 2) That in Paul's words, "if righteousness comes through the Law, then Christ died needlessly" (2:21). In other words, if Man had the ability to live in a perfect faith, empowered completely in God's strength, and thereby achieve a personal righteousness through his own effort by observing the Law, then what would be the need for Christ to be crucified? The fact that Christ came to earth in order to sacrifice Himself on the Cross for our sins is an indication that we do not

---

[34] Smith, *Dead to Sin*, 51.

possess the ability to save ourselves—that we are all, Paul concluded, sinners.

Obviously, those passages represent powerful realities for all Believers. They are even more powerful when compared with other Pauline statements that seem to express an ability of faith that can empower a Believer to resist Satan's temptations. One of those is found in Paul's first letter to the Corinthians. There he stated profoundly the following:

> *No temptation has overtaken you but such as is common to man; and God is faithful, who will not allow you to be tempted beyond what you are able, but with the temptation will provide the way of escape also, so that you will be able to endure it.* (10:13)

An initial reaction to that passage might be "Did I read that right" or "Let me check another translation." Even with a second reading, we come face-to-face with an interesting concept regarding our sins—that God provides us a "way of escape" and that we, with His indwelling power, are "able to endure it." Applying a literal interpretation of the text, a Christian could conclude that we are able to live a sin-free life. However, if we are all sinners, if we all have a sin nature that will lead us, unwaveringly, to yield to temptation and commit sins, then how is that possible? Before we begin an attempt to answer that question, let me throw another monkey wrench into the whole scheme of things by adding the belief that the Bible is the inspired Word of God, making that passage a literal, God-given Truth for His people. So, how do we synchronize the two, apparently opposing, presentations noted above?

The answer, obviously, comes from a correct interpretation of the passage as it pertains to the question at hand—Man as a sinner and our relationship with God as a result of our sins. As many scholars deduce, Paul's proclamation was not a declaration that Man will never be tested or that he can live a sin free life. Instead, Paul's position is that the people of faith accept God as omnipotent and as such He possesses a power that is greater than any temptation. Applying that concept to our life, the conclusion would be that within a Christian's perfectly developed spiritual life (i.e., empowered with God's strength) we each would be able to resist whatever temptation Satan might throw in our path.[35] A position supported in the literature that several different Christian denominations developed, supplied, and taught through the years.

It is a generally accepted truth that Man does not have the ability within his present earthly existence to live a "perfectly spiritual" life. Two points in Scripture acknowledge that truth. The first is the concept of faith, or, in this perspective, a lack of it. Jesus was often critical of the disciples' faith and numerous times inquired about their lack of faith and their doubts (see Matthew 8:26, 13:31-32, 14:31; Mark 4:30-32; Luke 13:18-19; et. al.). As a result of Jesus' bodily resurrection, the disciples began to have and demonstrate an extraordinary faith. Of course, without the empowerment of God that comes with a personal faith, it is impossible for Man to have the ability to resist Satan. We may have a saving faith; but may not have a "perfect" faith, a faith that would demonstrate a perfectly empowered life capable of resisting temptation.

The Corinthians passage is just one example. Another comes from his letter to the Ephesians. In that letter, Paul provides an illustration of the Armor of God which is designed to protect the people of faith against the evil influences of the world and, specifically, of Satan. Paul writes the following to the Ephesians:

> Be strong in the Lord and in the strength of His might. 11 Put on the full armor of God, so that you will be able to stand firm against the schemes of the devil. 12 For our struggle is not against [e]flesh and blood, but against the rulers, against the powers, against the world forces of this darkness, against the spiritual forces of wickedness in the heavenly places. 13 Therefore, take up the full armor of God, so that you will be able to resist in the evil day, and having done everything, to stand firm. Stand firm therefore,

---

[35] C. K. Barrett, *A Commentary on the First Epistle to the Corinthians* (New York: Harper and Row, 1968), 229.

> *having girded your loins with truth,*
> *and having put on the breastplate of*
> *righteousness, and having shod your*
> *feet with the preparation of the*
> *gospel of peace; in addition to all,*
> *taking up the shield of faith with*
> *which you will be able to extinguish*
> *all the flaming arrows of the evil*
> *one. And take the helmet of*
> *salvation, and the sword of the*
> *Spirit, which is the word of God.*
> (Ephesians 6:10-17)

At face value, the passage presents a clear Truth. According to the passage, equipped with our personal "shield of faith" we can resist the temptations (the "flaming darts") of Satan. However, with the acknowledged Truth from other passages of the New Testament, something seems a little amiss. The answer is that Paul's "Armor of God" illustration again presents a picture of a life demonstrating a perfect faith. Within that capacity, Man possesses a shield of perfect faith which, by the power of that faith, can resist Satan's temptations.

Unfortunately, while some Christians may exemplify stronger faith than others and resist sins that adversely affect so many, no Man can manifest a perfect faith in every situation and possess the power to resist all temptations in his life. The earlier exegesis makes that point abundantly clear. However, if one wanted to boil this down to one definitive word that clearly identifies why Man cannot successfully employ the "shield of faith" to resist Satan, that word would be "pride." Theodore Wedel, a noted preacher and lecturer in the Episcopal Church, concluded that Man's pride is the enemy of his faith and is the answer as to why Man cannot effectively handle the shield of faith.[36]

In addition to the proclamation from the pulpit, scholars within the world of academia champion that same point. One noted: "We are ruled by sin, by principalities and powers, by Satan, by the law and death."[37] For Thompson, who served as a

---

[36] Theodore O. Wedel, "Exposition on Ephesians" *The Interpreter's Bible, Vol. 10* (New York: Abingdon Press, 1953), 742.

[37] William M. Thompson, *The Jesus Debate: A Survey and Synthesis* (New York: Paulist Press, 1985), 294.

professor of Systematic Theology at Duquesne University, Man possesses a sinful nature and within this world he is powerless to resist the temptations of Satan. Even in the East, where sin is not considered to be the "nature" of Man but the consequence of the Fall, the bottom line is the same: Man is separated from God as a result of his sinfulness (nature or consequence) and is powerless to alter that reality.

Others echo that sentiment. In Thomas Nagel's interesting book, *A Brief Inquiry into the Meaning of Sin and Faith*, Robert Adams provided an essay that acknowledged differences in conceptual points but concluded with "the inevitability of sin" for all of Mankind.[38] Mosher and Marshall, in their *Sin, Forgiveness, and Reconciliation* book, made the point that sin is "irreplaceable for the diagnosis of the human condition and its self-interpretation."[39] And finally, Andrew Finstuen, dean of the Honors College at Boise State University, compiled an argument that compared the theological perspective of three giants of the Christian faith: Reinhold Niebuhr, Paul Tillich, and Billy Graham. He noted that all three disagreed on some conceptual ideas of Man as sinner, especially as it related to the idea of original sin. On the other hand, they all agreed that Man lives in a sinful state of being.

Even within the psychology of religion arena, we find similar conclusions. As noted earlier, Wayne Oates was a renowned scholar on the psychology of religion. He proclaimed a similar truth when he noted that "Man soon learns that he is not only finite as an individual; he also lives among a people of finitude, a people of sinfulness."[40] Oates goes on to express the psychological perspective of Man's sinfulness and the reality that we must all accept and acknowledge that we are, indeed, sinners. Oates also added an interesting twist to the truth of Man's sinfulness when he stated that "sin is the antithesis of faith."[41] In other words, the act of sin for the Believer is a commitment to act in a manner that he understands is contrary to his professed faith in God as the director for his life.

---

[38] Robert Adams, The Theological Ethics of Young Rawls and Its Background" in *A Brief Inquiry into the Meaning of Sin and Faith* by Thomas Nagel (Cambridge: Harvard University Press, 2009), 79.

[39] Mosher, *Sin, Forgiveness, and Reconciliation*, 23.

[40] Oates, *The Psychology of Religion*, 51.

[41] Ibid, 205.

Perhaps that is enough evidence to support Man's proclivity to sin, but one additional resource adds a personal perspective to the mix. Matthew Stanford, the CEO for the Hope and Healing Center & Institute in Houston, authored the book, *The Biology of Sin: Grace, Hope and Healing for Those Who Feel Trapped*. In that book he asked his readers if anyone believed that they could live free from sin. He continued by asking, "Are you up for the challenge?" and concluded that "Adam and Eve were unsuccessful. The Pharisees tried and failed. And I am also confident that neither you nor I would be successful."[42]

The point is obvious: Man became a sinner. Whether as a result of his nature, or the consequence of his Fall, it is proclaimed as a Truth in the Bible and professed as a fact by theologians and psychologists. The Bible does make some interesting statements regarding Man's ability to live sin free through a demonstration of a perfect faith. However, it also makes it clear that since we live in this physical world, we do not possess the power within ourselves to resist Satan's influence at every step throughout our life. The very presence of Christ and his crucifixion (whether from the East or West perspective) is evidence that we cannot accomplish a perfection God requires for our eternal salvation.

That being the case, we move to the next chapter that addresses the result of that Truth: Man's separation from God.

---

[42] Matthew Stanford, *The Biology of Sin: Grace, Hope and Healing for Those Who Feel Trapped* (Westmont, IL: Intervarsity Press, 2012), 9.

CHAPTER 10

MAN'S SEPARATION FROM GOD

Therefore, the Lord God sent him out from the garden of Eden, to cultivate the ground from which he was taken. So He drove the man out; and at the east of the garden of Eden He stationed the cherubim and the flaming sword which turned every direction to guard the way to the tree of life. (Genesis 3:23-24)

In the beginning, Man enjoyed a unique relationship with God. Man was on Earth and God still reigned in Heaven; but the Bible makes a case for God appearing with Adam and Eve on Earth. We can read that after their sin they hid themselves from God and Adam reported to Him that "I heard the sound of You in the garden, and I was afraid" (Genesis 3:10). The passage provides some indication that God routinely walked in the Garden with Adam and Eve to the extent that they could recognize the sound of His footsteps. It makes you wonder what kind of sound God made when He walked through the Garden, but maybe that is a discussion for seminarians to debate in the systematic theology classes they take. For our purpose, let it suffice to say that God maintained a very specific and personal relationship in the Garden with Adam and Eve during the period prior to their sin.

113

That relationship became severed as a result of the first sin: Eating fruit from the Forbidden Tree. The result, as noted in the passage highlighted at the beginning of this chapter, was God casting Adam and Eve out of the Garden and establishing a guard at the entrance to the Garden and near the Tree. The outcome did not occur as a complete surprise. God made it clear to Adam that he could eat from any tree in the Garden except the one, forbidden, tree. God further explained that if he did eat of that tree, he would surely die (see Genesis 2:15-17). Now, some might ask, "Why didn't Adam and Eve die after committing their sin?" Some may even question the integrity of God by claiming "He said they would die and then they did not die." What's up?

The answer to the apparent contradiction, as with most of the supposed "contradictions" in the Bible, rests on a proper interpretation of the passages in question. On one front, Adam and Eve did "die" in that the life they experienced in the Garden died. They lived in a perfect world where they enjoyed every possible provision and even had a personal, face-to-face, relationship with God. The Genesis account gives no indication that either Adam or Eve would ever grow old and die. In fact, the evidence is that if they did not disobey God (i.e., sin), they would live in the Garden, with God, for eternity. That reality died when they sinned. On another front, we could inject the concept regarding the mercy and grace of God. With this point, we understand that even though God proclaimed a set punishment for their sin, as God He certainly maintained a character that allowed for a merciful handling of Adam and Eve's iniquity.

A similar situation occurred on Mount Sinai when God became angry with the Hebrew people for creating and worshipping a golden calf as they waited for Moses to return. We can read about the account in Exodus 32. It states:

> *Then the Lord spoke to Moses, "Go down at once, for your people, whom you brought up from the land of Egypt, have corrupted themselves. They have quickly turned aside from the way which I commanded them. They have made for themselves a molten calf and have worshiped it and have sacrificed to it and said, 'This is your god, O Israel, who brought you*

> up from the land of Egypt!'" The Lord
> said to Moses, "I have seen this
> people, and behold, they are an
> obstinate people. Now then let Me
> alone, that My anger may burn against
> them and that I may destroy them."
> (Exodus 32:7-10)

God desired, and even proclaimed to Moses, that He intended to destroy the Hebrews because of their sinful activity. Of course, God did not destroy them at that point and actually changed his mind. Through Moses' defense of the people, we are told that "the Lord changed His mind about the harm which He said He would do to His people" (Exodus 32:14). In essence, God proclaimed the punishment and then decided to act in a more merciful way towards the sinfulness of the Hebrews. Such is the understanding we have with the demonstration of God's mercy towards the sin of Adam and Eve. His justice demanded a judgment against them and, as a result of their sin, they lost their place in the Garden and their direct, personal relationship with God. However, the mercy of God decided to soften His previously proclaimed punishment for them. God, in a demonstration of love for His creation, was able to respond to their sin with mercy.

God allowed Adam and Eve to live but separated them from the communal presence they enjoyed in the Garden because of their sin. Additionally, we need to understand that the result of sin for us, as it pertains to Man's relationship to God, is that sin creates a separation between the two entities. Although the omnipresence of God still maintains his "presence" with us, we need to understand the point that sin did create a separation from Him for Adam and Eve. And, everyone since Adam and Eve realizes that same sense of separation from God as a result of sin. So, a separation from God, in some respect, was the case for Adam and Eve, for the Hebrew people and for all of Mankind. In His perfection, God could not continue the type of relationship enjoyed by Adam and Eve; nor can sinful Man experience that type of relationship with Him today.

The prophet Isaiah proclaimed that Truth to the people when he spoke to them regarding their sin. He stated:

> Behold, the Lord's hand is not so
> short that it cannot save; nor is His

> *ear so dull that it cannot hear. But*
> *your iniquities have made a separation*
> *between you and your God and your sins*
> *have hidden His face from you. (Isaiah*
> *59:2-3)*

Interestingly, Isaiah noted a certain omnipotence of God, at least from the standpoint that He can always hear and save His people. Unfortunately, the prophet also noted that because of their sin they were estranged from God. The sins of the people caused a "separation between you and your God" and that God had "hidden His face from you." Understand that this was not a prophetic statement about some time that Isaiah saw would come to the people; but, instead, was a proclamation to the Hebrew people regarding their current condition. Their sins brought about a separation from God.

Moving to the New Testament, Paul wrote a letter to the Galatians and specifically discussed the idea of justification under the Law as it related to circumcision. In that context, Paul wrote that many of the Galatians "have been severed from Christ, you who are seeking to be justified by law" (5:4). Of course, the point here is that no one can be justified under the Law, since no one can keep the Law due to the sinful Nature of Man. Therefore, those who "seek to be justified by the Law" find themselves "severed from Christ" (from God) because of their sin.

And finally, in Paul's letter to the Ephesians, we find him again dealing with the idea of the Law and circumcision. In that context, he wrote the following:

> *Remember that formerly you, the*
> *Gentiles in the flesh, who are called*
> *"Uncircumcision" by the so-called*
> *"Circumcision," . . . remember that*
> *you were at that time separate from*
> *Christ, excluded from the commonwealth*
> *of Israel, and strangers to the*
> *covenants of promise, having no hope*
> *and without God in the world.*
> (Ephesians 2:11-12)

I do not know if it can get any clearer than that. Paul, of course, gave no credence to the concept of circumcision. He referred to it as something performed in the flesh by human hands, giving a sort of "idol" label to the idea. Still, the reference to circumcision identified the Gentiles as those who were outside the Faith, at least from the Jewish perspective. And, being outside of the Faith (i.e., still in their sin), they had "no hope and were without God." For Paul, and the entirety of the biblical Truth, when we are living in our sins we are estranged, separated from God.

Beyond the biblical evidence of God's separation from Man, scholars substantiate that Truth. Samuel Clarke was a British philosopher and Anglican theologian of the late seventeenth and early eighteenth centuries. He wrote a short essay entitled "Can God Do Evil?" In his compelling essay, he surmised that the omnipotence of God did not allow Him to perform acts contrary to His character. According to Clarke, God functioned in "justice, goodness, and truth."[43] With that reality, Clarke concluded that God "cannot possibly do anything that is evil."[44] Carrying out that position to a rational conclusion and the point is obvious: God cannot do, nor associate with, anything that is evil or is contrary to His personal attributes of justice, goodness, and truth. That being the case, Man's sinfulness would create a natural alienation from God.

Looking at this topic through another lens, Oates stated the whole idea from a psychological point of view. He noted that sin reflects an alienation from God and then further stated that the "alienation from God and Man is the composite and end result meaning of sin."[45] Oates used that as an introduction to a discussion provided in his book on the psychology of Man's alienation. He made several observations about alienation, but the salient point for our discussion is that alienation from God is the result of Man's sins.

The other side of the theological coin is the point that because of the separation God continued to work throughout history to bring about a reconciliation with Man. That Truth becomes obvious as one examines the breadth of the Old Testament, although often missed by many Christians. To illustrate that point, ask someone "What is the essence of the Old Testament?" Many people, including scholars and

---

[43] Samuel Clarke, "Can God Do Evil?," in *Philosophy of Religion: Selected Readings*, edited by William Rowe and William Wainwright (New York: Harcourt, Brace, Jovanovich, Inc., 1973), 75.

[44] Ibid.

[45] Oates, *Psychology of Religion*, 211.

ministers, will respond to that question by saying, "It is a recorded history of the Hebrew people." Others, those who understand the direct correlation between the Old and New Testaments, might answer the question with something about it being a historical account leading to the coming of Jesus as the Christ. Both of those replies are accurate, to a point. The Old Testament does represent a history of the Hebrew people and it does chronicle the period leading up to (and points directly to) the coming of Christ. Nevertheless, it misses a theological perspective that represents another Truth. Along a theological line, the Old Testament is an accounting of God's desire to restore the broken relationship that resulted as a repercussion of Man's sins.

The illustration of that position is obvious throughout the Old Testament. We know that some association existed between God and Man after the Fall. In Genesis 4 we can read that the sons of Adam and Eve (the first generation after their parent's expulsion from the Garden) offered sacrifices to God. The passage states,

> *So it came about in the course of time that Cain brought an offering to the Lord of the fruit of the ground. Abel, on his part also brought of the firstlings of his flock and of their fat portions.* (Genesis 4:3-4)

The passage further states that God accepted the offering of Abel but had no regard for Cain's. The indication here is that God provided the "First Family" a directive for offering proper sacrifices and for worshipping Him. In fact, it appears that they maintained a close relationship with God in that Cain spoke to God directly after he killed his brother. That conversation is depicted a few verses later (see Genesis 4:9-15). So, at least initially, God provided a means by which Man could still enjoy some semblance of connection to God.

That connection did not last very long. God watched as Man struggled through life and experienced the challenges of trying to understand God's presence in the world. Through those years, Man continued his sinful ways, culminating in two major events highlighted in the first dozen chapters of Genesis. The first is found in Genesis 6-7 and is described in history as "The Great Flood." The chapters describe God's

118

disappointment about the sinfulness of Man and decided to "blot out man whom I have created from the face of the land" (Genesis 6:7).

A few chapters late, in Genesis 11, we can read the "Tower of Babel" narrative. In that story, Man attempted to build a tower that could reach Heaven. Although it might be tempting to assign a spiritual quality to their attempt (i.e., the people wanted to be close to God), it seemed to be a sense of arrogance that concerned God. The point here is that God needed to thwart the idea that sinful Man can make it to Heaven through his own effort or merit. That Truth represents the main message of God's Word and ultimately the need for God to come in the flesh and make secure that reality.

Amidst the setbacks of Man's continued sinfulness, God did continue to speak directly to people of faith. A case in point is the story of the Flood, as God recognized the righteousness of Noah and directed him to build an Ark. When the flood waters receded and Noah was able to leave the Ark, God established a covenant with Noah and his family. A passage tells us that God spoke directly to Noah and said, "Now behold, I Myself do establish My covenant with you, and with your descendants after you" (Genesis 9:8). In addition to that statement, God pledges a covenant with the world that He will never again cut off all flesh by a flood and then places a "bow" (i.e., rainbow) in the sky as a sign of that covenant pledge that God made to Noah (see Genesis 9:11-17). Even though Man's sin severed the perfect relationship he had with God, God was still trying to salvage some element of their previous association.

All of that is biblically true. However, perhaps the real nature of God's effort to renew Man's broken relationship with Him began with Abram. It was at this point that God facilitated two things that indicated to Abram His desire to re-establish His bond with Man. God directed both components to Abram at the same time, solidifying the covenant's full scope between he and God. The first was a calling of Abram as the father of many nations, God's chosen people. As a sign of that covenant, God changed Abram's name to Abraham. He also instituted a second sign, one that required Abraham's commitment. The other one was the practice of circumcision. We can read the story of that account in Genesis 17 as follows:

> *God said to him, "As for me, this is
> my covenant with you: You will be the
> father of many nations. No longer
> will you be called Abram; your name
> will be Abraham, for I have made you
> a father of many nations. I will
> establish my covenant as an
> everlasting covenant between me and
> you and your descendants after you
> for the generations to come, to be
> your God and the God of your
> descendants after you. Then God said
> to Abraham, "As for you, you must
> keep my covenant, you and your
> descendants after you for the
> generations to come. This is my
> covenant with you and your
> descendants after you, the covenant
> you are to keep: Every male among you
> shall be circumcised. You are to
> undergo circumcision, and it will be
> the sign of the covenant between me
> and you." (Genesis 17:3-5, 7, 9-11).*

Scholars debate the nature and substance of this covenant from every possible angle. Entire monoliths are dedicated to the examination of God's covenant with Abraham. Many of them acknowledge the covenant represents a new era in the God-Man relationship. Gerhard Von Rad, a noted German theologian and professor of Old Testament at the University of Heidelberg in the mid-twentieth century, concluded that the Jewish covenant with Abraham instituted a "new relationship with God and the land."[46] Indeed, scholars often set the covenant God established with Abraham as a new beginning in the relationship between God and His Creation.

From that new beginning, God and Man went through a myriad of ups and downs. God rescued His people from a dreaded famine by providing a means for them to receive food and protection in Egypt. The Bible is not clear on God's reasoning, but we know that the Egyptians enslaved the Hebrews and that they spent the next several centuries in bondage.

---

[46] Gerhard Von Rad, *Genesis* (Philadelphia: Westminster Press, 1974), 200.

God ultimately answered their prayers and called Moses to lead the people out of Egypt and to the "Promised Land" where God would create for them a great nation. That set up the period of the Judges who served during a time when God used them to provide proper spiritual leadership for His people. After some three hundred years, the people came to a decision that they wanted to have a king instead of Judges. Against God's directives, the people continued to persist. As a result, God granted their petition and the kings remained until the destruction of Israel (721BC) and Judah (586BC). During the time of the kings, God also called on prophets to proclaim His message to His people.

It was all designed to maintain God as their God and the Hebrews as God's people. As stated in I Chronicles 7:14,

> If My people who are called by My name humble themselves and pray and seek My face and turn from their wicked ways, then I will hear from heaven, will forgive their sin and will heal their land.

In that statement is the essence of God's covenant and His expectation for His people. He will be their God and have a specific and direct relationship with them if they will continue to live and serve Him as their one and only God.

The problem with this new covenant resulted from the same thing that caused the first sin in the Garden of Eden—Man is a sinner. All you need to do is run through the following examples: Abraham lied to Abimelech that his wife, Sarah, was his sister (Genesis 20); Joseph's brothers sold him into slavery and lied to their father, Jacob (Genesis 37); Moses struck the rock at Meribah without God's approval (Numbers 20); Samson committed a sin with Delilah (Judges 16); and David, proclaimed as "a man after God's own heart" (I Samuel 13), had a sinful night with Bathsheba (II Samuel 11). These examples seem to be the rule rather than the exception.

The Old Testament, God's inspired Word provided for the benefit of His people, is not simply a testimony to the history of the Hebrew people. It is a proclamation of God's Truth that Man is a sinner, will always be a sinner, and as such is incapable of maintaining a covenant relationship with God based on his own efforts. Given that reality, Man will always fail.

121

Therefore, a new covenant had to be established. It had to be a covenant orchestrated by God, based on His grace, and one that did not rely on Man's spiritual perfection. Enter Jesus as the incarnation of God and the "Suffering Servant" prophesized by Isaiah (see Isaiah 42:1-4; 49:1-6; 50:4-7; and 52:13-53:12). A traditional passage (noted earlier, see Chapter 7) states:

> *Surely our griefs He Himself bore and our sorrows He carried; yet we ourselves esteemed Him stricken, smitten of God and afflicted. But He was pierced for our transgressions, He was crushed for our iniquities. The chastening for our well-being fell upon Him and by His scourging we are healed.* (53:4-5)

The point regarding the establishment of a new covenant to reconcile the broken relationship between God and Man is a valid one for this discussion. However, the nature of that new covenant relates to Jesus ("the new covenant in my blood," II Corinthians 11:25) and the Atonement through His crucifixion.

With that Truth in place, this discussion needs to move to the next chapter, "Jesus and Atonement."

CHAPTER 11

JESUS AND ATONEMENT

But God demonstrates His own love toward us, in that while we were yet sinners, Christ died for us. Having now been justified by His blood, we shall be saved from the wrath of God through Him. For if while we were enemies we were reconciled to God through the death of His Son, much more, having been reconciled, we shall be saved by His life. (Romans 5:8-10)

One specific definition ascribed to "atonement" is "the reconciliation between God and Man thus brought about by Christ."[47] With that definition, how could there be any debate within the Church as to what atonement means for Christians. However, some debate does exist and it has since the earliest period of Christianity. The early Church Fathers debated the concept of Atonement. The debate raised the question of whether Man's sin was completely forgiven by Christ's death on the Cross. At issue was whether the Christian needed to share in the Atonement through some commitment, as if sharing in Christ's crucifixion, in order to complete the process of forgiveness offered by God.

---

[47] Webster's II: New Riverside Dictionary, s.v. "attonement."

Given the fact that the idea of Atonement still stirs a significant debate throughout Christianity, it is possible that this chapter presents one of the great challenges to the premise for a unity of faith within the Christian Church. The problem is that many denominations profess several, seemingly conflicting views on the Atonement of Christ. That reality makes finding a unifying compromise exceedingly difficult. Now, some may debate the point, but the conclusion here is that the Christian Faith proclaims three main positions on the question of Atonement. They are: the Satisfaction Theory; the Ransom Theory; and the Penal Substitutionary Theory. A basic examination of each theory should provide a clear understanding of the differences they express and the challenge one faces trying to establish a unified position for all denominations within Christianity.

Satisfaction Theory

The Satisfaction Theory of Atonement argues that God, as the Sovereign, required a "satisfaction" for Man's rebellion. Offered primarily by Anselm of Canterbury, this theological position maintains that Jesus suffered on the Cross as a payment of a debt Man owes to God because of the dishonor he shows to God as being the One True and Living God. Jesus' complete obedience to God, represented in His being crucified, was a demonstration of sincere honor and satisfied the Sovereign's requirement that He demands for Man's rebellion against His authority. The Satisfaction Theory of Atonement finds its main support within the Roman Catholic, Lutheran, and Reformed Churches.

Ransom Theory

Perhaps first articulated by Irenaeus and later by Origen, this theory postulates that Man's sin requires a payment of a ransom. The theological position is that Man is enslaved to Satan who holds him in spiritual slavery because of his sin. To be free from that slavery, Satan requires a ransom payment. God provides Christ's sacrifice as that payment, which brings about the Atonement Man needs. It is a concept supported in Christ's own words as recorded in Matthew when Jesus stated, "Just as the Son of Man did not come to be served, but to serve, and to give His life a ransom for many" (20:28).

An interesting twist to that "payment" motif is the position that Satan demands a payment for Man's sin. This revision focuses on God's pronouncement in the Garden of Eden when He told Adam, "But from the tree of the knowledge of good and evil you shall not eat, for in the day that you eat from it you will surely die" (Genesis 2:17). Other passages (i.e., Romans 6:23, "The wages of sin is death") also support the relationship between the act of sin and the reality of death. The conclusion is that God's justice demands death as a result of sin and Man's yielding to the temptations of Satan. With that requirement, Christ came to "pay the price" (i.e., the ransom) to death, to Satan, or both for our sins and we are set free by the price He paid.

Penal Substitutionary Theory

This idea is like the Ransom Theory but differs on a major point. That point is that in the Penal Substitutionary Theory, God (or Satan) is not calling for a payment (a ransom) from us. Instead, the motivation is God's desire to bring a reconciliation to the broken relationship between He and Man that exists as a result of sin. This is the position of many mainstream Protestant Churches of Western Christianity. Those churches will point to several passages that they feel support their theological position. Three of those are:

> *He Himself bore our sins in His body on the cross, so that we might die to sin and live to righteousness; for by His wounds you were healed. For you were continually straying like sheep, but now you have returned to the Shepherd and Guardian of your souls. (I Peter 2:24-25)*

> *For Christ also died for sins once for all, the just for the unjust, so that He might bring us to God, having been put to death in the flesh, but made alive in the spirit. (1 Peter 3:18)*

> *if anyone sins, we have an Advocate with the Father, Jesus Christ the righteous; and He Himself is the propitiation for our sins; and not for ours only, but also for those of the whole world. (I John 2:2)*

Even as early as Johnathan Edwards, a pillar of faith during the First Great Awakening in the New World, many of the Christian faithful raised question about the theory. Edwards, although considering the theory was theologically sound, did confess that he felt a "compelling need to reframe the doctrine of atonement along a more scientific or consistent line, seeing that the Old Calvinist notion of Penal Substitutionary Atonement was particularly offensive to modern thinkers."[48]

In more contemporary times the debate has received some renewed attention within the scholarly circles of Christianity. The criticism normally centers on the universally held Christian concept that "God is love." In that respect, many will reach a conclusion that God, being love, could not direct His own Son to die on a Cross for the sins of Man. For those who champion that point, they hold that the theory is simply not theologically sound nor philosophically logical.

While one might agree on the philosophical point that a loving father would not be willing to sacrifice his only son for the sins of strangers, they miss completely the theological point expressed in Christ's crucifixion. As discussed in an earlier chapter, Jesus was not a literal son of God as much as He was God, Himself. He was the incarnation of God. As stated in the Gospel of John: "The Word was God and the Word became flesh and dwelt among us" (John 1:1, 14). As we understand that the Word *was* God and that the Word became flesh in the form of Jesus Christ, we can begin to realize that God did not offer Jesus, His only begotten Son, as a sacrifice for Man's sin. To the contrary, God offered Himself as the sacrifice of sin. With that theological point established, the Penal Substitutionary Atonement Theory remains intact, regardless of the debate that still raises its head periodically.

The various denominational positions create something of a dilemma, especially when you add the Eastern Orthodox concept of "Theosis." It is a theological position that proclaims a "closeness with God" view of the Atonement and creates a whole new debate within the Christian community. Just to provide some clarification for our discussion on this point, the Eastern position on the Atonement focuses on the resurrection of Christ, rather than simply His crucifixion, as often expressed in many Western denominations. Frederica Mathewes-Greene, who is considered by many in the United States as the

---

48 Brandon James Crawford, *Johnathan Edwards on Atonement: Understanding the Legacy of America's Greatest Theologian* (Eugene, OR: Wipf and Stock, 2017), 9.

First Lady of American Orthodoxy, stated that the Eastern view of the crucifixion establishes Jesus as the "Hero of the Cross" and identifies the resurrection as the atoning power that rescues sinners from the gates of Hell.[49] She continued by noting that God's salvation of the Hebrews from Egypt through the Exodus represents a perfect parallel to the atoning process of Christ in His resurrection.[50]

At face value, the whole presentation so far would seem to present an impossible dilemma that scuttles this entire project. But not so fast! The key to this presentation is to express that which unifies us in the tenets of faith, not what divides us as we try to defend our own denominational camp. With that concept intact, we should note that the theological construct of Jesus and Atonement does have a unifying point: Man's reconciliation with God. For instance, even though many Christians seem to fall on both sides of the theological argument expressed above in Penal Substitutionary Atonement, the theory also makes perfect sense from a biblical standpoint. Most Christians may view the Old Testament as a history of the Hebrew people; and, it is difficult to refute that point. Obviously, the Old Testament does document a historical account of God's people leading up to the coming of Christ. However, from another perspective, it represents an attempt by God to bring Himself back into fellowship with Man.

As noted earlier, Man's sin in the Garden of Eden brought about his separation from a direct, personal relationship with God. The confrontation God had with them after the Fall depicted a direct question and answer session where Adam and Eve spoke with and to God. The result of their sin was banishment from Eden. Although God banished them from the Garden, He did not banish them from His providence and care. Indeed, God continued to speak directly to Man. He spoke to Abel, Noah, Abraham, Jacob, Moses and all the prophets. In fact, the point was made that one could argue that the entirety of the Old Testament is an effort by God to re-establish a broken covenant relationship with Man. However, nothing seemed to work. The Law, the Judges, the kings, and the prophets were ineffective because Man continued to sin. The only option for establishing a lasting (even eternal)

---

[49] Frederica Mathewes-Greene, "Orthodoxy and the Atonement" a video presentation of TheoriaTV, taken fromhttp://www.theoria.tv./orthodoxy-and-the-atonement on 08/08/2019.
[50] Ibid.

covenant with Man was for God to do it Himself. In that way, the covenant was not contingent on the possibility of Man's perfect obedience, but on God's redemptive sacrifice on a Cross: on Atonement! So, apart from the noted theological debate regarding the various theories of Atonement that may separate us denominationally, perhaps we should examine "Jesus and Atonement" from a purely biblical perspective.

That next step would include the relationship between God's love that offers forgiveness for sin and the understanding that it is God's love that offers Atonement through His crucifixion. While the West may focus on the sacrifice of Christ on the Cross, the East will highlight the resurrection as the rescuing of Man from the condemnation of Hell. Even though they differ in proclamation, both perspectives reach the same conclusion: the demonstration of God's love. On another front, even from a biblical standpoint, it is possible to throw another problem into the discussion. That problem comes from a position that questions the whole Atonement issue. The question is: If Man receives forgiveness of his sins through a sincere repentance, does he not already possess a reconciliation with God? Baillie recognized that question when he asked, "Why do we speak of Atonement? Is not forgiveness enough?"[51] He made the argument even more pronounced when he offered two additional questions as he posited, "What room is there for an atoning sacrifice? Does not God's forgiveness cover everything?[52] Although the East's perspective on the Crucifixion represents a victory over death and Satan, Baillie presents an intriguing theological question that any discussion seeking agreement on the Atonement should address.

Therefore, as we attempt to address the issue of God's forgiveness and its relationship to Atonement, the argument can present two possible viewpoints. The first is the hypothesis that the forgiveness provided by God through repentance covers Man's specific sins. In other words, repentance brings God's forgiveness for an act of sin. Christ's death on the Cross for our atonement reflects God's willingness to remove even the nature of Man's sinfulness, his rebellion against God. A second presentation, perhaps as a theological explanation of the first, notes that repentance brings forgiveness for this life and Atonement brings a union

---

[51] Baillie *God Was in Christ*, 171.
[52] Ibid., 172.

with God for eternity. We can see in this respect that repentance establishes a righteousness for the penitent in this life. Forgiveness then becomes the means by which God sees us as righteous in this life, while Atonement is the perfect righteousness provided for eternity.

That dual understanding of the dispensation of God's grace (His righteousness) opens the door to another possibility for discussing the Atonement as it relates to God's righteousness. The righteousness element rests on the understanding of the difference between "imputed" and "imparted" righteousness. A definition of terms will help in understanding their application to the discussion. A definition for "impute" is "to ascribe or to attribute."[53] Looking at the word "impart," one can find that it means "to grant a share of; to bestow upon."[54] Applying the definitions to the theology of righteousness can bring us to a reasonable conclusion. The repentance for specific sins results in God's imputed (ascribed) righteousness to the penitent Believer. In that respect, God "ascribes" to us a label of righteousness; even though we are still sinful creatures and possess a sinful aspect in our life. Atonement provides the opportunity for God to "bestow" upon us a true and full imparted righteousness. In a true biblical sense, it "grants us a share of" Heaven. Sinful, corrupt Man cannot inherit (share) the perfect (righteous) Heaven. On the other hand, he cannot be perfectly righteous no matter how many penitent prayers he offers. Both concepts, imputed and imparted righteousness, are necessary to represent the full understanding of God's atoning righteousness towards the Believer.

As we continue, a still closer examination might shed some more light on the idea of "Jesus and Atonement." A basic, even elementary, way to establish the difference is to highlight the meaning of "sins" versus the meaning of "Sin." The difference is obvious, even to the casual reader. One is plural and lower case and the other is singular and capitalized. And, that is exactly the point that one can make between the two words, even from a theological standpoint. The plural, lower case "sins" gives reference to the individual and the specific sins that every Man routinely commits. The capitalized "Sin" indicates a proper noun which identifies Man's "State of Being" as a sinner. Repentance

---

[53] *Webster II: New Riverside Dictionary*, s.v. "impute."
[54] Ibid, s.v. "impart."

covers our personal sins. Faith in the sacrifice of Jesus (as the Christ) on a Cross is what covers that aspect of our sinfulness. One is necessary for union with God now and the other provides a union with God for all eternity.

As Paul Leithart, American theologian and the President of Theopolis Institute for Biblical, Liturgical, & Cultural Studies in Birmingham, Alabama, stated:

> Not that God's righteousness is manifest in the belief of the believers. Rather . . . that God's righteousness is evident in what God did through Jesus. By Jesus' death, God manifest his seriousness in dealing with sin.[55]

His statement implies the Truth regarding the two important points relative to this discussion. The first is that God's perfect righteousness is not manifested to Believers through simple belief. In contrast, his second point stipulated that the complete manifestation of God's righteousness came from the death of Jesus on the Cross. That is the exact Truth that all Christians should be able to accept. The Atonement, Jesus (as God) sacrificed on the Cross, brings Man to a full and complete righteousness before God that grants him eternal union with the Father.

So, the theological position presented so far recognizes that God manifests His righteousness in two distinct ways and as the result of two separate, but related, events. The first is the righteousness that "covers" our specific sins that is received as a result of a faithful repentance. The second is the complete, or perfect, righteousness that "removes" the Sin from our lives that we might be in union with God for eternity. That righteousness is the result of our faithful belief, which we demonstrate through our life (see James 2:26) with our acceptance of Jesus' sacrifice (or Victory) on the Cross.

Now, beyond all the theological posturing, the Bible makes a clear case for the covering of sins through repentance and the provision of God's righteousness through a sacrificial Atonement. The first illustration comes from the Old

---

[55] Paul J. Leithart, *Delivered from the Elements of the World: Atonement, Justification, Mission* (Downers Grove, IL: IVP Academic, 2016), 157.

Testament and relates to the practice of the Hebrew people regarding the offering of sacrifices. Now, before we dip our toe too far into this quagmire, let me note that I understand the difficulty in discussing the sacrifices of the Old Testament. Let's just acknowledge as an impossibility the attempt to answer every who, what, when, where, how question that relates to the practice of sacrifices in the Old Testament. So, to save you from reading (and me writing) five hundred more pages to discuss sacrifices among the Hebrew people, let's simply confine our discussion to the point that the Hebrews people did offer sacrifices. They did so in part for the forgiveness of sins. The following passages note the reality of that Truth:

> *When the nation of Israel disobeys me without meaning to, the whole nation is still guilty. Once you realize what has happened, you must sacrifice a young bull to ask my forgiveness. Lead the bull to the entrance of the sacred tent, where your tribal leaders will lay their hands on its head, before having it killed in my presence.* (Leviticus 4:13-15)

> *Now this is the law of the Nazirite when the days of his separation are fulfilled, he shall bring the offering to the doorway of the tent of meeting. He shall present his offering to the Lord: one male lamb a year old without defect for a burnt offering and one ewe-lamb a year old without defect for a sin offering.* (Numbers 6:13-14)

Each passage represents the offering of sacrifices for the forgiveness of sins. The first passage relates to the sins of the nation and requires the priest to offer sacrifices on behalf of the people in order to receive God's forgiveness. The point that the priests continued to offer the sacrifices makes it clear that God did not bestow a perfect righteousness to the people. The sacrifices covered those immediate sins, but the people still maintained a sinful context within their lives.

The second passage references a personal sacrifice for the forgiveness of sins. In Numbers 6, the instruction is given to one wanting to become a Nazarite (a dedicated individual seeking to accomplish God's purpose, as with Samson). Obviously, that person needed to possess some measure of righteousness if they desired to serve God. As such, God required a sacrifice for forgiveness of their sins before being commissioned to His service. As before, that person does not become perfectly righteous because of the sacrifice. The example of Samson and his sin with Dalilah is all the proof that is necessary to support that point. However, for Samson and others, a specific sinfulness is covered by means of the sacrifice.

As we move into the New Testament, the concept of penitent people receiving forgiveness for their sins is apparent in the ministry and mission of John the Baptist. John came to "prepare the way" for the coming of the Lord (see Isaiah 40:3 and Mark 1:3). That preparation required the forgiveness of sins, being that receiving the presence of God in an unforgiven state was considered impossible. To that point, Mark recorded in his Gospel (1:4) that, "John the Baptist appeared in the wilderness preaching a baptism of repentance for the forgiveness of sins." Again, the baptism of John did not create a perfectly righteous individual. It simply covered their sins and prepared them for the coming of Christ.

All of that being scripturally True, one must now attack the second part of the equation: The righteousness bestowed on the Believer through faith in the sacrificial Atonement of God. This is a righteousness that doesn't simply cover, but removes, the "Sin" that would eternally separate us from God. The Bible is clear on the need for such righteousness and on the means by which God bestows it.

The fact that Man needs to receive a righteousness from God is an easy biblical Truth to present. Besides for the symbolic separation from God depicted in the banishment of Adam and Eve from the Garden of Eden, the Bible is specifically clear that Man is eternally separated from God as a result of Sin, as his rebellion against God. Perhaps no better proclamation of that Truth is available than that found in the third chapter of the Gospel of John. That reference will, undoubtedly, suggest John 3:16, "For God so loved the world that He gave His only begotten Son, that whoever believes in Him should not perish but have everlasting life." Although that is a familiar passage and does fit this point, it is a verse after John 3:16 that provides the Truth pertinent to this discussion. John 3:18 states,

> He who believes in Him is not condemned; but he who does not believe is condemned already, because he has not believed in the name of the only begotten Son of God. (New King James)

In the same context where Jesus proclaimed the Truth for the Atonement (John 3:16), He also provided a chilling reality. He indicated that we are all condemned if we do not believe in Him and accept His sacrifice/payment for our sins. It is as if all of life has a default setting and that default is for Man's condemnation, for Hell. Although God created Man in His own image and then proclaimed it to be "very good," sin destroyed the perfect relationship with God and set Man on a course for condemnation. It is, therefore, an imperative that we come to a saving faith in the Atonement from God offered through Christ's crucifixion and resurrection. Without a true faith and subsequent righteousness provided by God, we are "condemned already."

Although that is a definitive passage, it is be no means the only biblical reference to our need for God's righteousness. A listing of other passages could include, but certainly are not limited to, the following:

> And you He made alive, who were dead in trespasses and sins, in which you once walked according to the course of this world, according to the prince of the power of the air, the spirit who now works in the sons of disobedience. (Ephesians 2:1-2)

> For many walk . . . that they are enemies of the cross of Christ, whose end is destruction, whose god is their appetite, and whose glory is in their shame, who set their minds on earthly things. (Philippians 3:18-19)

> For it pleased the Father that in Him all the fullness should dwell, and by

> *Him to reconcile all things to Himself, by Him, whether things on earth or things in heaven, having made peace through the blood of His cross. And you, who once were alienated and enemies in your mind by wicked works, yet now He has reconciled in the body of His flesh through death, to present you holy, and blameless, and above reproach in His sight.* (Colossians 1:19-22)

Each passage proclaims a similar point: The need for God's Atonement to remove our Sin. The Ephesians passage uses the idea of being "dead in trespasses and sins" as a reference to the point that the nature of Sin is death. The Ephesians reference goes on to note that it is a condition "in which we once walked." That phrase highlights the point that Paul wrote in his letter to the Christians in Ephesus in order to establish the Truth that they were no longer "dead," having accepted the saving gift of Atonement through the sacrificial death of Christ (see Ephesians 2:3-10).

Paul's statement in Philippians referred to people who lived as "enemies of the cross of Christ." Unfortunately, with just a cursory examination of this passage, a reader could completely misunderstand and misinterpret its application. In the simplest of terms, we believe the reference identifies those individuals who are directly and adamantly opposed to the Christian Faith. That they are "enemies" of the Christian Faith. However, when you read the full context and see the demonstration of what Paul means by "enemies" is a reference that applies to everyone who "sets their mind on earthly things." That is the very nature of Sin, which applies to everyone apart from God's righteousness. As Jesus stated, "No one can serve two masters; for either he will hate the one and love the other, or he will be devoted to one and despise the other. You cannot serve God and wealth" (Matthew 6:24). Paul's point for the Philippians, as for the Ephesians, was that prior to the coming of Christ and our acceptance of His sacrificial Atonement, all lived as enemies of the cross of Christ.

And finally, in Colossians, Paul brought the entire Truth together in one proclamation. He noted that even though we were "alienated" from God and lived as "enemies", God reconciled us to Himself "in the body of His flesh through death." The phrase was a clear reference to His sacrifice on the Cross. Paul then demonstrated the fullness of that reconciliation noting that it presented us as "holy and blameless." The theological and biblical Truth here is that it is impossible for Man to be holy and blameless apart from God's "imputed" righteousness. A righteousness that He "imparts" to us for eternity through His Atonement.

Beyond the question of Man's need to be reconciled to God is the direct presentation of Jesus' crucifixion as being the means through which God accomplished that reconciliation. The passages are too numerous to list and the earlier discussion of Penal Substitutionary Atonement already highlighted three of them (I Peter 2:24-25; 3:18; and I John 2:2). Not to belabor a point, but a couple of others might prove important to establish the relationship of the Cross to the Atonement granted by God to all Believers.

The first is the proclamation of John the Baptist. As you should know by now, John had a dual purpose in his ministry. The first was to prepare the people for the coming of the Messiah. The second was to identify Him when He appeared. In John 1:29, we can read that pronouncement as John proclaimed, "Behold, the Lamb of God who takes away the sin of the world!" Although one might be quick to point out that John did not reference the Cross, he certainly implied that reality. John referred to Jesus as the "Lamb of God." The lamb was a sacrificial animal and the illustration is that here is the One who has come to be the sacrifice for Man. He solidified that notion by indicating that Jesus, the Messiah, "takes away the sin of the world." "Sin" in that passage is singular and, as discussed earlier, can refer to Man's sinfulness. In that capacity, John made a clear pronouncement regarding Jesus and Atonement. He came as the atoning power of God to remove the consequence of Man's Sin.

Of course, we find most of the passages referencing Jesus and Atonement from the Gospels and Paul's Epistles, but a passage from another book provides an important reference. It comes from the book of Hebrews. There we can read, "Otherwise, He would have needed to suffer often since the foundation of the world; but now once at the consummation of the ages He has been manifested to put away sin by the sacrifice of Himself" (9:26).

Understanding that the passage does present something of an apocalyptic context, it still has an element relative to the

Atonement. The context provides a reference to the "cleansing" Christ brings. The phrase "would have needed to suffer often" seems to note that if Christ had to individually cover (suffer for) every sin, he would need to do that quite often. Instead of a continual act to address the continual sins of Man, the author of Hebrews stated that "He has been manifested to put away sin by the sacrifice of Himself." Man's Sin was "put away," not simply "covered," by His crucifixion.

God came to earth in the flesh to be sacrificed on a Cross in order to atone for Man's Sin and provide him His complete righteousness. The result is a unity between God and all who believe and receive His righteousness that will last for all eternity. Father Patrick Reardon, an Orthodox minister and author of several books, presented an interesting dialogue regarding the unity between God and Man. He stated that

> the truth is that God is drawn to us by love—that he has forcefully thrown in his lot with us, to the point of becoming one of us. This act of God—his deliberate assumption of our historical experience in order to make it his own—is what theology calls Divine Revelation, and its defining manifestation is the Mystery of the Incarnation. In the person of his Son, God has united humanity to himself by an indissoluble bond.[56]

After all the theological and biblical discussion, in the end it may be a simple animation that can express the Truth better than the theologians, or even a few selected passages from the Bible. The diagram in question shows two sides of a wide gulf. Man stands on one side and God resides on the other. Man can call to God and God can hear and respond to him, but the two remain separated by the gulf. Man can be repentant and receive God's forgiveness. This allows God to see Man as righteous and develop a personal relationship, but the two remain separated. It is only in the final frame,

---

[56] Patrick H. Reardon, "The Lover of Mankind," Orthodox Christian Network, October 13, 2016. Reviewed on 16 October 2019 at https://myocn.net/the-lover-of-mankind.

when you see the symbol of the Cross stretched across the divide, that Man can receive the true righteousness of God and achieve a relationship with Him for all eternity.

Jesus and the Atonement offered through the Cross is a Truth, regardless of the differing theological viewpoints, that unites the Christian Faith. We, as Believers, understand the biblical presentation of the need for God's righteousness, for we are all sinners. But God's desire for an eternal, permanent relationship with His Creation demanded more than a forgiveness for Man's personal sins. The very nature of Man's Sin needed to be cleansed. In his continual and perpetual state of sin Man could not achieve that end. Indeed, thousands of years of history proved that to be true. It was up to God to provide the perfect provision. So, He came in the flesh to accomplish for Man what Man could not accomplish for himself. The result was a perfect righteousness for Man and an eternal bound with all who accept the offer through their personal faith.

Question #4

Was Jesus Actually Resurrected?

CHAPTER 12

REQUIREMENT FOR RESURRECTION

Now My soul has become troubled; and what shall I say, 'Father, save Me from this hour'? But for this purpose I came to this hour. Father, glorify Your name." Then a voice came out of heaven: "I have both glorified it, and will glorify it again." So the crowd of people who stood by and heard it were saying that it had thundered; others were saying, "An angel has spoken to Him." Jesus answered and said, "This voice has not come for My sake, but for your sakes. Now judgment is upon this world; now the ruler of this world will be cast out. And I, if I am lifted up from the earth, will draw all men to Myself." (John 12:27-32)

I t seems like it should be beyond comprehension that Christians could argue over the reality of the resurrection of Jesus Christ . . . but argue they do. Of course, we all know of churches splitting over the color of the carpet and the idea of whether flowers or the Bible should be placed on the altar table. So, I guess it makes some sense that Christians are likely to argue about anything, even something as basic to our Faith as Christ's resurrection from the dead. And, let there be no doubt that the reality of the resurrection of Jesus, as the Christ, represents an important tenet of the Christian Faith.

To set the stage more formally, let me ask, "What *is* the essence of the Christian Faith?" Now, granted, this may be one of those situations where you ask three people the same question and get four different answers! So, we need to be willing to accept that although the answers may vary in scope and depth, they should present a universal concept in their core presentation. In some capacity the answer should state something like, "God came to Earth as a man to cover our sin and bring victory over death in order that all who believe in Him might have eternal life in Heaven." That answer presents an important Truth regarding a foundational aspect of Christianity, the availability of Eternal Life! So, we recognize that Christianity proclaims a faith in eternal life and, in that respect, conclude that resurrection from the dead is a reality for all Believers. With that being true, it only follows that Jesus was raised from the dead.

So, the next three chapters will examine three aspects of that resurrection. This first chapter examines the requirement for the resurrection, in that it is not simply a belief, but a necessity for the Faith. The next two chapters will look at the Truth of the resurrection relative to the evidence available and the assurance provided to the Believer. The analysis will look at the evidence that supports the reality of the resurrection, while the last chapter in this section examines the assurance of resurrection for all who believe in Jesus as the Christ and His death on the Cross.

Earlier chapters discussed the requirement for Christ's sacrifice on the Cross, noting that the separation that exists between Man and God demanded it. The discussion included the point that the purpose of the sacrifice was for the Atonement of Man's Sin. That Atonement provided a means for eternal life to all who would believe in that Truth. Since eternal life is part of the Christian Truth of Atonement, it must also apply to the One making the sacrifice—Jesus Christ. And, indeed, it did. As we will discuss the evidence of the resurrection in the next chapter, let us direct our attention in this chapter to the requirement for the resurrection. And, one cannot understate the significance of the resurrection of Jesus as a requirement for the Faith, for Him and for His followers who accepted Him as the Christ.

In relationship to His followers, D. M. Baillie provided an interesting presentation regarding the requirement of Christ's resurrection as related to the First Century commitment of His followers. Baillie noted the fear and disbelief the disciples possessed following the crucifixion of Jesus.[57] They believed in Him as the Christ and perhaps believed that once on the Cross He would save Himself and make clear that He was the Messiah. That did not happen. Instead, the resurrected Jesus found them all fearful, disbelieving and sequestered in an isolated room not knowing what to do. Looking at the situation logically, it makes perfect sense. The Pharisees wanted Jesus dead. They worked their influence with the people and the Roman authorities in order to accomplish that task. It also made perfect sense that their next targets would be Jesus' followers, especially the disciples. We can recognize a little of that hostility in the arrest of Peter and John (see Acts 4). Therefore, it is understandable that immediately following the crucifixion, the disciples didn't know what to do and so they went into hiding and waited.

Baillie expressed the magnitude of the situation when he noted that as a result of their witnessing the crucifixion of Jesus the "doubt and rebellion increased a hundredfold" within the disciples.[58] He followed that enlightening statement with the following:

> *If the followers of Jesus did not feel*
> *like that, was it because the tragedy*
> *of the crucifixion was soon followed*
> *by the experiences of Easter morning?*
> *(And that the resurrection) had been*
> *brought about by the purpose of God.*[59]

For Baillie (et.al.), the resurrection became a requirement of God's purpose as a means of motivating Christ's followers. In that concept it was designed to move them past the realities of the crucifixion, but also to support them through the period of persecution of the Early Church that would attempt to destroy their message and the Faith.

The resurrection was a requirement as a logical provision for the support necessary for the followers of Jesus to become whom God needed them to be. That certainly qualifies as a requirement, especially as Baillie ascribed it as a purpose of

---

[57] Baillie, *God Was in Christ*, 185.
[58] Ibid., 184.
[59] Ibid., 185.

God. However, it becomes difficult to hang one's hat on that type of conclusion. Throughout history, Man did all sorts of things (some not at all pleasant) through a sense of religious motivation. Therefore, it seems we must move back to the actual basis on which this book examines each tenet—the Bible. It is in the biblical text that the Word of God clearly delineates the requirement for the resurrection.

A primary support for a resurrection requirement argument is the point that biblical evidence acknowledges through Jesus. Passages highlight Jesus' proclamations that His resurrection would take place following His death. In the Gospel of Matthew, two separate passages express two incidents where Jesus predicted His death and resurrection. Those references state:

> *From that time Jesus began to show His disciples that He must go to Jerusalem, and suffer many things from the elders and chief priests and scribes, and be killed, and be raised up on the third day. Peter took Him aside and began to rebuke Him, saying, "God forbid it, Lord! This shall never happen to You." But He turned and said to Peter, "Get behind Me, Satan! You are a stumbling block to Me; for you are not setting your mind on God's interests, but man's." (Matthew 16:21-23)*

> *And while they were gathering together in Galilee, Jesus said to them, "The Son of Man is going to be delivered into the hands of men; and they will kill Him, and He will be raised on the third day." And they were deeply grieved.* (Matthew 17:22-23)

These passages establish Jesus as a prophet, proclaiming the Word of God to His followers regarding His ultimate death and resurrection. Even though Peter tried to intercede in the picture Christ painted of His future, Jesus rebuked him. He said to Peter "Get behind me Satan," as a statement that Peter's influence was contrary to God's purpose. That purpose was for Jesus to die on the Cross and be raised from the dead on the third day. Six days later, according to Matthew and following the Transfiguration, Jesus came to Capernaum and made the same prediction: He will die and be raised on the third day.

The significance of Christ's statement (and the supporting passages in the other Synoptic Gospels) is obvious. Jesus made His proclamation as a Truth. If His resurrection failed to materialize following His death, where would that leave the disciples and His followers who accepted Him as God incarnate, the Messiah? If the proclamation Jesus provided regarding His resurrection proved false, a legitimate question among His disciples becomes, "What other aspects of His ministry could (should) be discarded?" The resurrection of Jesus as the Christ was required because of the pandora's box that springs open if the resurrection proved to be false.

Interestingly, some scholars raise serious questions about the Matthew passage. They believe the prediction by Jesus of His impending death and resurrection was a later addition. They surmise that the Gospel writers included Christ's prediction of His resurrection in order to provide some supportive documentation to substantiate that He was the Christ. One such scholar was Sherman Johnson, who wrote the exegesis on the Gospel of Matthew for *The Interpreter's Bible*. In his analysis of the passage above, he noted the following:

> *If Jesus predicted his suffering, death, and resurrection in such explicit terms, it is difficult to see why in the Gospels the disciples are portrayed as crushed by the Crucifixion and surprised by the Resurrection.* [60]

Sherman's statement poses something of a dilemma. It makes some logical sense and does require some type of response. The easy answer would be that the Bible is the inspired Word of God, therefore I believe that the prediction by Jesus is true. That will cover the bases a little, but that is an argument for the last question (Section 5, "Is the Bible the True Word of God?"). Actually, Sherman answered his own

---

[60] Sherman E. Johnson, "Exegesis on the Gospel According to St. Matthew" *The Interpreter's Bible*, Vol 7 (New York: Abingdon Press, 1953), 454.

question by stating that even though He predicted His resurrection, He did not indicate that the disciples, or others, would see Him in a resurrected form.[61] That provides some satisfaction and certainly maintains the viability of the prediction as being from Jesus, as the Christ and, therefore, truthful.

Another possibility is that the disciples were too shaken, distraught, and fearful following the crucifixion to remember what Jesus said about His resurrection. This possibility goes back to Baillie's argument regarding the mental and emotional condition of the disciples. And, one must admit, it has some merit. Throughout Christ's ministry the disciples routinely failed to understand His teachings and often asked for some clarification about one thing or another. Even when the times were relatively easy, they often missed the significance of what Jesus said. Fast forward through the months and years to a time when the disciples were fearful for their very lives. It now becomes completely understandable that during that time they did not completely comprehend the concept that Christ's resurrection was possible or remember that He proclaimed it during His ministry.

Beyond the proclamation of Christ's own words, the first people to arrive at the tomb received a confirmation for the validity of Christ's prediction regarding His resurrection. The women who arrived at the tomb on that first Easter Sunday found the stone rolled away and the tomb empty. They also encountered an angel at the tomb. According to the Gospel of Luke, they had some communication with the angel. A portion of that discourse indicates that the angel said to the women, "He is not here, but He has risen. Remember how He spoke to you while He was still in Galilee" (Luke 24:6). Since Capernaum is in Galilee (and since the account in Matthew 17 specifically identified Galilee as the location of Jesus prediction), the angel's statement to the women draws a straight line back to Jesus and His pronouncement regarding His death and resurrection.

Perhaps it is enough to accept that Jesus foretold of His death and resurrection. That Truth alone would confirm the requirement for resurrection. After all, Jesus said it. As the Christ, there now came a requirement that the resurrection came to fruition. For many, that would be adequate. It falls into a type of "the Bible says it, I believe it, that settles

---

61 Ibid.

it" kind of category. And, while we can applaud the demonstration of faith in God's Word, more support regarding the requirement of the resurrection is available in the Scriptures. Apart from Christ's own words, the very nature of Christianity requires an acknowledgement of the reality for the resurrection. Paul made the point very succinctly in his first letter to the Corinthians (15:12-19) when he noted the following:

> Now if Christ is preached that He has been raised from the dead, how do some among you say that there is no resurrection of the dead? But if there is no resurrection of the dead, then Christ is not risen. And if Christ is not risen, then our preaching is empty and your faith is also empty. Yes, and we are found false witnesses of God, because we have testified of God that He raised up Christ, whom He did not raise up—if in fact the dead do not rise. For if the dead do not rise, then Christ is not risen. And if Christ is not risen, your faith is futile; you are still in your sins! Then also those who have [c]fallen asleep in Christ have perished. If in this life only we have hope in Christ, we are of all men the most pitiable.

As we move through this passage, it becomes obvious that Paul established a vibrant case for the requirement of Christ's resurrection. In fact, the first line sets up the rest of the argument with a perfect rhetorical question. Paul asks the Corinthians how they can deny the resurrection of the dead if the proclamation of God's Truth, the preaching of the risen Lord's disciples, made it clear that Jesus experienced a resurrection from the dead. Paul followed that question with a definitive statement that if one considers resurrection to be impossible, then "not even Jesus has been raised."

Now, we know that many people during this period rejected the concept that resurrection was a possibility. Jesus had an encounter with the Sadducees over accepting the reality of a resurrection from the dead. All three Synoptic Gospels record the meeting where they stated that the Sadducees did not believe in the resurrection (see Matthew 22:23, Mark 12:23, and Luke 20:27). The situation was set up as a test of Jesus. The Sadducees presented Jesus with a hypothetical situation where a woman remarried after each of her first six husbands died. The Sadducees then posed a question to Jesus as to whose wife she would be in the resurrection. That is not to say that some of the people reading Paul's letter to the Corinthians were of a Sadducean background. However, it is certainly plausible that an influence from that group existed in Corinth at the time that Paul wrote his letter.

Regardless whether that is true, while the readers of Paul's letter were trying to recover from their dismay at his questioning the truth of the resurrection, he played his hole card, an ace! He made a profound statement that mandated the requirement for Christ's resurrection by stating that "if Christ has not been raised, then . . . your faith also is vain." That is an incredible declaration and one that made the significance, and requirement, of the resurrection of Jesus Christ quite clear. For Paul, the issue was that without the resurrection of Jesus Christ the Christian Faith falls apart. Certainly, that is a Truth that all Christians can, even must, accept.

However, Paul was not finished presenting his side of the resurrection debate. He proclaimed that if preachers continue proclaiming that resurrection is impossible, while the biblical Truth is that Jesus was raised from the dead, then they become "false witnesses of God." Paul's point here follows a logical path. For him, the scriptural evidence supported God's Truth that resurrection was a reality and that Jesus, Himself, was raised from the dead. That being the case, anyone who believed, and subsequently preached, that resurrection from the dead was an impossibility would be preaching a false doctrine and would be considered a false witness.

That, certainly, was a serious charge. The Greeks in the city of Corinth did not stand under the Law of Moses, but the book of Deuteronomy provided punishment for the one who brings a false witness (see 13:1-5). And, Jesus referred to the false prophets as "ravenous wolves" (Matthew 7:15). For Paul, the requirement of the resurrection dictated a proclamation of God's Truth; both for the preacher and the ones receiving a truthful proclamation from them.

148

Requirement for Resurrection

As the passage continued, Paul turned his attention to a more logical and reasonable argument. Here he noted that the requirement of the resurrection of Christ centered on the Faith of the Christian. He argued the truth of Christ's resurrection from one side, while relating it to the reality of resurrection on the other. The result is that without the security of the truth regarding the resurrection of Jesus Christ "our faith is worthless" . . . worthless! Keeping that roll going, he added that we are still in our sins, meaning that we have no hope of eternal life and as such are just muddling through this earthly existence.

His final remark proclaimed that if we live with only a faith for this life, with no possibility of the eternal life promised through Christ, "we are of all men the most pitiable." This is a powerful, but a most disturbing, picture of what life and the Christian Faith would be apart from the resurrection of Jesus Christ. Without the reality of the Resurrection, Man simply plods through the chaos of life clinging to a faith that has no validity and cannot accomplish or provide what it claims. The Believer possesses no hope, because none is available without Christ's Resurrection. It is no wonder that Paul referenced such a life as being "pitiable." Is there anything more pitiful than a person living in a conviction for which there is no reward or benefit for the dedication of his faith that he blindly follows?

Numerous scholars, the biblical record, and Christ's own words establish a definitive presentation for the requirement of the Resurrection. It would be enough to conclude the discussion at this point with the assurance that all Christians must accept the requirement for the Resurrection as a true element of the Faith. However, perhaps one additional passage will put some icing on the cake and not leave any stone unturned. The passage comes from Paul's letter to the Romans and states,

> *Do you not know that all of us who have been baptized into Christ Jesus have been baptized into His death? Therefore we have been buried with Him through baptism into death, so that as Christ was raised from the dead through the glory of the Father, so we too might walk in newness of life.*
> (Romans 6:3-4)

Most people, as they examine the context of the passage will reach an immediate conclusion related to this discussion. That conclusion, rightly identified, is that Paul was not speaking of Christ's resurrection, specifically; but, instead, was addressing the subject of baptism. That conclusion is certainly true. The chapter begins with Paul confronting the Christians in Rome who professed a theologically skewed view about the dispensation of God's grace. They surmised that the more they sinned the more forgiveness they would receive. That being true, even from a scriptural standpoint, it meant they would also receive a greater measure of God's grace.

Paul directly and emphatically rejected their distorted theory by presenting a short statement on the nature of baptism. Now, everyone take a deep breath, sit back and relax. This is not an examination of the doctrine of baptism. Everyone can appreciate that Baptism is one of those "practice of faith" issues that divide us denominationally. The questions of who, when, how, produce different answers from all the different denominations. The answers are so varied and intriguing that I took a dedicated course at seminary on the biblical principles of baptism within the Christian Church.

All that being said, it does not seem like a passage that references Man's sins and the dispensation of God's grace; nor does it seem to relate directly to the question of the requirement for the Resurrection. Still, Paul referenced a link between baptism and resurrection when he stated, "so that as Christ was raised from the dead through the glory of the Father, so we too might walk in newness of life" (Romans 6:4). Since Paul created the link between baptism and the resurrection, it offers an opportunity for an interesting analysis that is pertinent to the question at hand.

Paul noted that baptism signifies a burial and resurrection for the Believer. Again, this is not a discourse on baptism, but the point is obvious that some symbolism, regardless of the purpose, mode, or any other denominational considerations, does exist in baptism as applied to the Resurrection. For Paul, the point was that just as the old life that was the "God in the flesh" died and was resurrected to a new life; so, too, baptism becomes a "death and resurrection" experience for the Believer. His old life of sin "died" and he receives a "resurrection" to a new life of spiritual awakening in Christ and is no longer a slave to sin (Romans 6:3-7).

150

The point here is that Paul's passage in Romans related the symbolism of a sanctified life directly to the resurrection of Jesus Christ. In a way, Paul established a requirement for the Resurrection. It was necessary in order to set the example for what a life of faithful conviction truly meant: A rejection of the old life of sin for a resurrected life of faith. Paul reiterated that point in a more definitive way when he stated that "if anyone is in Christ, he is a new creature; the old things passed away; behold, new things have come" (II Corinthians 5:17).

A Believer's new life in Christ is the result of a spiritual resurrection. One that is made even more understandable as a result of the actual resurrection of Christ. In that capacity, one might even note the requirement for the Resurrection. Even if some consider that a little bit of a stretch, the requirement for the Resurrection rests on three legitimate arguments: the scholars that acknowledge it, biblical passages that proclaim it, and Christ's own words that substantiate it. As Paul noted, without the Resurrection, then there is no resurrection and we live in this world with a faith that is worthless.

CHAPTER 13

EVIDENCE OF RESURRECTION

When she had said this, she turned around and saw Jesus standing there, and did not know that it was Jesus. Jesus said to her, "Woman, why are you weeping? Whom are you seeking?" Supposing Him to be the gardener, she said to Him, "Sir, if you have carried Him away, tell me where you have laid Him, and I will take Him away." Jesus said to her, "Mary!" She turned and said to Him in Hebrew, "Rabboni!" (which means, Teacher). Jesus said to her, "Stop clinging to Me, for I have not yet ascended to the Father; but go to My brethren and say to them, 'I ascend to My Father and your Father, and My God and your God.'" Mary Magdalene *came, announcing to the disciples, "I have seen the Lord," and that He had said these things to her. (John 20:14-18)

As the title proclaims, this chapter is an examination of the evidence surrounding the Resurrection of Jesus Christ. In short, it represents a monumental task. The scholarly works which reference the Resurrection of Jesus rival the amount of ink dedicated to the search for the historical Jesus. And, the detractors do exist. One author compiled a collection of essays on the resurrection accounts in the Gospel of John and highlighted the problem trying to answer the question as one of "imaginative implausibility."[62] In one of the collected essays, John Newman, an influential Anglican (and later a Roman Catholic) priest in Nineteenth Century England, attempted to try and provide a definitive answer to the question regarding the reality of the Resurrection. Although he acknowledged the presence of some obstacles, he continued his essay by expressing a certain dismay that Christians "have developed serious hesitations about the absolute and exclusivist claims of the Church for Jesus' uniqueness as the sole survivor and only way of salvation for all peoples."[63]

Apart from that evolution of Christian thought and the magnitude of the task at hand, some scholars continue to attack the notion of Christ's Resurrection. Besides for the criticism that no verifiable historical record exists, they substitute other considerations as plausible possibilities. One of the conclusions offered the premise that the Resurrection was meant as a spiritual event, not a literal one. One scholar, Gerald O'Collins (a Jesuit priest and theologian), responded directly to that position. He stated:

> *Are we to imagine that the first century Christian authors were deliberately deceptive in their use of the language? Or were they remarkably incompetent? . . . These are the only plausible alternatives open to us if we allege that their assertions about Jesus' Resurrection were merely assertions about themselves.*[64]

O'Collins notwithstanding, the Resurrection was not just about the disciples.

---

[62] Sandra M. Schneiders, *Jesus Risen in Our Midst: Essays on the Resurrection of Jesus in the Fourth Gospel"* (Collegeville, MN: Liturgical Press, 2013), 9.

[63] John Henry Newman, "The Bodily Resurrection of Jesus and Xn Spirituality" in *Jesus Risen in Our Midst*, by Sandra M. Schneiders (Collegeville, MN: Liturgical Press, 2013), 24.

[64] Gerald O'Collins, *Believing in the Resurrection: The Meaning and Promise of the Risen Jesus* (New York: Paulist Press, 2012), 43.

Evidence of Resurrection

Beyond the debate, a truth exists in some scholarly circles that no amount of "evidence" would ever be enough to convince some of the bodily resurrection of Jesus Christ. Through the years, many scholars and philosophers express a position that refuses to accept the Resurrection regardless of the evidence. O'Collins acknowledged that point by noting that David Hume believed "in principle there could never be enough historical evidence to justify accepting Christ's resurrection from the dead."[65] That, and the other points, certainly make for a daunting task as one attempts to offer some evidence for the Resurrection.

As we move into the actual presentation of the evidence for the Resurrection of Christ, the most prolific understanding the Christian community offers as proof for the resurrection is the empty tomb. For many Christians, the reality of the empty tomb becomes the focus of their faith in the Resurrection. During the Church's Easter celebration, every cantata, passion play, hymn, and sermon uses the empty tomb as its focus.

It also is the basic theme of a story that many preachers use during their Easter sermon. It tells of a young boy named Johnny, who was something of a problem for his Sunday School teacher. He was a smart child, but always had weird ideas and you never knew exactly what he might say or do. It was in Sunday School one Easter season that the teacher gave each child a plastic egg to take home with instructions to place something inside the egg that represented the story of Easter. The next Sunday, the teacher would open the eggs and discuss how each item related to the crucifixion and the story of Easter. The next Sunday arrived and all the children brought their eggs, but the teacher had a concern when Johnny put his egg in the basket. She opened each egg and discussed its contents. One egg had a nail in it for the nails in Christ's hands during the crucifixion. In another egg, the teacher found a rock for the stone covering the tomb. She went through all the eggs and kept Johnny's tell the end, not knowing what to expect and what she might need to explain. When she opened it, she found that it was empty. She thought that Johnny had forgotten to put anything in the egg. As she tried to put the egg aside, Johnny immediately spoke up and said, "You didn't talk about my egg." The teacher then told the young boy, "But Johnny, there is not anything in your

---

[65] Ibid., 92.

egg." "That's right," he said, "It's empty. It's just like the tomb on Easter morning." Even through the faithful innocence of a child, we can understand the reality of that first Easter morning: the tomb was empty!

An adage that is the rewording of a biblical text states, "Out of the mouths of babes comes wisdom" (see Psalm 8:2 and Matthew 21:16). Stating that "The tomb is empty" is a simple Truth, but it represents a basic proclamation of the Christian Church's acknowledgement of the resurrection of Jesus Christ. For the Church, the empty tomb brings the Believer to accept the only logical conclusion of faith: that Jesus was raised from the dead. However, does the fact that the tomb was empty on that first Easter morning when the women arrived to complete the anointing of Jesus' body allow for a legitimately logical conclusion that he was raised from the dead? Is it possible that other events or conditions caused the tomb to be empty? If so, what might those issues be?

As one begins to examine the empty tomb evidence available, any number of people or groups are standing by ready to offer their theories. Although, we must begin by accepting that the tomb was, indeed, empty when the woman arrived that first Easter morning. Beyond that starting point, the cynics present three theories for the empty tomb. They are: The Theft Theory, that the body of Jesus was stolen; The Swoon Theory, that Jesus was not dead but only passed out; and The Hallucination Theory, that the people who saw Jesus only hallucinated His appearance. Josh McDowell, a Christian apologist and evangelist, offered an explanation of each theory in his critically acclaimed book, *Evidence that Demands a Verdict*.[66] The book is one of over 150 that he authored or co-authored and was ranked by *Christianity Today* in the top twenty of the most influential Christian books published since World War II. A close look at his analysis of each theory should help clear the air a little.

Theft Theory

Interestingly, many point to a passage in the Gospel of Matthew as support for the Theft Theory. In Matthew 28 we read:

> *Now while they were on their way, some*
> *of the guard came into the city and*

---

[66] Josh McDowell, *Evidence that Demands a Verdict* (Orlando: Campus Crusade for Christ, 1977), 241-265.

> *reported to the chief priests all that*
> *had happened. And when they had*
> *assembled with the elders and*
> *consulted together, they gave a large*
> *sum of money to the soldiers, and*
> *said, "You are to say, 'His disciples*
> *came by night and stole Him away while*
> *we were asleep.' And if this should*
> *come to the governor's ears, we will*
> *win him over and keep you out of*
> *trouble." And they took the money and*
> *did as they had been instructed; and*
> *this story was widely spread among the*
> *Jews.* (Matthew 28:11-15)

The Matthew account gave the Jews some ammunition against the resurrection fervor of Jesus' followers. And, as Matthew noted, the story "was widely spread among the Jews." McDowell made a reference that the story "was popular among the Jews for some time (as) seen in the writings of Justin Martyr, Tertullian, and others."[67] However, a closer contextual criticism of the passage reveals that a theft of the body did not take place. According to Matthew, the chief priests and elders bribed the guards to testify that the body was stolen. Therefore, the empty tomb still exists as a testimony to the Truth that Jesus was raised from the dead.

Now, before being able to address this first theory in an adequate manner, a pertinent question needs to be asked: If someone stole the body of Jesus, then who did it? Only three potential "body-snatching" groups present plausible answers to that question. Those three entities are the Pharisees, the Roman soldiers, or Jesus' followers. It is a simple process to element two of the groups. The Pharisees, literally, had no advantage to gain with an empty tomb. They wanted Jesus dead and worked out a plan to ensure that He would die. They also, as noted above, paid to perpetrate the claim while knowing (if they stole the body) that it was false. The Scriptures are quite clear on that Truth. The Gospel of John recorded a chilling account of the inner working of the Pharisees as they discussed the popularity of Jesus. In John 11, we can read,

---

[67] Ibid., 241.

> *Therefore, the chief priests and the Pharisees convened a council, and were saying, "What are we doing? For this man is performing many signs. If we let Him go on like this, all men will believe in Him, and the Romans will come and take away both our place and our nation." But one of them, Caiaphas, who was high priest that year, said to them, "You know nothing at all, nor do you take into account that it is expedient for you that one man die for the people, and that the whole nation not perish." So, from that day on they planned together to kill Him. (John 11:47-50, 53).*

The Pharisees represented the religious hierarchy of their day. They controlled the synagogue and, as such, the ability to influence the people. The story of the man born blind (see John 9) related the fear the common people possessed in the presence of the Pharisees. In the passage from John 11, the Pharisees questioned their viability in reference to the popularity of Jesus, stating, "the Romans will come and take away our place." That fear led the Pharisees to develop a plan that would result in the death of Jesus and, in their estimation, a death to the rabble that followed Him.

Even with their plan fully in place and functioning like a well-oiled machine, there was a lone moment when it looked like the wheels would come off. Pilate could find no fault in Jesus and sought to release Him back to the people. According to all four of the canonical Gospels, the Governor would release one prisoner as a goodwill gesture to the Jews during the period of Passover. Pilate brought out Jesus and a murderer by the name of Barabbas. The Pharisees knew that Jesus had a following in Jerusalem, having witnessed the masses celebrating His arrival into the city just five days ago. They needed to ensure the crucifixion of Jesus, so they began to influence the crowd to demand that Pilate release the murderer, Barabbas, and crucify Jesus (see Matthew 27:20 and Mark 15:11). The biblical record documents the hatred the Pharisees had for Jesus, specifically, and for His followers, generally. With that Truth in hand, what possible motivation did the Pharisee have for stealing the body of Jesus, making

Evidence of Resurrection

it appear that His resurrection from the dead was a reality? The answer to that question is easy, "None!" Therefore, the Pharisees do not stand up very well as a group that stole the body of Jesus and produced the empty tomb that proclaimed Jesus as risen.

So, let's move to the second group, the Romans; or, more specifically, the Roman soldiers guarding the tomb. This answer becomes even more problematic than the first for one very clear point: The Roman soldiers were ordered to guard the tomb so that no one would steal the body. Failure to fulfill one's duties as a Roman soldier could, and often would, result in the execution of the soldier. That point is made clear in an account of Paul and Silas with a Philippian jailer. The account stipulates that the prison doors miraculously opened. The jailer, seeing the open doors and thinking the prisoners escaped, drew his sword to kill himself. Paul interceded by acknowledging to the guard that they were all still in the cell (see Acts 16:25-28). Granted, it is something of a speculation, but one possessing some sound logic. The conclusion is that the jailer was attempting to kill himself because he knew that if a prisoner escaped from his jail on his watch his execution was inevitable.

Now, is it conceivable that the guards would risk their own lives to steal the body of Jesus in order to substantiate His claim of Messiahship? The answer to that question is as easy as the last, "Hardly!" Not only would the resulting empty tomb be evidence that could result in their own execution; but what would they do with the body? The notion that the soldiers stole the body from the tomb is totally illogical and beyond the realm of possibility. So, neither the Pharisees nor the soldiers offer a plausible conclusion for those who might want to steal the body of Jesus. That leaves only one group as having any vested interest in Christ's body and a presentation of an empty tomb. That final group is the followers, perhaps specifically the disciples, of Jesus.

Unlike the previous two groups, this group did posses a legitimate reason for stealing the body of Christ. They could use the empty tomb as evidence that Jesus was the true Messiah. Although it sounds like it came from the pages of a B-novel "who dun it" plot, it may seem to make some sense that the disciples masterminded a plan to steal the body of Jesus and then proclaim Him as the Messiah. Unfortunately for those who would like to disprove the resurrection of Jesus by using "the disciples stole the body" theory, the argument has multiple flaws. The first flaw is the presence of the guards. These men were Roman soldiers, trained killers whose expertise in that arena allowed them to conquer most of the known world at that time. Are we to believe that a small band of untrained laborers overpowered the Roman soldiers? Even if we accept, for argument's sake, that the disciples were able to put together a plan to steal the body of Jesus, it is highly unlikely it possessed any reasonable possibility of success. So, let's simply accept it for what it is, fiction, and move to the next point.

Another major roadblock exists for the "disciples stole the body" theory. If the disciples stole the body of Jesus, then they were complicit in perpetuating a fraud. In other words, accepting this theory as the answer means that the disciples knew that the empty tomb was a hoax. Of course, that means the entirety of Christianity is a hoax. As disturbing as that scenario might seem, there is no need to fret, it has no basis in reality for an obvious reason: all the disciples (save John) died a martyr's death. Of course, John suffered the fate of being boiled in oil, but did not die. That means they died for a cause they knew was false! Does that make any sense to anyone, including the cynics?

Consider for a moment how the disciples, including Matthias, who was chosen to replace Judas, died. Of course, one can find many reports and rumors regarding how the disciples met their fate. Some accounts are more reliable than others, but it is safe to say that they each met some type of brutal end. The list below comes from a reputable source related to the Christian Faith and Christian Church tradition.[68]

1. Andrew: Crucified
2. Bartholomew: Reports he was martyred, but not how
3. James (son of Alpheus): Stoned, then clubbed to death
4. James (son of Zebedee): Killed by a sword (Herod)
5. Judas: Suicide by hanging
6. Matthew: Some reported he was executed by stabbing
7. Matthias: Burned to death
8. Peter: Crucified
9. Philip: Received cruel death by a Roman Pro-counsel
10. Simon the Zealot: Martyred, but not reports of how
11. Thomas: Pierced through with spears

---

[68] Taken from https//www.christianity.com, 12/18/2018

The concepts of being burned, pierced through with spears, bludgeoned to death and crucified do not seem to support a theory that these men went to their cruel deaths in order to maintain a hoax. The Theft Theory is like a sieve that cannot hold water. Likewise, the "Theft Theory" does not hold the Truth.

One final tidbit needs to be added at this point. Sandra Schneiders serves as professor emerita at the Jesuit School of Theology at the Graduate Theological Union in Berkeley. She wrote in her book, *Jesus Risen in Our Midst: Essays on the Resurrection of Jesus in the Fourth Gospel* that

> *a telling argument for the historicity of the empty tomb is the fact that only women are associated with the story of its discovery. If the early Church had invented the story in order to prove the Resurrection, they would surely have established its facticity by the testimony of legal witnesses, i.e., males.* [69]

That certainly sounds like a chauvinistic statement, especially in today's politically correct climate, but one that expresses a truth as it applies to the New Testament period. Schneiders' conclusion was that if the disciples wanted to falsify a story about the empty tomb and the Resurrection, the women were not the instrument to accomplish the task in that Age of the New Testament nor within the Hebrew culture.

Swoon Theory

The next theory is The Swoon Theory and claims that Jesus did not die during His crucifixion. Instead, as a result of the loss of blood from the scourging and the nails through His hands and feet, he "swooned" death, taken down from the Cross and then buried. The theory goes on to stipulate that the coolness of the tomb revived Him to the point that he emerged to appear to His disciples as being raised from the dead. The disciples, having watched Him "die," were able to touch His hands and His feet (see Luke 24:36-40). With that "proof," they accepted His resurrection, even though unbeknownst to

---

[69] Schneiders, *Jesus Risen in Our Midst*, 32.

them they were touching His actual body, not a resurrected one.

Again, the Scriptures become the focal point for the cynics supporting documentation for this theory. In Mark 15:44, when Joseph of Arimathea asked Pilate for the body of Jesus, Pilate wondered if Jesus was truly dead and even summoned a centurion to verify the fact. Even though the passage stipulated that the centurion confirmed the death, it still became a prominent part of the support for The Swoon Theory. In addition to that point, the "Swoonists" make the case that Jesus "died" quicker than expected. Although the biblical account acknowledges that Jesus died before the other two being crucified with Him, the Scriptures also provide an obvious reason why. Passages point out that He received a scourging from the Roman soldiers prior to his crucifixion (see Matthew 27:26, Mark 15:15, Luke 23:16, and John 19:1). The scourging alone often resulted in death. So, it would confirm that Jesus was certainly in a weakened condition before His crucifixion which would account for his relatively quick death.

Regardless, the Swoon Theory possesses as many holes as the Theft Theory, although these are more easily delineated. Two primary points refute this theory. The first is the fact that the Roman soldiers, as noted earlier, were professional killers. They executed thousands, even tens of thousands, and knew how to accomplish the task. The second identifies a soldier that took a spear and pierced the side of Jesus. The passage in John that recorded this act states that "one of the soldiers pierced His side with a spear, and immediately blood and water came out" (John 19:34).

The major problem with The Swoon Theory is that it presumes that a swooning (i.e., fainting) person could fool the Roman soldiers into believing that he was dead. In that light, we need to understand that even though these men did not have a doctor's degree or study the medical practices of the day, they still knew how to tell if a man was dead. They learned the art of killing on the battlefield and applied it well in the routine executions they conducted. Basically, it meant that when a man stopped breathing, or his heart stopped beating, he was dead. They did not learn CPR in the First Century, nor did they have an AED Defibrillator nailed on a post at Golgotha.

The point here is that when a person "swoons" it means they faint, pass out. It is not a drug-induced state that imitates death, so that someone may be fooled into believing a person was dead. In Jesus' situation, if he fainted, he would still be breathing; which, in that time was the determining factor in concluding whether a person was dead. To further support that point, the Gospel of John reports that the soldiers came to break the legs of those being crucified in order to hasten their death. But, when the soldiers came to break Jesus' legs, they discovered that he was already dead (see John 19:31-33). In other words, the soldiers, the trained killers, those who knew how to execute a man, examined Jesus and determined that Jesus was dead. It seems logical (in fact, it seems definitive) to conclude that Jesus was, indeed, dead when they took Him from the Cross and placed Him in the tomb. Simply stated: the Roman soldiers knew what they were doing.

Going back to the passage in John, we can illustrate another flaw in this improbable Swoon Theory. As noted, at one point during the Crucifixion, a soldier took a spear and pierced the side of Jesus and both blood and water ran from the wound (John 19:34). Many scholars try to invoke some medical application to that issue in order to substantiate the reality of Christ's death. Whether those determinations are true or false is not a major consequence to this discussion, because the interpretation of the passage clearly establishes the Truth that we need at this point. Wilbert F. Howard, writing "The Exegesis of the Gospel John" for *The Interpreter's Bible*, concluded that a primary reason John recorded the event was that "It is an emphatic declaration that the death of Jesus was no mere semblance."[70]

For Howard, and many others, Jesus died on the Cross. It is an established fact supported by biblical passages and by the refuting of the false theories that do not present any logical alternative. It is also refuted by pure scientific evidence. The scourging produces significant blood loss that undoubtedly led to severe shock. His weakened condition was exemplified in his inability to carry the crossbar of the Cross to Golgotha. The injuries caused by the nails in his feet would have made walking out of the tomb extremely painful, if not impossible. Additionally, the hours He spent on the Cross also produced additional aspects of shock and ultimately asphyxiation. The soldier's thrusting a spear into his side was simply a further acknowledgement that Jesus suffered enough personal injury to clearly conclude that He was dead.

---

[70] Wilbert F. Howard, "Exegesis for the Gospel of John," *The Interpreter's Bible*, Vol. 8 (New York: Abingdon Press, 1952), 787.

The Swoon Theory reflects a completely implausible explanation on several fronts, even from a clearly medical perspective.

Hallucination Theory

The discussion now turns to the Hallucination Theory: the idea that the people who saw Jesus simply thought, or hallucinated, that they saw Him. This theory requires an examination of the eyewitness accounts of the Resurrection. Granted, the testimony at this point falls into the concept of faith, as they all appear in biblical references. However, that should not discount the legitimacy of the presentation.

The first person, according to Scripture, to see Jesus after His resurrection was Mary Magdalene. The next eyewitness encounter occurred with two travelers on the road to Emmaus. Then, Jesus appeared to the eleven disciples. According to Paul, the next appearance was to more than five hundred people at one time. After other appearances, the final event took place on the Damascus Road with Paul's epiphany of the resurrected Christ. Each event represents a significant element in the evidence that supports Christ's resurrection.

The account of Mary Magdalene's experience is unique in that, even with the empty tomb, she did not immediately realize that Jesus had been raised from the dead. John was the only Gospel writer that included this event and noted that Mary concluded that the body was stolen, making that point to Jesus whom she thought was the gardener. Once she became aware of the reality that the man was Jesus, she came to the disciples to tell them "I have seen the Lord" (John 20:18). Mary Magdalene saw the risen Lord and proclaimed that truth as an eyewitness to others.

It is interesting to note that the chronology in both Mark and Luke sets the next appearance to two travelers on the road to Emmaus (see Mark 16 and Luke 24). One of the two is named Cleopas, according to Luke 24:18, but the other one remained anonymous. They both encounter Jesus as they walked to Emmaus to inform the Christian brothers there that it was now the third day with no sign of the risen Lord (Luke 24:21). They talk with Jesus for a while, never recognizing Him. When they get to Emmaus, they convince Jesus to stay with them and in the course of the subsequent conversation "their eyes were opened and they recognized Him" (Luke 24:31). The passage goes on to state that they returned to Jerusalem that very night to tell the others what they experienced at Emmaus.

Beyond Mary and the travelers to Emmaus, all four of the Gospels include accounts of resurrection appearances to the disciples. The Gospel of Matthew provides only a small section of Jesus appearing to the disciples; but does provide the Great Commission passage (Matthew 28:19-20). Mark includes Jesus' appearance to the disciples in a disputed section of material not found in the oldest manuscripts (Mark 16:9-20). Still, the passage appears in most versions of the Bible and includes a similar commissioning of the disciples to spread the Christian message to the world. The Gospel of Luke provides two important events from the Christian Faith perspective. Christianity does declare a bodily resurrection of Christ. The passage in Luke, unlike the first two Gospels, references the physical quality of the risen Lord. In Luke 24:38, Jesus told the disciples to "touch Me and see, for a Spirit does not have flesh and bones as you see that I have." The second passage is in the same context, a couple of verses later, when Jesus asked the disciples if they had something to eat and the passage tells us that He ate some boiled fish. Both of those passages give an indication of the bodily resurrection of Christ, in that He presented Himself with "flesh and bones" and "ate some boiled fish."

However, it is in the Gospel of John that we find the most active appearances of Jesus with the disciples. Although the Synoptics limit the resurrection activity with the disciples to only a few verses, John used the last half of chapter 20 and all of Chapter 21 to report the appearances of the risen Lord with the disciples. John recorded Jesus "breathing" on the disciples to "receive the Holy Spirit" (John 20:22). He also included the "doubting Thomas" (John 20:26-29) narrative where Jesus offered His hands and side to Thomas as a testimony that it was really Him. And, the accounts at the Sea of Galilee when Jesus cooked the fish and addressed Peter's love for Him are found in John 21:12-16. These accounts and the others that run throughout the Gospels depict Jesus being with the disciples, not as a hallucination, but as the true resurrected body.

The final two passages that proclaim the Resurrection of Jesus Christ are noteworthy because of the magnitude of the event. The first is incredible because of the number of people involved; while the second results in a complete transformation of the individual that encountered the risen Lord. Although the typical appearance of Jesus was to a person here, a couple there and then to the disciples, in I Corinthians 15, we can read that Jesus appeared to more than five hundred people at one time (15:6). Paul noted that many of those who saw Jesus are still alive, implying that they can provide a personal, eyewitness testimony to the fact that Jesus was, indeed, raised from the dead.

Scholars make a case that the event, regardless of the specifics surrounding exactly what happened, represents a significant experience for those present. C. K. Barrett, a noted British theologian and recognized expert on the New Testament, noted in his commentary on Paul's first epistle to the Corinthians that "it has been suggested that this event should be identified with that described in Acts 2 as the gift of the Holy Spirit."[71] As such, Barrett ascribes the appearance of Jesus in this situation as an event that dramatically changed the lives of those present at the time.

And, as noted above, the appearance provided a plethora of personal testimony to support the Faith's contention regarding the Resurrection of Christ. Sterling Sexton, who produced a commentary on First Corinthians, concurred with that point. His position was that Paul mentioned the appearance in order to provide greater support for the Resurrection than just that of His closest followers. He noted that "Paul mentions this large number who hold no special office . . . that can be interrogated, because most of the five hundred remain."[72] Certainly, the testimony of five hundred people makes for a very convincing case.

The final passage we will examine that highlights an eye-witness encounter with the risen Lord is Paul's experience on the Damascus Road. Found in Acts 9, the account represents a dramatic example of a resurrection appearance of Jesus.

> *Now Saul, still breathing threats and murder against the disciples of the Lord, went to the high priest, and asked for letters from him to the synagogues at Damascus, so that if he found any belonging to the Way, both men and women, he might bring them bound to Jerusalem. As he was traveling, it happened that he was approaching Damascus, and suddenly a light from heaven flashed around him;*

---

[71] Barrett, *Corinthians*, 343.
[72] Sterling Sexton, *A Commentary on First Corinthians* (Stone Mountain, GA; Vista Publications), 240.

and he fell to the ground and heard a voice saying to him, "Saul, Saul, why are you persecuting Me?" And he said, "Who are You, Lord?" And He said, "I am Jesus whom you are persecuting, but get up and enter the city, and it will be told you what you must do." The men who traveled with him stood speechless, hearing the voice but seeing no one. Saul got up from the ground, and though his eyes were open, he could see nothing; and leading him by the hand, they brought him into Damascus. (Acts 9:1-8)

Several points represent the incredible nature of this event and make it unique among the resurrection appearances of Christ. First, Saul (his name before this experience) was a Pharisee and committed to destroying the followers of Jesus. The first two verses express the seriousness with which Saul attempted to complete that commitment. Given that reality, in what sense did Jesus find an avenue for good in this man? It is a difficult question to answer, but one that demonstrates the powerful nature of this appearance. In a "desperate times calls for desperate measures" concept, Jesus confronted Saul in a dramatic fashion. He, literally, knocked him to the ground by a flash of light. As a direct result of the experience, Saul is left blind. It is interesting that the men traveling with him heard something but could not see Jesus. The epiphany was for Saul and for Saul, only. The men carried Saul to Damascus and, as they say, the rest is history. The experience changed Saul's life to the point that he changed his name to Paul and through his service to the Kingdom, helped to change the world.

So far, this chapter established the empty tomb as a basic proclamation of the Christian Church for the Resurrection of Jesus Christ. It accomplished that in two ways. First, it refuted the various theories that try to explain the empty tomb apart from the Resurrection. With that defense in place, it highlighted the eyewitness accounts that clearly support the empty tomb as the symbol of Christ's resurrection. Now we come to the final tile in this mosaic: the testimony of various scholars that reached a logical conclusion for the Resurrection.

One scholar claimed that the "empty tomb, the multiple apparitions, and the seismic change in the followers of Jesus" amounted to all the proof necessary to acknowledge the reality of the Resurrection.[73] A scholar in another forum substantiated that point with the following: "The only way to account historically for the emergence of the Christian movement in the particular form it took is to affirm Jesus' resurrection."[74] Other scholars find themselves ringing that same bell. Going back to Schneiders' book, she provided a compelling evaluation of the evidence and reached a positive conclusion regarding the Resurrection by noting that

> *the data about the appearances is extensive and diverse and suggests by its quantitative and qualitative variety that we are not dealing with a single or private experience that was multiplied by psychological "contagion" or literary replication. We are dealing with something that "happened."*[75]

And to that, O'Collins adds:

> *After a public career that lasted at most three or four years, Jesus was abandoned by nearly all of his close followers, crucified, as a messianic pretender and apparently rejected by God who he proclaimed as "ABBA" or "loving father". Yet within a few years the reform movement he had led within Judaism spread explosively to become a world religion. How can one account for this documented effect without accepting an adequate cause, namely, Jesus' resurrection from the dead?*[76]

---

[73] Gary Wills, *What Jesus Said* (New York: Penguin Books, 2006), 124.

[74] Matthew Levering, *Jesus and the Demise of Death: Resurrection, Afterlife, and the Fate of the Christian* (Waco: Baylor University Press, 2012), 32.

[75] Schneiders, *Jesus Risen in Our Midst*, 30.

[76] O'Collins, *Believing in the Resurrection*, 93.

Evidence of Resurrection

Looking to a more philosophical approach, we could turn to classic philosophers of the Middle Ages. Matthew Levering, who holds the Perry Chair of Theology at Mundelein Seminary in Chicago, referenced Aquinas' argument. He noted that Aquinas gave five specific points for the necessity of the Resurrection. They are: 1) Vindication of God's justice, settled through Christ's resurrection; 2) Confirms our faith that Jesus is the Son of God, acknowledged through the demonstrated power of the Resurrection; 3) Inspires our hope that we, too, will be resurrected, indicative of Pauls' words in II Corinthians 4:14; 4) That power of the risen Jesus enables us to become holy, empowering His Believers as "children of God;" and 5) That God will exalt those who follow the risen Jesus, "delivering us from evil."[77]

In a more contemporary philosophical setting, we can find Richard Swineburne, an emeritus professor of philosophy at the University of Oxford. He wrote and delivered an essay for a symposium on the Resurrection. As a philosopher, he examined the Resurrection from a philosophical and a historical context, not as a theologian. The concluding remark in his essay stated that "the historical evidence is quite strong enough, given the background evidence, to make it considerably more probable than not that Jesus Christ rose from the dead on the first Easter Day."[78] "More probable than not" is not totally definitive, but coming from a philosopher you can take that to the bank.

"The tomb is empty, praise the Lord!" That is a statement that represents the universal proclamation of faith for the Christian Church regarding the Resurrection of Jesus Christ. Even though the critics abound who offer their theories for the empty tomb, they all come up short. The only plausible conclusion to the reality the women experienced at the tomb on that first Easter morning is that Jesus was raised from the dead. The eyewitness accounts in Scripture clearly support that Truth, as do the positions of numerous scholars and theologians. Basically, the reality of the resurrection of Jesus represents a main pillar on which the entirety of the Christian Faith stands. As one Christian apologist stated,

---

[77] Levering, *Jesus and the Demise of Death*, 36.
[78] Richard Swineburne, "Evidence for the Resurrection," in *The Resurrection: An interdisciplinary Symposium on the Resurrection of Jesus*, edited by Stephen Davis, Daniel Kendall, Gerald O'Conner (Oxford: Oxford University Press, 1997), 207.

"Without the resurrection, the Messianic and Kingly position of Jesus could not be convincingly established."[79]

With that Truth intact, we move to the second half of the resurrection equation that Paul expressed in his second letter to the Corinthians when he wrote, "knowing that He who raised the Lord Jesus will raise us also with Jesus and will present us with you" (4:14). With the Resurrection of Jesus came the power to raise all who believe in Him as the Christ and receive Him as Savior.

And with that we have a perfect introduction for the next chapter . . . The Assurance Provided by Resurrection.

---

[79] McDowell, *Evidence*, 187.

CHAPTER 14

ASSURANCE PROVIDED BY RESURRECTION

One of the criminals who were hanged there was hurling abuse at Him, saying, "Are You not the Christ? Save Yourself and us!" But the other answered, and rebuking him said, "Do you not even fear God, since you are under the same sentence of condemnation? And we indeed are suffering justly, for we are receiving what we deserve for our deeds; but this man has done nothing wrong." And he was saying, "Jesus, remember me when You come in Your kingdom!" And He said to him, "Truly I say to you, today you shall be with Me in Paradise." (Luke 23:39-43)

One of the dramatic characteristics regarding the life of Jesus and a basic principle of the Christian Faith is the fact surrounding His resurrection from the dead and its application to the life of the Believer. Without the reality of the resurrection, Jesus becomes simply another messianic figure that the Romans executed as an insurrectionist and the possibility of a resurrection for all of those who believe in Him vanishes. It is true that He brought a new message to the people and performed miracles that confounded the religious establishment at the time, most notably the Pharisees. In that respect, He would fall into a similar classification with many other

171

religious leaders and enjoy a following of disciples who believed in His message. However, without an assurance of a resurrection to a new and glorified life, the concept of eternal life would cease to be part of the Faith. In fact, it is the resurrection that stands as the dividing line that separates Jesus from all other Faiths. So incredible is the reality of the resurrection, it established the focus on which the calendar for the entire world was set.

That is a true statement, even though political correctness dictated a change in that acknowledgement. Historically, the abbreviations "BC" and "AD" denoted the period "Before Christ," or "Before Christianity," and "Anno Domini" (Year of the Lord). Today, historians almost universally ascribe the use of "BCE" (Before the Common Era) and "ACE" (After the Common Era) in the dating of historical events. I believe it is obvious that many may consider the "common" designations more agreeable to the community at large because they do not express a distinctly religious context. However, no matter how one might change the terminology for our calendar, the reality remains the same: the dating is the result of the life, including the resurrection, of Jesus as the Christ.

With that little soapbox speech out of the way, let us turn back to the question at hand and discuss the assurance provided by the resurrection. Chapter 13 provided the evidence for accepting the fact that Jesus was, indeed, raised from the dead. The point here is that God accomplished the resurrection of Jesus through His direct Will. As a result, Christ's resurrection established two important points. First, it substantiated the reality of resurrection. Second, it created a basis on which the power of God could accomplish that same resurrection for Man.

For the numerous doubters, even those of Jesus' time who debated the reality of a resurrection from the dead, it is important to set the record straight. All three of the Synoptic Gospel authors recorded a familiar confrontation regarding the question of resurrection. Taking the account from Matthew, we can read the following:

> *On that day some Sadducees (who say there is no resurrection) came to Jesus and questioned Him, asking, "Teacher, Moses said, 'If a man dies having no children, his brother as next of kin shall marry his wife, and*

*raise up children for his brother.'
Now there were seven brothers with us;
and the first married and died, and
having no children left his wife to
his brother; so also the second, and
the third, down to the seventh. Last
of all, the woman died. In the
resurrection, therefore, whose wife of
the seven will she be? For they all
had married her."   But Jesus answered
and said to them, "You are mistaken,
not understanding the Scriptures nor
the power of God. For in the
resurrection they neither marry nor
are given in marriage, but are like
angels in heaven."   (Matthew 22:23-30)*

Like many of the encounters Jesus had with the Sadducees and
Pharisees, this one was an attempt to trap Jesus with trying
to answer a hypothetical situation regarding the resurrection.
The exact discourse and the Sadducees' motivation for the
debate is not important.   What is important in the
confrontation is the identification of a group of people, the
Sadducees, who did not believe in a resurrection from the
dead.   The passage is also important because Jesus made a
clear argument for the reality of resurrection stating that
"in the resurrection they neither marry nor are given in
marriage, but are like angels."   The resurrection of Jesus
made a definitive statement on both of those fronts: 1)
Resurrection was established as a reality; and 2) The
availability of a resurrection for anyone.

That second point represents the crux of the presentation in
this chapter—the assurance that resurrection provides for all
Believers.   At this point, many people might surrender to a
position that resurrection is a matter of faith and that no
empirical evidence exists to prove its reality.   On the other
hand, in a dramatic statement from the Cross, Jesus provided
clear evidence for the availability of resurrection for all
who would believe in Him as the Christ.   That statement
appears only in the Gospel of Luke and provided the words of
comfort Jesus offered to the thief.   The entirety of the
discourse is as follows:

173

> *One of the criminals who were hanged*
> *there was hurling abuse at Him,*
> *saying, "Are You not the Christ? Save*
> *Yourself and us!" But the other*
> *answered, and rebuking him said, "Do*
> *you not even fear God, since you are*
> *under the same sentence of*
> *condemnation? And we indeed are*
> *suffering justly, for we are receiving*
> *what we deserve for our deeds; but*
> *this man has done nothing wrong." And*
> *he was saying, "Jesus, remember me*
> *when You come in Your kingdom!" And*
> *He said to him, "Truly I say to you,*
> *today you shall be with Me in*
> *Paradise."* (Luke 23:39-43)

Unfortunately, this passage is often cited during some of the denominational debate on the practice of baptism. Since some denominations believe baptism is essential to salvation, others are quick to point out that the individual being crucified with Jesus received salvation without the benefit of baptism. The question of whether baptism is essential for salvation is an interesting one which can cause deep denominational division. However, that issue is more of a "Practice of Faith" concept than a true tenet for the entirety of the Christian Faith. As such, it does not fall within the scope of the discussion in this chapter.

Specifically, the focus for this chapter is the assurance of salvation for all who believe in Jesus as the Christ. That is the Truth expressed in the passage from Luke 23. The passage noted that one thief verbally abused Jesus, while the other challenged him to appreciate the dynamic of what was happening. That thief then turned to Jesus and asked to be remembered when Jesus came into His kingdom. Jesus responded that not only would He remember the thief but would take him that day so that he might be with Jesus in paradise.

Of course, the story does possess a certain theological hiccup that one ought to address. The issue is the lack, or apparent lack, of any confessional statement. In other words, the thief received resurrection and an eternal life in heaven but was he a true Believer? If not, does that throw the proverbial monkey wrench into the whole "believe on the Lord Jesus Christ and you will be saved" (Acts 16:31) salvation

174

element of the Christian Faith? Perhaps, if that conclusion represents the faith condition of the thief. Granted, the thief's faith perspective of Jesus as the Christ is hard to recognize; but not impossible. He did refer to Jesus by name and referenced His kingdom (v.42). In that respect, the thief recognized Jesus for who He was and the description for which He was being crucified. The other part of the equation is that the passage may not include the entirety of the dialogue. Did the thief make other, more definitive, statements of faith? That is certainly possible. Regardless, the passage provides a clear presentation that resurrection is available and Jesus, as the Christ, can provide an assurance of that resurrection to all those who believe in Him.

That represents the position of the Christian Church. As a basic tenet of the Faith, the Church acknowledges that the resurrection of Jesus confirmed the belief that all Believers will receive a similar resurrection. McDowell noted plainly that "the Resurrection of Jesus is a promise of our Resurrection also."[80] In addition, Thompson, although he raised some questions regarding the historical evolution of the Easter event within the Church, noted that the resurrection appearance "illustrates that we cannot separate Jesus from the gift of salvation."[81]

Indeed, the Christian Church proclaims a resurrection to eternal glorification for all those who believe. Therefore, it is understandable that the biblical authors recorded numerous statements acknowledging that Truth. Several passages reveal Jesus' own words regarding the resurrection that God will bestow on His followers. One of the most significant is found in the Gospel of John as Jesus spoke to His disciples as they met for the final time before His crucifixion. At that time, Jesus told His disciples the following:

> Do not let your heart be troubled;
> believe in God, believe also in Me. In
> My Father's house are many dwelling
> places; if it were not so, I would
> have told you; for I go to prepare a
> place for you. If I go and prepare a
> place for you, I will come again and

---

[80] McDowell, *Evidence*, 202.
[81] Thompson, *The Jesus Debate*, 233.

> *receive you to Myself, that where I am, there you may be also.* (John 14:1-3)

The context of a passage is always important and that is certainly true regarding this statement by Jesus. As noted, He spoke to His disciples near the end of His life. In fact, this speech took place following the institution of the Lord's Supper and prior to Christ's Garden of Gethsemane experience. The context reflects the imminent death of Jesus and permanent departure from the disciples. In that setting, one would expect Jesus to speak words of comfort to them. And, He did. He provided that comfort through a message that assured them of the reality of their resurrection and, by implication, that which was available for all Believers.

Two statements in Jesus' words are specifically important. The first is found in Christ telling His disciples that He was going to "prepare a place" for each one of them. Since in the context of the passage Jesus spoke about His death, His idea of "going" was a clear reference to His resurrection and to a place that would be in Heaven. The second significant comment in the passage is the connection between Christ's going and the future arrival of the disciples to live with Him. In that moment He emphatically stated "that where I am, there you may be also." Jesus issued those words as a guarantee that the disciples would receive a similar resurrection. Even without Jesus' physical resurrection, but certainly confirmed by it, the disciples received a Truth that life after death was a reality and that they would spend that resurrected life with Jesus.

The John passage is compelling, but not the only passage that proclaims the assurance of resurrection for all who believe in Jesus as the Christ. Paul provided several such assurances in the numerous letters he wrote to Christian communities in Asia and throughout the known world. One such passage is found in his second letter to the Corinthians. In that letter, Paul provided the following to the Christians at Corinth:

> *But having the same spirit of faith, according to what is written, "I believed, therefore I spoke," we also believe, therefore we also speak, knowing that He who raised the Lord*

Jesus will raise us also with Jesus and will present us with you. (II Corinthians 4:13-14)

In this portion of his letter, Paul described the rigors of the Christian life. His main point was that the Christian may experience hardship (i.e., "afflicted in every way"), but should remain strong and not suffer defeat. He then introduced the focus of this passage about how his faith provided a direct relationship to how he spoke. In other words, Paul possessed a conviction that his proclamation was Truth due to his faith. The idea was that his speech matched his faith and so allowed the people to accept his testimony as True. Therefore, as a result of his faith, Paul made a definitive statement regarding the assurance of resurrection for all Believers. His "He who raised the Lord Jesus will raise us also" proclamation connected His faith with his words and ultimately united one's faith to the reality of a resurrection from the dead.

Beyond that general assessment of Paul's words, scholars note that Paul revealed the emphatic nature of his conviction regarding that resurrection when he included the word "knowing" in his statement. Floyd Filson, a New Testament scholar of the mid-twentieth century, noted in his exegesis of II Corinthians that the word "knowing" is a casual participle. However, he added that it also established "the fact that God has raised Jesus and is taken as solid ground for confidence that He will likewise raise those who believe in the Lord Jesus."[82] Paul confirmed that point, noting in the passage that the Believers would experience a resurrection with Jesus and be present with Him.

Other passages provide additional supporting documentation for the assurance of resurrection for all Believers. The first is from Paul's letter to the Romans and one I noted in an earlier chapter. He stated:

For if we have become united with Him in the likeness of His death, certainly we shall also be in the likeness of His resurrection, knowing this, that our old self was crucified

---

[82] Floyd V. Filson, "Exegesis on the Second Letter to the Corinthians" *The Interpreter's Bible*, Vol 7 (New York: Abingdon Press, 1953), 322.

> *with Him, in order that our body of*
> *sin might be done away with, so that*
> *we would no longer be slaves to sin.*
> (Romans 6:5-6)

The context of this passage is Paul's response to some Believers who accepted a convoluted application of God's grace. He addressed the concept that a Believer might consider a sinful lifestyle that would result in the further expression of God's forgiveness and, therefore, a further measure of God's grace. Paul responded to that distorted perspective by referencing a certain theological aspect of baptism: as a burial ("baptized into His death", 6:3) and as a resurrection (raised to "walk in newness of life," 6:4). Of course, as I promised earlier, I am not going to undertake an examination of what constitutes New Testament baptism. However, Paul concluded the idea of a "burial and resurrection" symbolism within the baptismal event with the proclamation that "certainly we shall also be in the likeness of His resurrection" (6:5).

Scholars agree that the passage confirms the reality of Christ's resurrection and the provision that in His resurrection lies the assurance of a resurrection for all Believers. C. K. Barrett stated in his commentary on the passage: "Paul has simply elicited the fact that Christian existence is rooted in a death and resurrection dependent upon Christ's."[83] In other words, Barrett indicated that the basic concept of Christianity lies in the acceptance of the reality of death and resurrection for the Believer. A reality linked, inextricably, to the death and resurrection of Christ.

Paul offered an additional assurance of resurrection in his first letter to the Christians at Thessalonica. In the fourth chapter of that letter, Paul stated

> *But we do not want you to be*
> *uninformed, brethren, about those who*
> *are asleep, so that you will not*
> *grieve as do the rest who have no*
> *hope. For if we believe that Jesus*
> *died and rose again, even so God will*
> *bring with Him those who have fallen*

---

[83] C. K. Barrett, *The Epistle to the Romans* (London: Adams and Charles Black, 1973), 124.

asleep in Jesus. (I Thessalonians 4:13-14)

The context of this Thessalonian passage is eschatological, as the reference relates to the end of time and the resurrection of the saints. Paul offered words of comfort to those still living regarding the death of their fellow Christians (as "those who are asleep"). Again, as with the previous issue of baptism, this is not going to be a discourse on the Eschaton. The focus for our discussion is the statement within the context that "God will bring with Him those who have fallen asleep." Paul provided a definitive statement of faith to the Thessalonians that all who die with a conviction of faith in Jesus as the Christ will receive a resurrection with Him.

Of course, the astute reader will note that the passage solicits an additional question regarding our resurrection. Namely, when does the Believer receive that resurrection? Is it immediately after his death; or, as seemingly indicated by this passage, at the second coming of Christ? It is an interesting and challenging question, but one that is not germane to this discussion and one that could easily take volumes to properly examine. The easy answer is that all Christians receive an immediate resurrection, per Jesus' "today" confirmation to the thief during His crucifixion. Additionally, we are resurrected a second time to a glorified body at the end of time, per Paul's passage in Thessalonians. Be that as it may, we will leave the questions concerning the Eschaton to the seminary classroom and simply acknowledge for our purpose that Paul's statement to the Thessalonians clearly delineates an assurance of resurrection for all Believers.

Beyond Paul's statements, John also joins in the assurance provided to Believers when he stated in his first epistle that

> *And the testimony is this, that God has given us eternal life, and this life is in His Son. He who has the Son has the life; he who does not have the Son of God does not have the life. These things I have written to you who believe in the name of the Son of God, so that you may know that you have eternal life. (I John 5:11-13).*

179

The passage makes three important statements relative to the point in question. The first is the emphatic proclamation by John that "God has given us eternal life." What greater assurance do we need? God's power accomplished the resurrection of Jesus and grants that power to all Believers. The second is John's explanation of the previous statement. For him, the possibility of eternal life is found "in His (God's) Son." John then concluded that the one who "has the Son has the life." Now that just makes sense. Those who are "in Christ" share in what Christ can provide to them, eternal life. The final statement is found in verse 13 where John proclaimed that he wrote his words in order that the Believers reading his letter would "know that you (the Believers) have eternal life." John's first epistle, and specifically this passage, provided a clear assurance of resurrection for all who would believe in Jesus as the Son of God.

It is at this point that we may need to chase a little rabbit. Actually, it is not a "little" rabbit, but represents a vital part of the Christin Faith and a significant aspect of the salvation theology expressed in Paul's Letter to the Romans. It is the idea of "Justification by Faith" and it represents an integral part of the assurance of resurrection discussion that is pertinent to this chapter on two fronts. The first is the idea of "justification" and the second is the understanding of "faith."

Justification, by definition, is "the act of declaring free from blame."[84] To attach a religious context to the definition we could state that justification is setting a person free from the penalty of their Sin. Therefore, when the Bible speaks about the Justification by Faith, it means the willingness of God, through His mercy, not to hold Man accountable for his Sin. Of course, the question of Justification by the Law was an important concept for the Hebrew people, given their dedication to the Decalogue and the Old Testament Law. However, Paul made it clear that no one could become justified by the Law, since it was impossible to keep every aspect of the Law. As he stated in his Letter to the Romans, "by the works of the Law no flesh will be justified in His sight for through the Law comes the knowledge of sin" (Romans 3:20). For Paul, the Law brought a knowledge of sin and through that knowledge Man realizes his sinfulness as a result of his obvious disobedience. The point here is

---

[84] *Webster's New Riverside University Dictionary*, s.v. "Justification" (with "Justify").

that the Law provided a realization of Man's sinfulness and the idea of being justified before God as a result of the Law was impossible.

Paul noted a couple of verses later that "all have sinned and fallen short of the glory of God" (Romans 3:23). Therefore, since Justification by the Law was impossible due to Man's sinful nature, another avenue for justification became necessary for God to accomplish His purpose—Man's freedom from the penalty of his Sin. The result was God's presentation of Justification by Faith. Numerous passages in the New Testament provide a direct, or an implied, reference to the idea of a Justification by Faith. Paul presented the specific passage regarding the idea in Romans 3-4. A part of that passage states that

> being justified as a gift by His grace through the redemption which is in Christ Jesus; whom God displayed publicly as a propitiation in His blood through faith. This was to demonstrate His righteousness, because in the forbearance of God He passed over the sins previously committed . . . so that He would be just and the justifier of the one who has faith in Jesus. (Romans 3:24-26)

As noted, the context of the passage expresses the impossibility of obtaining a righteousness by means of the Law, since "all have sinned" and disobey the Law. It continues by noting that justification is a "gift by His grace . . . through Christ Jesus" and that He (Jesus) became the "propitiation" for our sins that one receives through faith—Justified by Faith.

However, many will claim that faith is not an easy topic to discuss effectively in such a limited scope as this one chapter. Indeed, throughout academic circles many scholars continue to compile tome after tome on faith and in the process find it difficult to reach any definitive conclusions. As one scholar stated, "taken out of context, therefore, statements about faith may be ambiguous or even misleading."[85]

---

[85] Monika K. Hellwig, "A History of the Concept of Faith," in *Handbook of Faith*, edited by James Michael Lee (Birmingham, AL: Religious Education Press, 1990), 3.

Of course, the approach for our discussion is not meant to be "misleading."

However, McDowell expressed one aspect of that misleading quality when he related a story about a debate between himself and a professor of philosophy at a reputable university in the Midwest. During a discussion on faith, the professor noted that a consideration of something that happened (the reference was the resurrection of Jesus) was not all that important. For that professor (and others, no doubt) the important factor was a matter of whether the Believer *believed* that it (resurrection) happened. McDowell claimed that he immediately responded to that statement with the following: "Sir, it does matter what I as a Christian believe, because the value of Christian faith is not in the one believing but in its object (the reality of Christ's resurrection)."[86] McDowell's perspective was that the "value" of Christian faith is in the object of the Believer's faith, not simply the faith. In that respect, the reality of faith's focus (in this case, resurrection) becomes the imperative. Therefore, the concept of being Justified by Faith represents the act of God declaring Man free from the penalty of his sin which becomes based on the faith in the reality of the resurrection.

That leads us to the final digit in the combination that will unlock the otherwise fuzzy picture regarding the assurance of resurrection for the person demonstrating a faith in Christ. That final digit is the nature of our justification that leads the Believer to realize eternal life through a resurrection from the dead. At the heart of this point is the righteousness that God imputes as the result of the justification that the Believer receives through faith. God exists in a perfect righteousness. Man, as a result of his Sin and subsequent unrighteousness, is currently (and eternally) separated from God. That point is the spiritual focus of the Fall. Prior to the Fall, Man lived in a righteousness and in a direct, one-on-one relationship with God. The Genesis narrative acknowledges that Adam had direct and personal conversations with God. When Adam and Eve sinned, they fell into an unrighteousness and God cast them out of the Garden and out of His direct presence. With the coming of Jesus and His sacrifice on the Cross, God established a means for covering Man's sins. With that covering, God presented Man with the opportunity to be brought

---

[86] McDowell, *Evidence*, 5.

back into a presence with Him today and for eternity. We receive that covering (the righteousness) through a profession of faith in Jesus as the Christ. That concept is representative of the concept of a "Justification by Faith."

It brings to mind a simple analogy. The sin of Man is obvious. We are all sinners and have no ability to be good enough to establish our own righteousness and bring ourselves back into fellowship with God. We are, quite literally, out in the cold. However, there is a "cover" that is being offered to us. It is a cover that will provide protection for our entire body. And, it is being offered as a free gift. All we need to do is reach out and accept it. The choice is clear. We can remain in the cold and freeze to death; or accept the free gift and live. Ephesians 2:8 states, "For it is by grace you have been saved, through faith—and this is not from yourselves, it is the gift of God." God's grace is a free gift. All we need to do is accept it, "through faith," receiving God's justification that results in our righteousness, that brings us life . . . now and forever!

That interpretation brings out one important difference that exists between denominations regarding the salvation of Man through the "free gift" provided by God as noted in the passage from Ephesians. At issue is the doctrine of Predestination, the belief that God "predetermined" the salvation for each Believer. At the heart of this debate is the question of who would accept His gift and what constitutes the gift. Is grace the gift, or is it faith? Predestination denotes the "gift" of Ephesians 2:8 to be faith. Various interpretations provide a different context, but the basic premise is that God provided the gift of faith that activates His saving grace to whom He chose would receive salvation. The other side of that coin is the position that God's Grace is the "gift" expressed in Ephesians 2:8. As such, God's grace is freely available to everyone and therefore requires an individual decision of faith in order to accept the gift. In this salvation model, Man is personally responsible for accepting or denying the gift and whether, or not, he receives salvation.

The doctrine of Predestination is a theology associated with John Calvin and linked primarily to Calvinist denominations like the Presbyterian Church. The Congregationalist churches, like Baptists, accept the "personal faith" doctrine as essential for Man's salvation. Regardless of the specific theological model a specific church accepts for salvation, the

Christian Church universally accepts the Truth presented in Scripture that Man is "saved by grace through faith."

At the close of this section on Jesus' resurrection, three conclusions become an imperative for every Believer. First, we must accept the importance of the resurrection. Without the resurrection, Jesus is simply another messianic figure and an interesting personality of the time. The main point here is that the resurrection of Jesus set a precedent that resurrection was a possibility and something that all Believers could accept as a reality. The second Truth is that the faith of a Believer in the resurrection is not a blind faith. Through the evidence afforded from the biblical accounts of eyewitnesses and even the confirmed logic presented in this discussion, one can have a conviction in the reality of Christ's resurrection from the dead. Finally, the positive presentation of the first two brings an assurance of resurrection for all Believers. As a result of their faith, the Believer receives a justification from God which results in a righteousness that brings the assurance of an eternal union with God . . . a glorious resurrection from the dead.

Question #5

Is the Bible the True Word of God?

CHAPTER 15

THE HISTORY OF THE BIBLE

And there are also many other things which Jesus did, which if they were written in detail, I suppose that even the world itself would not contain the books that would be written. (John 21:25)

The Bible stands as, arguably, the greatest book ever written. According to one resource, an estimate establishes the total number of Bibles at over six billion ("billion," with a "b") and a downloadable application reached 300 million at the end of 2017.[87] That seems incredible, but as one reference stated,

> "The Bible's value, above all, is as a guide to lives. And, we mean to all lives, whether one is religious or not, whether one is Christian, Jewish, or from another religion, or no religion . . . now finds many who have never read or studied the Bible, who still share a cultural sense of its

---

[87] From the "Bible Answers" website, https://thebibleanswer.org, on 18 April 2019.

importance as a foundation of morality and virtues."[88]

However, one of the truly great challenges of Christian Apologetics is represented in the questions related to the formation and inspiration of the Bible, the sacred text of Christianity. The individual denominations illustrate that challenge by the nature of their specific acknowledgement of what constitutes the Bible. The Protestant denominations accept the Old and New Testaments, while the Roman Catholic Church adds several books (referred to as the Apocrypha) and the Orthodox Church adds even more. An additional challenge is seen in the historical reality that it took over three centuries before Christianity had a Canon in the form the Church accepted as the Bible that we know today. Such is the daunting task reflected in the attempt to answer the question posed for this last section.

And so, regardless of the pitfalls, let us press on as I am reminded of Admiral David Farragut's words during the Battle of Mobile Bay, "Damn the torpedoes, full speed ahead." With those words of encouragement, the next three chapters will attempt to address, and even answer, the major questions surrounding the Bible as the Holy Scriptures of the Christian Church. The first chapter will focus on the difficult historical question regarding the development and acceptance of what would become the Bible. A close examination of the struggle within the Church through those early centuries can leave some Christians shaking their heads and has the potential of producing more questions than answers.

The second chapter tackles the always tricky subject of biblical inspiration. Since the Bible proclaims itself to be inspired, the consensus is that the Bible *is* inspired. In that respect, the Christian Church accepts that the Bible is the Word of God. However, as it is with many things within the Christian Church, that statement simply raises another question. That question is: "How was the Bible inspired?" The dissemination of several different inspiration theories makes this chapter an interesting read for every Christian. And, the result may even challenge a preconceived concept on the inspiration of the Bible as God's Word.

---

[88] Richard Elliott Friedman and Shawna Dolansky, *The Bible Now* (New York: Oxford University Press, 2011), xi.

The third chapter reflects a "where the rubber meets the road" concept. Accepting the history of the Bible as being God's preservation of His Word and the inspiration by Him to secure His Truth for His people, the final chapter examines how the Bible is still, after thousands of years, applicable to the life of the Believer. The point here is that as Christians we must accept the premise that God cares for us, provides for us, and that the Bible represents a means by which He accomplishes that care and provision.

With that brief introduction, I must provide one disclaimer and establish one "given." The disclaimer is one that seeks to limit the size and complexity of this endeavor by dealing with the Bible from a purely Christian perspective. In other words, this section will not examine the specific development of the Hebrew Scriptures; but instead will explore the history that resulted in the adoption of a Holy Scriptures, collectively. That perspective also means that the research will not proceed beyond the scope of canonization. In other words, this chapter will not attempt to address the development of the Bible through the last two thousand years. In the 1960s, Cambridge University in England attempted to present a monolith on the history of the Bible from its beginning to the modern-day. The result was a three-volume tome of over 1500 pages. That is not the focus nor the intent of this section. Instead, it is limited to answering the question "Is the Bible the True Word of God?" A look at how the Early Church formed the Holy Scriptures into a Canon should be adequate to provide an answer to that question.

The idea of a "given" is a concept a student of geometry would understand. In geometry the student tries to prove some problem. The "proof" provides the student with a beginning point and a conclusion. Students then use various postulates and theorems to progress from the beginning to the conclusion. The beginning of the proof is called "the given." It represents the foundation of the problem and it cannot be changed. In his book on the formation of the Bible, Thomas Bokedal, who served as Lecturer at the Lutheran School of Theology in Sweden, stated that "the fact that they (Scriptures) have been formed into a single volume is certainly not accidental."[89] Arthur Pink, one of the most influential Christian authors of the mid-twentieth century,

---

[89] Thomas Bokedal, *The Formation and Significance of the Christian Biblical Canon: A Study in Text, Ritual, and Interpretation* (London: Bloomsbury, 2014), 7

stated that "Christianity is based upon the impregnable rock of Holy Scripture."[90]   Both of these men acknowledged the inspiration of the Christian Bible. Bokedal stated it as a concept that could not be considered as "accidental."   In other words, it possessed some measure of divine inspiration. Pink, referenced the Bible as "Holy" Scripture, referring to the divine quality of the biblical text and thereby presenting the importance of that "impregnable rock" as realized through the inspiration of God.

All of that is important as a means of setting the stage for a discussion on the Bible as the Holy Scriptures of the Christian Faith.   We can reserve most of the discussion regarding the inspiration of Scripture to Chapter 16.   Still, as we begin to examine the history of the Bible, the given in the process must be an understanding that a basis of Christianity accepts the Bible as the inspired Word of God. Regardless of the historical challenges that the topic uncovers, the bottom line for the Christian Faith is that the Bible became what it is today as a matter of divine direction— God working His Will through the hearts of imperfect men. With that "given," let us proceed.

The basic concept that we, as Christians, accept in our view of the Bible is that it *is* the Word of God. In that respect, it establishes its authority within the Church for "its role in theological or moral argument, its place in proclamation, (and) it's liturgical presence."[91]   Webster then added the conclusion of John Calvin regarding the presentation of the Canon as he noted:

> First, it is derived from the Spirit's
> presence in the Church, and therefore
> by no means autonomous . . . But
> second the Church's act with respect
> to the Canon is an act of faithful
> assent rather than a self-derived
> judgment.[92]

Calvin's defense of the Bible indicated that he believed the Bible did not take shape out of a single effort, or even out

---

[90] Arthur Pink, *Divine Inspiration of the Bible* (Swengel, PA: Bible Truth Depot, 1917), 2.

[91] John Webster, *Holy Scripture: A Dogmatic Sketch* (Cambridge: Cambridge University Press, 2003), 53.

[92] *Ibid.*, 62.

of the congregated effort of a single Council. Instead, he implied that God was its ultimate Creator. As such, the Church accepted the final form as not only God's Word, but as orchestrated by God, Himself.

Other scholars echo that sentiment. Luis Schokel, who was a Spanish theologian of the twentieth century with nearly forty books to his credit, stated in a book he published just before his death that "we (as Christians) do not proclaim the 'Idea of God' but rather the 'Word of God,' because first and foremost, Scripture transmits the divine Word, the communicative will of God to human beings."[93] For Schokel, a number of other biblical scholars, and certainly the Christian Church, "the reading of these texts (the early Church writings) as Canon, in one way or another, is a matter of great importance to every (emphasis added) Christian community."[94] Another scholar put it this way:

> The clear intention of the text is to help readers obtain knowledge and to touch them emotionally, to motivate the faithful to act upon God's commands. For centuries people of faith have believed the act of reading God's Word is the process whereby humans receive the thoughts of God.[95]

With that level of faithful consideration, it became an imperative to direct some sort of collection of the texts in order to establish an authoritative Canon for the Early Church. That sentiment became an imperative as Church leaders battled various heresies that attempted to thwart the development of God's True word. Two opposing factions were at the center of this debate. One side believed in a concise collection of authoritative books that the Church should accept as the True Word of God. The opposing viewpoint taught that the revelation of Scripture never ended. They did not believe in closing the door on the possibility that God might provide additional Truth. Certainly, they would argue, if God

[93] Luis Alonso Schokel, *A Manual of Hermeneutics* (Sheffield, England: Sheffield Academy Press, 1998), 25.
[94] Bokedal, *The Formation and Significance of the Christian Biblical Canon*, 4.
[95] Donald L. Brake, *A Visual History of the English Bible* (Grand Rapids: Baker Books, 2008), 21.

provided more Truth the Church should add that Truth to the Canon. As a couple of religious historians stated:

> *The reason Christians have twenty-seven books in their New Testament, many scholars say, is because early church leaders did not like the eleven that the theologian named Marcion approved. Nor did they care for the claim of another theologian, Montanus, that God's revelation was continuing and there should be no end to scripture.*[96]

Although noted earlier that a "Holy Scripture" for the Christian Church did not exist for centuries after Christ's death, it is not a true statement to proclaim that the early Christians of the First Century (and beyond) did not possess God's Word. The historical record provides several reasons to acknowledge that truth. The first is the presence of an oral tradition that was, for that period, a major conduit for passing along information. Stephen Miller and Richard Huber provide a statement in their book that makes the point abundantly clear.

> *For the first 100 years after Jesus, there did not seem to be a problem (with a written account). Christians were content with the eyewitness reports of Jesus' apostles and the second-hand reports from followers of the apostles. The living memory, passed on by word of mouth, had a powerful effect.*[97]

Oral tradition was a perfectly acceptable means for the early Christians to hear about the life of Jesus. However, that reality also created a vacuum. As the early apostles died and the stories became less familiar to those Christians who were

---

[96] Stephen M. Miller and Robert V. Huber, *The Bible: A History* (Intercourse, PA: Good Books, 2004), 92.
[97] Ibid.

still alive, a general concern for a written record emerged within the Church.

The second element that perhaps delayed a committed effort to collect specific accounts of Christ's life was the dedicated ministry and vociferous letter writing of the apostle Paul. Paul wrote numerous letters to the Christians in the churches he started during his three missionary journeys. Those letters, as well as a few personal ones to Timothy, Titus, Philemon, and the letter to the Christians in Rome, represent thirty percent of the entire New Testament. In addition, Paul began writing about Jesus as the Christ and His sacrifice for the sins of Man before the presence of the first written Gospel account appeared on the scene.[98] As such, oral tradition was not the only means of disseminating the truth about Jesus. Still, as the years passed and the followers of Jesus began to desire more than the personal stories from the apostles, a desire to compile the information about Jesus into a single collection began to evolve.

However, a final problem existed for the Christians during the Early Church period. That problem was persecution. The Roman Empire labeled the new religion as an enemy of the State and sought to destroy the foundation of the Faith by persecuting its followers. Historical accounts of Christians being torn apart by wild beasts, burned at the stake, and crucified by the tens of thousands are easily accessible. However, regardless of the dangers the early Church faced, the sincere and dedicated faith demonstrated throughout the early centuries resulted in a steady increase in the Church's influence and its numbers. In the second chapter of the Book of Acts we can read accounts of the effective proclamation ministry carried out by the apostles. In verse forty-one we read, "Those who accepted his message were baptized, and about three thousand were added to their number that day." And later, in verse forty-seven, it states, "And the Lord was adding to their number day by day those who were being saved."

Of course, those accounts took place prior to the period of the severest persecution of the Church within the Roman Empire. Still, even during the time of the ever-present threat of death, the Faith expanded. As early as the second century, the Church in Rome read Gospel narratives and

---

[98] Exact dating is difficult, but most scholars acknowledge Paul's first letter was I Thessalonians at about 50. By contrast, the first Gospel was undoubtedly Mark, which usually receives a dating in the early 60s (62-64).

portions of what is now the Old Testament. During that century, Marcion compiled for the Church a "Canon," composed of a Gospel and some of the letters of Paul. It was a start, but Marcion was a Gnostic and ultimately deemed a heretic. Still, one might argue that the heretics inspired the collection of what we now claim as the Bible. As the Church struggled with various doctrinal positions, it was inevitable that the question of what is right and what is wrong had to be answered. In a pastoral little book, the author concluded that "We could say, then, that a heretic (Marcion) planted the idea of a New Testament and heretics made it necessary to form a New Testament."[99]

Even though the Church understood the need for a collection of the Christian writings, how to accomplish that requirement was a challenge. Because of the Christian persecution within the Roman Empire, any attempt to overtly unite the different factions along any lines deemed to be an impossible, perhaps even suicidal, task. For centuries the Church, for the most part, operated independently and congregations worshipped in small, local assemblages. During the services, they read from whatever narrative manuscripts they had at their disposal.

It was not until the beginning of the Fourth Century and the rise of Constantine as Emperor that the persecution of Christians in the Empire came to an end. It was in 313 that Constantine issued an edict that declared that Christianity did not pose a threat to the Empire. Although church historians continue to debate the concept that Emperor Constantine was a true Christian, the historical record shows that the favor he provided to the Fourth Century Christians certainly added to the success for the cause of the Christian Church. In fact, we can read that the situation for the Church and Christianity improved tremendously as a result of the new emperor's perspective on the Christian faith. For instance, during the fourth century

> *most Christian communities existed within the Roman world, and earlier Roman victories against Jewish freedom fighters . . . led to the development of Christian centers away from Jerusalem, in Alexandria, Caesarea,*

---

[99] Charles Merrill Smith and James W. Bennett, *How the Bible Was Built* (Grand Rapids: Eerdmann, 2005), 62.

Antioch, Rome, Carthage, and with Constantinople.[100]

Now that Christianity was "legal" within the Empire, the Faith needed a divine text to facilitate its continual expansion throughout the world.

Unfortunately, the immediate move to establish a Canon for the Church was something of a mess. Numerous early Church Fathers offered a "canon" of Scriptures. Maricon, Irenaeus (second century), Tertullian (late second and early third century), Eusebius (late third and early fourth century), and Athanasius (fourth century) are just a few of those Early Church Fathers who provided a specific collection of Scriptures for the Church. So, with all the conflicting "canons" circulating throughout the world, how did the Church develop and accept the Holy Scriptures in the form that we know it today? A possible answer to that question is that God directed the process, as acknowledged earlier in this chapter. However, that answer sidesteps the historical record of what happened that brought the Christian Bible into reality. And, it is an interesting record.

Apart from the various individuals that created their own version of the Canon, the actual collection of the narrative accounts presented another problem. Some of the manuscripts existed in scroll form that could be rolled up for storage and then taken out in order to be read during a worship service. Others existed in codices that represented the collection of numerous "books" that included the narrative selections. The Codex Sinaiticus and Vaticanus represent what many consider "by far the oldest and best and most important copies of the Greek Bible extant"[101] In the case of the Sinaiticus, the codex contains all the books of today's Christian Bible and is typically dated to the fourth century.[102]

The Codex Sinaiticus represents an incredible historical record of what existed as a fourth century "Bible" for the Early Church. However, that still does not answer the question of how the Sinaiticus, or any codex/Bible came into being. For the answer to that question, we need to go back to the historical record of the fourth century. It is at that

---

[100] Margaret Davies, "The New Testament" in *The Oxford Illustrated History of the Bible*, edited by John Rogerson (Oxford: Oxford University Press, 2001), 43.

[101] Christopher De Hamel, *The Book: A History of the Bible* (London: Phaidon, 2001), 52.

[102] Davies, "The New Testament," 39.

point that we can begin to piece together the development of the Christian Bible. Of course, that record reveals the involvement of Man in the process and that is often a sign of trouble! Regardless, in order to answer the question from a historical perspective, it is necessary to place Man at the center of establishing the Holy Scriptures as a single, divine text.

To begin this examination, it is a consensus among many scholars that the Canon for the Early Church became adopted as the result of what Church considered "accepted, vice "disputed," Scripture. Understandably, that required a good deal of debate and effort to direct a collective consensus of what would be "accepted" and what would be "disputed" within the Christian Church. Basically, the "Accepted Scriptures" were those books that represented a broad recognition as an authoritative Word of God. Those classified as "Disputed" received that label because the Early Church believed they expressed a premise contrary to the accepted principles of the Faith. Along those lines we can read in a scholarly work an emphatic statement that

> *the books rejected from the Canon were rejected because they seemed to conflict with what the accepted books taught. Selection thus involved not only comparison among books, but also a comparison with a norm viewed as relatively fixed.*[103]

In other words, the decision as to which books would be included as part of the Canon was made on the declaration of what the Church considered as being authoritative, either by authorship or theological presentation. The fact that a group of men made that decision is often proclaimed as a criticism by some non-believers regarding the Bible. They note that if men made their decisions based on their own faith persuasion then the Bible is simply a man-made collection of books. It, therefore, does not warrant the title of "Holy Scriptures." To add some fuel to that fire, the historical record of the various Councils during the Early Church period often disputed

---

[103] R. M. Grant, "The New Testament Canon" in *The Cambridge History of the Bible: From Beginning to Jerome*, edited by P. R. Ackroyd and C. F. Evans, Cambridge: Cambridge University Press, 1970), 285.

what was a true word of God or what was theologically sound doctrine. One scholar championed that point by stating that "those who were deciding what constitutes the New Testament were also discussing what expressions of Christian belief were acceptable or not."[104]

As one might imagine, confrontations between conflicting ideas (and individuals) occurred often. It was even possible for one person to be cited as a heretic at one Council and then praised as a saint at a subsequent meeting. Without going through a litany of examples, let us look at the life of one man, Athanasius. Athanasius lived during the fourth century and served as the Archbishop at Alexandria. Although revered today as a pillar of the Early Church, he often found himself in conflict with his colleagues and even received a banishment from church leaders.[105] In fact, within some circles his title was *Athanasius Contra Mundum* (Athanasius Against the World). Still, his development of a Canon received widespread acceptance as representative of the Church. In fact, apart from the criticism of personal influence, Athanasius' Canon was not one of personal opinion; but it was a consideration of the established position of the Church.[106] That dedicated effort to preserve the Word of God (and not a personal opinion) resulted in Athanasius' Canon being accepted as authoritative at the Church Councils in Hippo (393), Carthage (397), and Carthage again (419).[107]

To look at the criticism from another perspective, we can examine the biblical history. In that history, we can certainly read where God demonstrated an ability to direct the actions of Man in order to accomplish His purpose. God was even able to instill His purpose in the lives of non-believers in order to affect His divine Will. With that clear biblical Truth, why is it hard for people to accept the point that God worked through the lives of the men attending those early Councils to preserve His Truth for His people. A valid point of faith that we will discuss in more detail in the next chapter on inspiration.

So, we arrive at two distinct points regarding the work to establish a Canon for the Early Church. The first point is the movement to have a codified "Holy Scriptures" for the

---

[104] Davies, "The New Testament," 46.
[105] Smith, *How the Bible Was Built*, 67.
[106] Miller, *The Bible*, 97.
[107] Ibid.

Church. The second is the divine Will that accomplished that purpose. It is here that the Early Church again owes a debt of gratitude to the emperor, Constantine. In 325, he ordered church leaders to meet in a council at Nicaea, an ancient city in modern-day Turkey. The Council met for the purpose of addressing what was a doctrinal Truth for the Church, specifically, as it related to the Arian dispute. At the heart of the disagreement was the question of the type of relationship that existed between God and Jesus. On one side, Arius (and the Arians) believed in a distinction between the nature of God and the nature of Jesus. On the other side, Athanasius (et. al.) believed that the two were identical, the same. For them, Jesus was distinctly God. The two possessed the same nature (refer to the homoousia and homoiousia discussion from Chapter 4, "The Trinitarian Nature of God").

As a result of the discussion, the Council ruled Arianism a heresy and adopted a creedal statement of faith that we recognize as the Nicene Creed. In part, the creed stated that Jesus was "God of God, Light of Light, true God of true God, begotten and not made; of the very same nature of the Father." Although the Council did not specifically address the issue of a Canon, the "bishops considered which Christian writings should be accorded most authority."[108] Eusebius attended that Council and as an aftermath of that meeting he wrote his Magnum Opus, *Church History*, in which he specified that which is and is not "Scripture."[109] With that, the road to developing a Canon for the Early Church was set in motion. As a result of a clearly established precedence, the Council set the parameters for the future considerations to develop a Canon for the Early Church. Perhaps unknowingly to the bishops attending the Council, their work and their conclusions established the concept of how the Church would ultimately adopt the books and epistles that would become what the Christian Church calls today "The Bible." However, it was not until the Council at Laodicea (363), nearly four decades after the first Council at Nicaea, that we find the first use of the word "canon" as the Council "encouraged the public reading of only 'canonical books' of the New Testament and the Old Testament."[110] Examining the record of this Council, one can find a list that corresponds to our modern-day New Testament

[108] Davies, "The New Testament," 43.
[109] Smith, *Built*, 66.
[110] Davies, "The New Testament," 44.

(minus John's Revelation).[111] It seems that the road to the establishment of "canonical books" into the Bible had finally begun in earnest.

I suppose at this point we could run through the entire history of the Church Councils, picking apart the pros and cons that each specific Council instituted. As interesting as that is from a historical perspective, I don't believe it adds much to the discussion at this point. Two conclusions are important to this presentation. The first is that the Early Church worked through the centuries to provide a collection of authoritative writings that the entirety of the Church could accept as the True Word of God. Through the threat of persecution and death and in the face of heresy debates and church dissension, the Church persevered. The Early Church Fathers collaborated to determine the most widely accepted and authoritative writings available for inclusion in the first "Bible." It took them four centuries to come to a consensus. However, the Christian Church expresses a faith that under the guidance of Almighty God, they got it right.

The overall presentation of this chapter leads the Christian to a recognized conclusion: It was God that directed the development and outcome of what we now have as the Christian Bible. In other words, the position of Christianity, and the position of any Faith Group, is that the Holy Scriptures represent God's Word for God's people. Therefore, as a matter of faith, what we have today is exactly what God intended for us to have. Even though imperfect Man made the decisions as to which books would be part of the Canon, that does not mean that the Bible we have today is not representative of God's divine Truth.

Of course, the rank and file faithful did not have a copy of the Bible. Even though the Church collected the various scrolls and letters into codices, individual Christians did not have direct access to that collection. In the mid-Fifteenth Century, Johannes Gutenberg changed that dynamic with the publication of the first Bible. His work laid a path for making the Bible available to every Believer. Now, as wonderful as that might seem (and it was an incredible gift to the Christian community), it created another problem. The printing of the Bible allowed for the personal interpretation of the Scriptures. That reality, of course, led to a competition between the various versions of the Bible. And,

---

[111] Ibid.

it is a competition that continues to this day. That competition exists between publishers that push their version as the most accurate and the individual Believer that has a version that they accept as authoritative. To add insult to injury, some publishers will even change the text in order to support a political correctness over the Truth. A case in point is a minister I heard read from a gender-neutral Bible that referred to God as "parent," vice Father, and Jesus as the "Child," vice the Son, of God.

Of course, all of that will create some immediate heartburn for some people. Apart from the political correctness debate, the basic problem comes from the fact that many people have their "cherished" versions of the Bible. As such, they may look to this chapter in hopes of confirming that the version they read is the true, "authorized" version of the Bible. In that light, let me reaffirm something I noted at the beginning. It is not the intent of this chapter to trace the development of the Bible from Christ's life to the twenty-first century. As one attempts to adopt the position regarding a perfect text, or an authorized version of the Bible, two important historical realities scuttle the whole idea.

The first point is that no "original biblical manuscripts" from the time of Jesus remain in existence. Shocking news, for some, I suspect; but true, nonetheless. Therefore, what we have are the manuscripts that date back to the Early Church period; but none that date back to the time that Jesus lived. As noted earlier, the oldest book in our New Testament is arguably First Thessalonians and Paul wrote it over a decade after Christ's death. Which leads us to the second point that notes that we have no specific writings from Jesus. That is an unfortunate truth, since it would be great to be able to read something that Jesus wrote in His own hand. Granted, we have the "words of Jesus" recorded for us in the Gospels and we accept those as His true words. However, it would seem to be something uniquely different to have a personal letter directly from Jesus that expressed His conviction on various issues.

All of that reflects back to the idea that some Christians accept different versions of the Bible as being more reliable, or "authoritative" than others. I remember one lady who made the statement that she only read a particular version of the Bible because "it was the one that Jesus wrote." Although she was a person of sincere faith, it was a little misguided.

Now, please understand, this is not an attempt to direct you to question your faith in, or even your allegiance to, a specific version of the Bible that you truly feel relates God's Truth.   Instead, it is an effort to bring us all to a level of appreciation for the difficulty the Early Church had in developing the Canon.   As we look through that difficulty, the only possible answer for a belief in what we have today as being the Word of God is a faith that God directed it.   And if God directed its composition, then God certainly possessed a desire to preserve it for the past two millennia.

That leads us into the difficult challenge of addressing the concept of biblical inspiration.   So, facing the challenge head-on and again using Admiral Farragut's famous words for our motivation, "full speed ahead!"

CHAPTER 16

BIBLE AS THE INSPIRED WORD OF GOD

All Scripture is inspired by God and profitable for teaching, for reproof, for correction, for training in righteousness; so that the man of God may be adequate, equipped for every good work. (II Timothy 3:16-17)

A s presented in the preceding chapter, the difficulty of sifting through the historical record that established the Bible as the Canon of the Christian Church is a significant challenge. It caused some significant angst within the Early Church, which continues to this day. A specific examination of how the Bible came into existence provides the information for some to question the method for, and even doubt the idea of, the Bible as authoritative. In that respect, it is hard to imagine a greater challenge facing the Christian apologist than the concept of biblical inspiration. One scholar acknowledged that point by concluding that a particular concept regarding the authority of the Bible is that "the Bible is an anthology of diverse writings that have been patched, stitched, and strung together over the course of a millennium . . . (And

203

that) the Bible was not simply given by God but written and edited by imperfect humans."[112]

Conversely, as early as Origen, the Church accepted the concept of biblical inspiration. As he stated, "The sacred books are not the works of men . . . (but) were written by the inspiration of the Holy Spirit at the will of the Father of all, through Jesus Christ."[113] It was also during that period that the Early Church developed a merging of the elements of biblical inspiration and the basic Truth proclaimed through the written word. In other words, the Church began to develop a "belief that the scriptures were received by inspiration of the Holy Spirit and have a deeper meaning than that which appears upon the surface of the record."[114] And, as noted in the previous chapter, the Second and Third Century Church struggled to incorporate just those books considered to be authoritative as representing the true Word of God. In their estimation, it was "not that other post-apostolic books were untrue . . . but that they were not wholly true."[115] It seems that from the beginning of the Christian movement the Church considered and accepted the position that the Bible was the inspired Word of God.

Not surprisingly, as with the answers to other questions posed in this book, the discussion of biblical inspiration is a contributing factor in the denominationalism that we know exists within Christianity. Some churches express a sincere conviction in a direct inspiration by God to the biblical authors and the inerrancy of what they wrote. Others have a more moderate, or even distinctly liberal, approach. Beyond that general point, it also caused (and continues to cause) rifts within specific denominations and churches. The Southern Baptist Convention addressed the issue during a movement in the late 1970s that steered the Convention to a more fundamental and theologically conservative direction. Nearly fifty years later, that issue is still a hot-button topic in many churches in the Convention. And, earlier in the

---

[112] Michael Satlow, *How the Bible Became Holy* (New Haven: Yale University Press, 2014), 1-2.

[113] Jeffery D. Bershears, *Bibliology: What Every Christian Should Know about the Origins, Composition, Inspiration, Interpretation, Canonicity, and Transmission of the Bible* (Eugene, OR: Wipf and Stock, 2017), 97.

[114] R. P. C. Hanson, "Biblical Exegesis in the Early Church" in *The Cambridge History of the Bible: From Beginning to Jerome*, edited by P. R. Ackroyd and C. F. Evans (Cambridge: Cambridge University Press, 1970), 461.

[115] Ibid., 105.

twentieth century, the Presbyterian Church confronted the same issue. The denomination tried to deal with the question of the inspiration of Scripture and the inerrancy of the biblical text, but instead the denomination copped out. During a 1927 meeting of the denomination, a report on the issue stated that "the General Assembly (of the Presbyterian Church) did not have the constitutional power to issue binding definitions."[116] That is certainly an interesting conclusion since it seems that within the Presbyterian Church the General Assembly possessed exactly that power and routinely provided "binding definitions" and directions they determined essential for the Church. As one might imagine, the conclusion from the General Assembly did not ease the tension. The historical record shows that throughout that century the Presbyterian Church struggled with the issue as "almost annually the church has been torn by controversies that are replayed in the terms of the fundamentalist-liberal dichotomy."[117] The question of Biblical inspiration represents a subject that is on the one hand essential to the Christian Faith, while on the other a point of continued debate and discussion.

The idea of biblical inspiration presented a significant problem for Southern Baptists, Presbyterians, and certainly many churches within the Christian Faith. Other denominations often struggled with the question of biblical inspiration and the idea that the Bible is inerrant. Interestingly, such division is not a contemporary matter. In the Seventeenth Century, Richard Farnworth, who was a Quaker and a Christian apologist, wrote numerous tracts on the Christian Faith. In a blistering pamphlet referencing those individuals who would propose to disagree with his conservative position regarding biblical inspiration and interpretation, he stated the following:

> Wherein they pretend to clear the truth of Scandals, but are found liars, and the lies is (sic) sent them back in a bundle or number, that they may flee their deceit, and Spirit of Lies, Error, and Slander."[118]

[116] Jack B. Rogers and John K. McKim, *The Authority and Inspiration of the Bible: An Historical Approach* (New York: Harper and Row, 1979), xix.
[117] Ibid.
[118] Richard F. Farnworth, "The Holy Scriptures from Scandals Are Cleared" (1655), 6.

In fact, this point is so divisive among Christians and theologians that Webster (an Anglican priest and theologian) noted, "Theorists in culture and religious studies, and more than a handful of modern theologians, seek to persuade us that there is not such a thing (as Holy Scripture).[119] An incredible statement and one that clearly establishes the daunting task before us: examining the historical record for the compilation of the Canon and then proclaiming it, through that process, as the inspired Word of God.

Perhaps the first question to ask in order to properly address the ultimate question of inspiration is what the idea of "inspiration" means. A precise dictionary definition would be a "stimulation of the mind or emotions to a high level of activity or feeling."[120] Taking the dictionary definition and relating it to the Bible seems to make the statement that biblical inspiration "refers to the enhancement to which the Bible instrumentally causes in persons and not to the Bible itself."[121] That is an interesting statement. At first glance, it seems to relate the idea of the Bible inspiring the reader, while negating the importance of the Bible itself as being inspired. Even if applied to the authors, it would provide more of an inspiration that a musician or poet or artist may receive before attempting to produce a beautiful masterpiece.

Of course, that is not the concept of biblical inspiration that is the focus of this chapter, nor does it adequately provide for the Believer to accept the written Word as the authoritative Word of God. The point here is that divine inspiration is not the same as simply "being inspired," like one might feel the urge or compulsion to do something. With that in mind, before we can move any further in this examination, we must establish the foundation for the discussion that "divine inspiration is supernatural (i.e., unlike poetic or artistic instances of inspiration) and different from 'ordinary' activity of the Spirit in conversion and sanctification."[122]

That statement clearly establishes the point: that beyond the dictionary definition, Christian scholars and the Church understand the nature of biblical inspiration for the

---

[119] Webster, *Holy Scripture*, 1.
[120] *Webster's New Riverside University Dictionary*, s.v. "Inspiration.".
[121] Kern Robert Trembath, *Evangelical Theories of Biblical Inspiration* (New York: Oxford University Press, 1987), 103.
[122] Ibid., 21.

Christian Church. In that environment, some tried to examine different types of inspiration, believing that so long as it is inspired the method was not important. Others tried to nail down a more specific construct for the acceptance of the Bible as the inspired Word of God. The Zondervan Dictionary provides a definition of inspiration as "The supernatural process whereby God influences the biblical writers to record the words of Scripture, thereby rendering it as the Word of God."[123]

In that respect, the Church accepted a wide range of defining statements and many of the explanations provided by scholars and theologians offered a general rendering of inspiration. N. T. Wright stated simply that inspiration "is a shorthand way of talking about the belief that by his Spirit God guided the very different writers and editors, so that the books produced were the books God intended his people to have."[124] McDowell tried to elaborate on that definition a little when he stated that "inspiration can be defined as the mysterious process by which God worked through human writers, employing their individual personalities and styles to produce divinely authoritative writings."[125]

Other scholars made statements to provide the best plausible application and understanding of biblical inspiration. One stated that inspiration was "the charisma or special impulse of the Holy Spirit given to the particular authors to compose and preserve in writing certain experiences of the event of divine revelation."[126] He then continued to elaborate, stating that biblical inspiration is "the direct and active impulse of the Holy Spirit, who acts upon authors during the entire process of a work's composition-from initial thought to final redaction."[127] He concluded his comments on the concept by stating that inspiration represents "the charism that enables human words to constitute the word of God that makes present the Word incarnate and living."[128] And finally, Alec Gilmore, a Baptist pastor and educator in England, provided a more

---

[123] Matthew DeMoss and J. Edward Miller, *Zondervan Dictionary of the Bible* (Grand Rapids: Zondervan, 2002), 122.

[124] N. T. Wright, *Scripture and the Authority of God* (New York: Harper One, 2011), 35.

[125] McDowell, *Evidence*, 334.

[126] Philip Moller, "What Should They Be Saying about Biblical Inspiration?: A Note on the State of the Question," *Theological Studies* 74, no. 3 (September 2013):607.

[127] Ibid, 609.

[128] Ibid, 618.

historic presentation on inspiration when he penned a definition of verbal inspiration as

> *a response to the rise of biblical criticism in the eighteenth and nineteenth centuries to reassert the authority of Scriptures by claiming that the Bible was divinely inspired with every word coming from the mouth of God.*[129]

Gilmore continued by stating that the acceptance of that theory of inspiration gave rise to the inerrancy movement, the concept that the Bible, in its entirety, expresses Truth without any measure of error.

Although challenged on some fronts, many scholars find the dual positions of "inspiration" and "inerrancy" to be congruous. As stated in one compelling volume,

> *the theological corollary of inspiration inerrancy, indicates that those writings have been thereby supernaturally protected from error, thus implying that scripture is entirely trustworthy & uniquely authoritative for a given community of faith.*[130]

Others address the question from the side of inerrancy and note that inspiration and inerrancy are two sides of the same coin. In fact, one scholar raised the bar by noting that the word inerrant is not adequate to relate to the divine inspiration of the Scriptures. He stated that "there can be inerrant phone books—with no errors—but they do not thereby have divine authority."[131]

In reality, it all represents a giant bed of quicksand. The point is that no matter how one tries to define and apply the

---

[129] Alec Gilmore, *A Concise Dictionary of Bible Origins and Interpretation* (London: T. T. Clark, 2006), 204.

[130] Bruce M. Metzger and Michael D. Coogan, eds., *The Oxford Companion to the Bible* (New York: Oxford University Press, 1993), 302.

[131] Norman L Geisler, "An Evaluation of McGowen's View on the Inspiration of Scripture," *Bibliotheca Sacra* 167 (2010): 17.

concept of biblical inspiration, a myriad of questions and alternate possibilities seem to raise their heads. That being duly noted, as with the examination of the history of the Bible, the history of its inspiration becomes a daunting and mammoth undertaking. Therefore, in order to keep this book to a manageable size, we probably need to move forward in the development of the debate regarding the inspiration of the Bible. In that respect, a good historical place to start would be the Post-Reformation period. According to many church historians, it was following the Reformation period when the Church began to accept the conception of the Bible as verbally inspired and inerrant.[132] A position that created some debate in the early Protestant movement.

As noted earlier, the Church confronted the issue of biblical inspiration during the second and third centuries as a main consideration for the development of the Canon; but it was during the Post-Reformation period that the text within the Bible became revered as the True Word of God. In fact, it was during the Post-Reformation that scholars searched for "a tangible, human certainty of the Bible's inspiration rather than for a divine certainty brought about by faith."[133] In other words, the quest was on to determine a legitimate construct to proclaim with certainty, apart from a simple expression of faith, the inspiration of all Scripture. As such, the period laid down the gauntlet that would become a defining topic for the Church throughout the centuries that followed and continues to this very day.

However, it is that exact expression of a simple faith that leads most Christians to an acceptance of the Bible as being inspired. Ask a Christian why they believe in the inspiration of the Bible as the Word of God and they will probably respond with a statement of faith. One possible response might be, "I believe the Bible is inspired, otherwise it's just a bunch of opinions." That Christian understands that without an inspiration of the Scriptures they lose their meaning as the Word of God. They become the word of Matthew, Mark, Luke, John, Paul, etc. Another Believer might say, "My Church teaches it and I accept it." That person believes in the authoritative presentation of the denominational persuasion of their Church as a matter of faith. Beyond those typical responses, the more mature Christian might argue that the

---

[132] Rogers and McKim, *Authority and Inspiration of the Bible*, 166.
[133] Ibid, 421.

inspiration of Scripture is based on the Bible, itself. These are the church-going Bible "scholars" that know the Bible from "cover to cover" and can quote chapter and verse for most any situation. As it pertains to inspiration, they have their verses ready.

The most familiar passage related to biblical inspiration is the one stated at the beginning of this chapter. In his second letter to Timothy, Paul stated that "all Scripture is inspired by God." The Greek word for "inspired" here is "theopneustia." The word is a combination of two Greek words into a single concept. The first half of the word is "Theo" meaning God, as in "theology," the study of God. The second is "pneustis" meaning air or wind, as in a "pneumatic," or air-powered, drill. The translation becomes "inspired," but it literally means "God-breathed." Therefore, the concept of inspiration from the perspective of Paul was that the Scriptures were God-breathed into the lives and minds of the various biblical authors. And, as one scholar stated, "Since 'all scripture is God-breathed,' logic dictates that the hallmark of divine origin, total accuracy and infallibility be ascribed to the Bible as the product of God."[134] A conclusion that certainly makes perfect sense.

Perhaps that one passage is enough to establish the Truth of biblical inspiration, but there are others. Paul made another statement regarding the inspiration of Scripture, this time to the Galatians. In the very first chapter, as Paul expressed his concern over the perversion of the Gospel message, he proclaimed,

> *For I would have you know, brethren, that the gospel which was preached by me is not according to man. For I neither received it from man, nor was I taught it, but I received it through a revelation of Jesus Christ.* (1:11-12)

Of course, the cynics are quick to point out that the passage referenced the "revelation" Paul received relative to his preaching the Gospel message and not the biblical account as being inspired. Still, one might ask why God revealed the

---

[134] John A. Witmer, "Biblical Evidence for the Verbal-Plenary Inspiration of the Bible," *Bibliotheca Sacra* 121 (1964): 245.

Truth to Paul for his ministry and then did not inspire the original authors in order to ensure that the entirety of the Gospel message was truthfully preserved.

Beyond the Pauline accounts, two additional passages are noteworthy. The first is II Peter 1:20-21 which states,

> *Know this first of all, that no prophecy of Scripture is a matter of one's own interpretation, for no prophecy was ever made by an act of human will, but men moved by the Holy Spirit spoke from God.*

Peter made his point as succinctly as Paul did, that God's Word is not a compilation of human will but directed by the movement of the Holy Spirit. The second passage comes from the book of Revelation. Again, from the first chapter, we can read,

> *I was in the Spirit on the Lord's day, and I heard behind me a loud voice like the sound of a trumpet, saying, "Write in a book what you see, and send it to the seven churches.* (1:10-11)

Here, John acknowledged that he heard a voice instructing him to write down what he saw and send it to the churches in Asia. When John turned around, he saw no one; but his "revelation" began at that very moment.

Those passages represent the main statements within the Bible that proclaim the inspiration of Scripture. Of course, the naysayers are ready to pounce on the idea that the Bible offering a Truth about itself cannot be considered a viable testimony and certainly not accepted as any empirical proof for inspiration. The idea is that a personal testimony may not be a reliable one. A person may possess an exceptional character, but a statement like "You have to believe me because I'm telling you the truth" does not warrant much respect as a basis for believing that person's proclaimed "truth." It is a circular argument that, in the attempt to prove itself truthful, proves nothing at all.

Bershears highlighted that very point when he referenced the concept of a self-referential argument as "rather obviously fallacious."[135]   He continued with his concluding remarks by pointing out that even though "there are good reasons to believe the Bible is true . . . it (self-reference) is nonetheless a flawed argument."[136]   It is a completely logical criticism; but, giving Bershears his due, he followed those statements with five clear points as to why it is important to accept the inspiration of Scripture as the Word of God.   They were: 1) Historically and Scientifically Reliable; 2) the Resurrection of Jesus Christ; 3) a Unified Theme; 4) a Rational and Plausible Worldview; and 5) the Fulfillment of Prophecy.[137]   A complete examination of each point is not necessary for this discussion.   However, it is important to note that for Bearshears, and others, the powerful elements within the Scriptures represent valid points for the acceptance of biblical inspiration.

Pink, in his classic piece, *Divine Inspiration of the Bible*, provided fourteen chapters that highlighted fourteen reasons why the Christian should accept the Bible as divinely inspired.   Twelve of the fourteen are: 1) the Presumption in Favor of the Bible being inspired (Man's need for God's revelation to be in written form); 2) the Perennial Freshness of the Bible Bears Witness to Its Divine Inspirer (the influence of the biblical passages for Man's need never fades); 3) the Unmistakable Honesty of the Writers of the Bible Attests to Its Heavenly Origin (the authors expressed God's Truth, not their own); 4) the Character of Its Teachings Evidences the Divine Authorship of the Bible (the Bible teaches us about God and Man's relationship to Him); 5) the Fulfilled Prophecies of the Bible Bespeak the Omniscience of Its Author (the Bible substantiates the fulfillment of divine prophecies); 6) the Typical Significance of the Scriptures Declare Their Divine Authorship (that the fundamental purpose of the Bible, Old and New Testaments, is to bring Man to redemption); 7) the Wonderful Unity of the Bible Attests Its Divine Authorship (it represents the same truth from cover to cover); 8) the Marvelous Influence of the Bible Declares Its Super-Human Character (the positive influence the Bible represented throughout all civilizations); 9) the Miraculous Power of the Bible Shows Forth That Its Inspirer Is the Almighty (affecting Man in a more powerful way than any other

---

[135] Bershears, *Bibilology*, 118.
[136] Ibid.
[137] Ibid, 119-130.

book); 10) the Completeness of the Bible Demonstrates Its Divine Perfection (no need to add anything to it); 11) the Indestructibility of the Bible Is a Proof That Its Author Is Divine (what human-authored book could survive through the centuries?); and 12) the Inward Confirmation of the Veracity of the Scriptures (the Bible provides absolute Truths).[138]

Obviously, they are all acceptable reasons and the idea of accepting them leads the Believer to a conclusion that the Bible was inspired. On the other hand, it does not provide an answer regarding the entire question of inspiration. Namely, it does not explain how the Bible was inspired. The Christian, as with any person of faith, should accept their sacred text (in this case the Bible) as the Word of God. That point demands some type of inspiration and the Christian should believe that the Bible is the inspired Word of God. The other side of that coin asks the question "How did the biblical writers receive the information they wrote?" In other words, we must attempt to answer the question of how the inspiration of the biblical authors took place.

Before we delve into the discussion on the various theories of how the biblical authors received their inspiration, perhaps we should heed the words of Ralph Earle, a Nazarene biblical scholar and founding Professor of New Testament at Nazarene Theological Seminary in Kansas City. He provided an interesting article for the *Bulletin of the Evangelical Theological Society* in which he stated that "no single view of inspiration conveys the total, or the true picture."[139] Although one might be willing to concede Earle's point, we should proceed along that path with some caution. While it is clear that no one can know exactly how God accomplished the inspiration of the Christian Scriptures, such a logical point should not throw the proverbial baby out with the bath water. The inspiration of the Holy Scripture represents an integral cornerstone of the Christian Faith. Even though the various denominations of the Christian Faith may disagree on how the inspiration occurred, few would disagree that inspiration was the means that produced the Bible we have today. The point being that regardless of the debate "two centuries of destructive Biblical criticism have failed to erase the identity of the Bible as the Word of God for the average

---

[138] Arthur Pink, *Divine Inspiration of the Bible* (Swengel, PA: Bible Truth Depot, 1917), 2-45.
[139] Ralph Earle, "Further Thoughts on Biblical Inspiration." *Bulletin of the Evangelical Theological Society* 6 (1963): 14.

Christian."[140]   Clearly, the concept of the Bible as inspired is a critical element of the Faith.

Even with the above being duly noted, we cannot simply proclaim the Bible as inspired and move on to the next chapter. As Jeremy Begbie, a renown biblical scholar and the Langford Distinguished Professor of Theology at the Duke Divinity School, stated, "Even if we take 'inspiration' to cover not only the origin but the process of scriptural formation (and the efficacy of Scripture today), serious consideration of the person and work of the Holy Spirit cannot be bypassed."[141]   For scholars like Begbie, the question of inspiration went far beyond a simple proclamation of faith. A significant element of the inspiration of Scripture rested on the "serious consideration of the person and work of the Holy Spirit."   In other words, any discussion of biblical inspiration must include an examination of the authors and how they received their inspiration to produce what the Church accepted as the inspired Word of God. Without understanding that specific point, we will miss a significant element of the question regarding the inspiration of the Bible.

Unfortunately, getting a good handle on the theories surrounding the inspiration of the Scriptures is a difficult task. It seems that every noted scholar proclaims a different theory based on their own insights and theological persuasion. And, to compound the problem, many of them overlap as to present concepts of biblical inspiration that, although not identical, are certainly quite similar. Add to that dilemma the point that scholars will often use different names to identify the exact same theory and the scope of the problem becomes even more evident. With that challenge in mind, let us examine four of the general concepts that various denominations present as to how the Holy Spirit inspired the original authors of the biblical text.

As we begin the endeavor, it is not the intention of the discussion to champion one theory, while denigrating another. The following presentation simply seeks to lay out distinctly different theories of biblical inspiration without any attempt to interject personal conviction. The premise for this chapter is to highlight the importance of understanding the Bible as being the inspired Word of Almighty God. As N. T.

---

[140] Witmer "Biblical Evidence," 243.
[141] Jeremy Begbie, "Who Is This God?: Biblical Inspiration Revisited," *Tyndale Bulletin* 43 (1982): 260.

Wright stated, "We should note that some kind of divine inspiration of Scripture was taken for granted in most of the ancient Israelite Scriptures themselves, as well as in the beliefs of the early Christians."[142] Another theologian made a similar statement when he said, "Almost all would agree that biblical inspiration is a special kind of inspiration; the task of interested people then becomes to define what is special about it."[143] In light of those points, the following presentation on the inspiration of Scripture is not meant to be an apologetic for any particular theory, but simply an examination of four specific theological positions on the inspiration of the Bible as the Word of God.

Partial or Spot Inspiration

Perhaps considered to be on the moderate, or even the more liberal side of the question, the idea of the Partial (often referred to as "Spot") Inspiration of the Bible is that the whole of the Bible is not inspired. As the name suggests, adherents to this theory believe that only a portion (or certain "spots") of the Bible are inspired. This position is convenient because it still allows the Believer to accept the Bible, at least in part, as the Word of God, while being able to dismiss some "difficult passages" that the average Christian might find difficult to explain or accept.

Interestingly, a further development of this theory includes the idea of a "Differing Inspiration." It represents an attempt, perhaps, to soften the criticism that the partial inspiration theorists often receive from their more conservative Brothers. While they would concur that only portions of the Bible are truly inspired, the "differing" quality allows for a belief that "all Scripture is inspired" (II Timothy 3:16), but not all Scripture is inspired with the same intention, direction, or influence. This is sort of the "have your cake and eat it too" approach to biblical inspiration.

The question posed to those advocating this position is "How do you know what is, or what is not, inspired?" It also raises a concern that once the Believer begins to question some of the Bible as being truly inspired, how does the same Believer come to a position that accepts any of it as inspired. A possible answer to that important criticism appeared in an article published in *The Westminster*

---

[142] Wright, *Scripture and the Authority of God*, 35.
[143] Trembath, *Evangelical Theories*, 6.

Theological Journal. In that article, the author stated his concept of inspiration "as extending to those parts of Scripture that are the product of revelation from God, while no such superintendence or direction extends to those parts that could be composed by the exercise of man's natural faculties"[144] Although not a completely sufficient answer, Murray basically stated that biblical inspiration applies to Scripture that relates to God's revelation and not to that which presents the authors' opinions, personal views or individual character.

Partial Inspiration does address some of the issues related to biblical inspiration, but it seems to create more holes than it fills. When carried to an extreme position, the Believer can simply discount any portion of the Bible that creates a personal conflict as not being truly inspired.

Intrinsic Inspiration

Intrinsic means natural, underlying, or innate. As such, this theory relates to the dictionary definition provided earlier, centering on the spiritual condition of the biblical writers. The proponents of this theory proclaim that the authors of the texts possessed a spiritual quality and strength of faith to have the *intrinsic* ability to provide a finished product that represented the true Word of God.

The Intrinsic Inspirationists believe that the theory gives them a win-win situation. On the one hand, they can continue to claim that the Bible is the Word of God. They would acknowledge that the authors of the divine texts had a clear understanding, as a result of their spiritual insight, to write what God needed them to write. On the other, as with the Spot Inspirationists, they could dismiss some of the more "difficult passages" of Scripture as being the result of the common failure of Man. Although the writers possessed a true faith, Man is still a sinner and can (and, for some passages of Scripture, did) create errors that appear in the final text.

To support their position, they point to their poster child for this theory: Peter. They highlight the passage where Jesus asked the disciples who they thought he was. Peter proclaimed that Jesus was "the Christ, the Son of the living God." (Matthew 16:16). Jesus responded to Peter's statement of faith that he did not make the claim by himself, but as a

---

[144] John Murray, "The Inspiration of the Scripture," *The Westminster Theological Journal* 2 (1940): 76.

result of the Holy Spirit revealing the Truth to him. Their point: Peter was able to make that confession because he had an *intrinsic* faith that the other disciples did not possess. And, as the adherents are quick to point out, the biblical narrative of Peter supports that conclusion. Peter, as a result of his significant personal faith, was able to walk on water (Matthew 14) and even raise an individual from the dead (Acts 9). And, since the Bible does not identify another disciple who demonstrated such *intrinsic* faith, it appears obvious that Peter possessed a spiritual quality greater than that of the others. That being the case, it is only a short hop, skip, and jump to formalizing that concept into the Intrinsic Inspiration theory.

Although, the theory presents a plausible concept, and even one that seems to have a biblical reference point, its flaw rests with the same problem as the Partial Inspiration theory. Namely, that the Believer has no definitive understanding of which passages contain the "intrinsic" side of the authors, vice the "human" side. Basically, the conclusion is left to each person's own "intrinsic" abilities. That being true, perhaps we should examine another possibility.

Dynamic Inspiration

The Dynamic Theory of inspiration proclaims a belief that God empowered (i.e., led) the authors in a dramatic manner to facilitate in them His Truth. Sometimes this theory is combined with, or explained as, the "Dictation Theory" of inspiration.

Regardless of how one tries to split the hairs in attempting to separate the two concepts, the bottom line for both is the same: the authors received the words they wrote directly from God. A popular theory for conservative churches in the 19th century, it did not gain much traction as a wide-spread answer to the question of biblical inspiration. Part of the problem was "the acceptance of conceptual and textual criticism . . . that forced the abandonment of the explicit theories of dictation."[145] Paul Tillich expressed the criticism Man leveled against dictation (or "mechanical inspiration" as he called it) in a blistering statement in his *Systematic Theology*. He stated, "In the last analysis, a mechanical or any other form of nonecstatic doctrine of inspiration is demonic."[146] Even

---

[145] Friedman and Dolansky, *The Bible Now*, 88.

[146] Paul Tillich, *Systematic Theology: Reason, and Revelation Being, and God* (Chicago: University of Chicago Press, 1951), 115.

with Tillich's condemnation, the Dynamic/Dictation Theory still holds a viable concept in some Christian circles and remains a part of the theological discussion on biblical inspiration.

Plenary-Verbal

That leads us to the final theory for our discussion, the Plenary-Verbal Theory. In the past, theologians discussed these two theories as separate concepts. However, the conservative denominations tend to combine the two theories into one. The result is a theory that expresses the whole of the Bible being verbally inspired by God.

That is the exact meaning of the two elements. The word "plenary" simply means that something is "full," "complete," or "whole." Of course, theology is not always that simple. One theologian tried to make the simple more difficult by defining plenary, as it relates to biblical inspiration, from two perspectives. He stated, "The first is that all parts of the Bible are equally inspired . . . (and) The second, or exclusive significance of plenary inspiration, is that only the Bible is assured of being the written Word of God."[147] That statement proclaimed the entirety of the Bible as inspired and that the Believer should not accept any other "biblical" writing as equally inspired.

Adding the word "verbal" to the mix became an obvious and reasonable combination. It provided an explanation of how God accomplished the "entirety of biblical inspiration." Simply stated, He did so verbally. In other words, the concept here is that God provided the Words directly to the authors. This is the true position of verbal inspiration, that every word that the authors wrote came directly from God. It is also the doctrine of many conservative churches which hold a belief that unless the entirety of the Bible is true the Christian has no guarantee that any of it is true. As Alan Richardson, who served as a past Professor of Christian Theology at the University of Nottingham, stated regarding the Conservative's acceptance of verbal inspiration,

> *The conservative evangelical reflects the spirit of the age in agreeing that there is only one kind of truth, namely the literal or scientific; if the Bible is true, it must be*

---

[147] Ibid., 92.

> *literally true, since there is no other kind of truth than literal. Hence, he feels that to admit that (say) the stories of Gen. i-xi are not literally true means that they are in fact false and that the Bible is therefore fallible and its claim to impart saving truth inadmissible.*[148]

Although a clear position of the early Christian Church, and specifically a position that gained prominence during and after the Reformation, it came under fire within the Roman Catholic Church. I suppose a church historian could argue that the Protestant movement away from the Catholic Church precipitated the criticism. That conclusion may not have a legitimate historical reference. However, a clear historical reference does acknowledge the presence of a Protestant Movement and within the period of that movement historians note that "there was a steady movement among Catholic theologians away from the theory of verbal inspiration of the Scriptures."[149] Still, the plenary/verbal theory became (and remains) a viable position on biblical inspiration for numerous conservative denominations. In that respect the serious debate of biblical inspiration continues within and throughout the many Protestant denominations.

Part of the criticism for this position, beyond the textual and other issues, was the sense of God speaking directly to the authors. Of course, the biblical record highlights several instances when God spoke directly to Man. However, that may not represent the consensus opinion of how God communicates with His people. The biblical accounts of God speaking directly to Man notwithstanding, the critics of the theory do ask a legitimate question: "What separates Verbal Inspiration theory from the defunct Dictation theory?"

The answer to the question comes from, as no surprise, the Bible. In that respect, the inspiration provided to the biblical authors was like that which God provided to the

---

[148] Alan Richardson, "The Rise of Modern Biblical Scholarship" in *The Cambridge History of the Bible: The West from the Reformation to the Present Day*, edited by S. L. Greenslade (Cambridge: Cambridge University Press, 1970), 308.

[149] F. J. Crehan, "The Bible in the Roman Catholic Church: From Trent to Present Day," in *The Cambridge History of the Bible: The West from the Reformation to the Present Day*, edited by S. L. Greenslade (Cambridge: Cambridge University Press, 1970), 217.

prophets. The prophets spoke what they understood was a direct word from God. Applying that to verbal inspiration, it would conclude that "as with the prophets, so with the writers of Scripture, biblical inspiration is by its very nature verbal."[150] The supporters of plenary/verbal inspiration would add Christ's words regarding the ministry of the Holy Spirit (John 14-16). In one of the five proclamations He made about the coming of the Holy Spirit, He stated, "The Helper, the Holy Spirit, whom the Father will send in my name, will teach you everything and make you remember all that I have told you" (14:26). By Jesus' own words, part of the ministry of the Holy Spirit was to bring to the Believer (and, one would conclude, to the biblical authors) the words of God. That does not mean that the inspiration came in some dictated form. On the other hand, it does profess a definite and distinct position that the inspiration of the biblical writers came directly from God.

Of course, this theory, like the others, has its critics. Some approach their criticism directly, stating that "the negative significance of plenary inspiration is that only the message of the writer is accorded the guarantee of divine infallibility and divine presence."[151] The author's point is that the theory does not allow for a continual inspiration or revelation from God, but restricts the Truth to a literal interpretation of the written word. Others criticize the problem with how plenary/verbal adherents apply their concept of inspiration. They highlight the fact that those proclaiming a plenary/verbal inspiration of the Bible do not properly address the issue of how the Church deals with Scripture. Even in the most conservative churches, some passages are elevated to a godly status, while others are deemed questionable. For instance, how many sermons have you heard preached from I Timothy 2:15? In that passage, Paul stated that "a woman will be saved through having children, if she perseveres in faith and love and holiness, with modesty." I do not believe many pastors would choose that passage for their next Mother's Day sermon.

Regardless of the criticism, one must acknowledge that Plenary/Verbal Inspiration remains a doctrinal pillar within the conservative churches of the Christian Faith.

---

[150] Ronald William Graham, "The Inspiration of Scripture," *Lexington Theological Quarterly* 22 (1987): 97-98.
[151] Trembath, *Evangelical Theories*, 15.

<u>Summary</u>

It is an imperative of Christianity that the Believer accepts the Bible as the Word of God. It is the same for every religion throughout the world: adherents to a faith accept their "sacred scriptures" as their god's word to them. The same is certainly true for Christianity. As one scholar stated, "even church leaders who deny and oppose this doctrine admit that it is the belief of the average Christian"[152] Therefore, it is important for us to acknowledge that the inspiration of Scripture, even if it is hard to grasps or put into a definitive doctrine, is a vital element of the Faith. The reality is that "the divine inspiration of Scripture is therefore a supernatural mystery, never fully comprehensible and always somewhat opaque to the human mind."[153]

Unfortunately, the nearly two thousand years of biblical interpretation has transformed the Bible into a myriad of versions and translations that even present a confusing truth when compared one to another. For instance, read Jeremiah 27:1 from various translations and try to answer the question: "Who was the king when the events of the chapter took place?" The King James Version states that it was Jehoiakim. The more modern translations, using early manuscripts that were not available in the Seventeenth Century, identify the king as Zedekiah. In that regard, we can conclude that even though the original authors received God's direct inspiration, Man, unfortunately, demonstrated a potential to manipulate that Truth.

So, how do we solve that modern-day problem. Perhaps we could learn something from Karl Barth who "distinguishes two phases of inspiration. The first came when the books of the Bible were written. The second, when the books are read."[154] The key here is to accept the doctrinal position that biblical authors received some inspiration from God in order to present to His people His divine Word. And, because the continual manipulation by Man potentially produces a less than inspired translation, it becomes an imperative that the inspiration of Scripture takes place as the Believer reads its passages.

Therefore, it is important to clarify that

---

[152] John A Witmer, "Biblical Evidence for the Verbal-Plenary Inspiration of the Bible." *Bibliotheca Sacra* 121 (1964): 243.

[153] Graham, "The Inspiration of Scripture", 98.

[154] Earle, "Further Thoughts," 14.

"whatever our understanding may be of the inspiration of Scripture, two things stand clear and must be held in tension and each given its due measure: the one, the sacred writers were genuinely and creatively active, God respecting their individuality and various powers; and the other, in the last analysis their every faculty was under the influence of God: they were borne along under the influence of God the Spirit."[155]

The Bible is the inspired Word of God; both in its original manuscripts through the inspiration of the biblical authors and in the personal reading of His Word as the Spirit directs our understanding. As such, it remains an authoritative book that the Believer can apply to their life in order to follow God's purpose and Will. And that point sets the perfect introduction for the next chapter.

---

[155] Graham, "The Inspiration of Scripture" 105

CHAPTER 17

BIBLICAL APPLICATION FOR LIFE

How can a young man keep his way pure? By keeping it according to Your word. With all my heart I have sought You; Do not let me wander from Your commandments. Your word I have treasured in my heart, that I may not sin against You. (Psalm 119:9-11)

And so, we come to the final chapter in this examination of what constitutes, from basically a biblical perspective, the true foundational elements of Christianity. Each section poses an important question about the nature of the Christian Faith. And, each chapter highlights an explanation of specific points that establish and clarify the question's importance as a basis for the Faith. Therefore, at almost every turn the reader may notice that the book declares the importance of the question or the points addressed in the chapters of that section. Often, the expression of that importance makes the case for that point being the most vital element for the foundation of Christianity. And, certainly, one can appreciate the truth in the statements. In fact, each of the five questions represent essential elements of the Faith; and hence, the subtitle of the book, *The Five Essential Questions of the Faith*.

However, one could argue that this chapter is the focal point of all the others. Obviously, the acceptance of a "One True and Living God" represents an essential aspect of the Faith, as is the reality that Jesus came to Earth as "the Christ," God incarnate, to suffer and die for Man's sin. In addition, His resurrection substantiated His life and sacrifice as the Christ. All of that is undoubtedly true, but without a divinely inspired Scriptures to preserve that Truth for the Believer, faith loses a basic foundational element.

Still, apart from the indispensable quality of each one of the questions raised in this book, if the Believer does not put faith into practice by applying God's inspired Truth to life, then what's the point? As James clearly pointed out in his epistle, "You believe that God is one. You do well; the demons also believe, and shudder. But are you willing to recognize, you foolish fellow, that faith without works is useless" (James 2:19-20)? James acknowledged that believing in "God as one" represented a good thing for the Believer, but also noted that even those who reject the Truth of the faith (i.e., the demons) believe that reality. The difference, as James noted, rests in the demonstration, the application, the working of that faith in the life of the Believer. Specifically, he stated that "faith without works (without application of that faith to a person's life) is useless." Therefore, it seems we need one final chapter to express the importance of applying the Bible to our lives as the Word of God.

Indeed, the Bible stands as the definitive text on how the Christian should proceed through this life. Countless books, study guides, and daily devotionals fill the shelves of bookstores all expressing a concept of how the Bible can become more relevant in the daily function of life. In short, it is an expression of a Christian reality that the faithful accept the Bible as a source of God's direction for life. As the editors of *The Oxford Companion to the Bible* perfectly stated it, the Bible is

> *more than a collection of ancient*
> *tales. Even before the canonical list*
> *of books considered sacred scripture*
> *or holy writ was established, the*
> *writings we now call the Bible were*

> *considered normative: they laid down
> the essential principles of how human
> beings should deal with God and with
> each other.*[156]

That is a concept supported by numerous other biblical scholars. Even in a book designed to examine only the King James Version of the Bible, the author noted that for the Christian community the Bible was "the word of God, an enormous, direct, vastly complicated, infinitely interpretable account of what God meant by and for His creation."[157] Although he noted plainly that the Bible is "vastly complicated" and that it presents a difficult task for interpretation, he also conceded that Christians accept it as an account of what God needs them to know and, by implication, how to use His Word to direct how they should live.

In three compelling articles, scholars from various traditions reinforced the position that the Bible stands as the authority for Christian conduct. John D. Woodbridge, Research Professor of Church History and the History of Christian Thought at Trinity Evangelical Divinity School, stated that "the Bible alone, the revealed written Word of God, is the final infallible authority for doctrine and practice and is a determining norm over all human opinions and church creeds and traditions."[158] In the article, Woodbridge made the case for a "sola Scriptura" approach to the Bible and then added that the concept of "only Scripture" dictates that the Bible becomes the authority for "all human opinions and church creeds and traditions."

Moving to a Greek Orthodox position, Philip Kariatlis, Academic Director and Senior Lecturer in Theology at Saint Andrews Greek Orthodox Theological College in Australia, provided an article on the Holy Trinity. Riding on the coat-tails of Woodbridge's statement that the Bible is the source of all "church creeds (doctrines) and traditions," Kariatlis stated that the Bible is "far from being lifeless doctrines, according to this understanding point of how human persons are called to live their life in relationship with God, one

---

[156] Metzger and Coogan, *Oxford Companion*, vi.

[157] Adam Nicholson, *God's Secretaries: The Making of the King James Bible* (New York: Harper-Collins, 2003), 122.

[158] John D. Woodbridge, "Sola Scriptura: Original Intent, Historical Development, and Import for Christian Living," *Presbyterion* 44 (2018): 5.

another and the entire created realm."[159] Although context of the quote referenced the doctrinal position of the Church as being the authority on how a Christian should "live their life," certainly we understand the position that the Church develops its doctrine from the biblical Truth.

Finally, an entry from a Christian education perspective that centered on the notion that compassion represents an element of Christian duty. In that context, the author stated that "the Bible also promotes compassion as a humane expression of neighborly love, something that Christ-followers are enjoined to show in their lives."[160] Obviously, the author presented a limited scope of the Bible as being authoritative for a person's life. Still, it provided the authority of the Bible for all Christians, even if within the one idea of being compassionate towards others.

One doesn't need to look to the theologians for conclusive evidence that the Bible serves as a guide, a light, for the Believer. The Old Testament presents the historical record of God trying to reestablish the broken relationship that existed with Man following the Fall in the Garden of Eden. The culmination of that effort, at least from an Old Testament point of view, rests in the provision of the Law, the Decalogue, the Ten Commandments. Beyond the Commandments, the Old Testament proclaims hundreds of additional directives, the Levitical Law, on how the people of God should live.

Of course, it is true that many people read the Old Testament as a history book which documents the progress of the Hebrew people leading up to the coming of Jesus. However, it is also a guidebook that reveals God's effort to bring a sense of personal responsibility to live one's life according to God's direction. Unfortunately, Man does not have the ability to accomplish God's desired union through the Law. As noted with Adam's first sin, Man demonstrated that he is a sinner and as such Man is incapable of following a prescribed law from God. That point and the discussion of it appeared in a previous chapter and established the need for the coming of Jesus as the Christ. Although that is a biblical Truth (see, Ecclesiastes 7:20, Romans 5:12, and 1 John 1:8), it does not mean that God does not possess an expectation on how His

---

[159] Philip Kariatlis, "The Mystery of the Holy Trinity: A Paradigm for Christian Living?" *Phronema* 33 (2018): 47.

[160] Alaster Gibson, "Meanings and Applications of Compassion in Teaching: A Practical Review of the Bible and Educational Literature," *Christian Education Journal* 12 (2015): 22.

people should live and so provides a pronouncement for how Christians ought to direct their lives.

Several biblical passages make the claim for the Church that the Bible declares God's direction for His people. The passage at the beginning of this chapter is one of them. Psalm 119:11 states simply, "Your word I have treasured in my heart, that I may not sin against You." The basic premise states that the Believer understands the importance of securing God's Word in their life (i.e., their "heart"). Interestingly, the passage goes on to express an intriguing theological concept: the idea of living a life without sin. Of course, no one can live a "sin free" life. As noted above and in an earlier chapter, Paul made that point abundantly clear when he stated in Romans 3:23 that "all have sinned and fallen short of the glory of God." The requirement for the coming of Jesus in order to be crucified for Man's sin proclaims the Truth that no one can live free of sin. Therefore, a proper interpretation of the passage becomes one of understanding the perfection of living totally in the Word of God. Indeed, if Man lived with God's true Word within his heart at every minute of every day, the Word would always dictate the perfect Will that the Believer should follow. Regardless of the hermeneutics, the understanding for our purpose is the directive for receiving and following the Word of God.

Three other passages that relate that same Truth are: Psalm 1:1-3; Psalm 119:105-106; and II Timothy 3:16-17. The first one, Psalm 1:1-3, states the following:

> How blessed is the man who does not
> walk in the counsel of the wicked, nor
> stand in the path of sinners, nor sit
> in the seat of scoffers. But his
> delight is in the law of the Lord, and
> in His law he meditates day and night.
> He will be like a tree firmly planted
> by streams of water, which yields its
> fruit in its season and its leaf does
> not wither; and in whatever he does,
> he prospers.

The passage divides easily into three sections, each one related to a single verse. The first verse identifies that which Man, the Believer, must avoid. The situations are

227

obvious and the Psalmist identified them as the "wicked," "sinners," and "scoffers." In other words, the proclamation is that in order to receive the blessings from God the Believer should avoid the advice of that which is totally opposed to God (the wicked), not follow the example of those living contrary to God's Will (the sinners), and not be a party to any anti-godly rhetoric (the scoffers). Instead, verse two states what the Believer should do—meditate on God's Word. Yes, it uses the word "law" in the passage, but the people considered the Law as the Word of God (see Exodus 20:1). And, that contemplation of God's Word should take place "day and night." The concept here is obvious. Man should reject that which is contrary to God and rely, instead, on the true Word of God. With that Truth intact, the psalmist proclaimed a result in verse 3 by stating that "he will be like a tree firmly planted by streams of water which yields its fruit in its season. Its leaf does not wither and in whatever he does, he prospers." The passage provided an acknowledged abundance that the Believer received by following the Word of God.

The second passage is Psalm 119:105-106. As noted, this chapter opened with an earlier passage from Psalm 119. This one is similar but states the Truth in a different way. In this passage, we can read, "Your word is a lamp to my feet and a light to my path. I have sworn and I will confirm it, that I will keep Your righteous ordinances." Two points help to clarify this passage for the application to the discussion at hand. First, the psalmist identified God's Word as a "lamp to my feet." The metaphor of the Word being a lamp refers to a "light" and is the opposite of the biblical dichotomy of "light" (God and goodness) to "darkness" (Satan and evil). For the psalmist, God's Word provided the light necessary to proceed in life according to the Word. The second point "confirms" the Truth and professes a dedication to "keep Your righteous ordinances." The key here acknowledges that by applying God's Word to our lives, we will live by the "light" of God's Word and possess the power to dispel the "darkness."

The final passage is from the New Testament and one that many consider the main passage related to the discussion in the previous chapter regarding the Bible as the inspired Word of God. It is II Timothy 3:16-17 and states that "all Scripture is inspired by God and profitable for teaching, for reproof, for correction, for training in righteousness; so that the man of God may be adequate, equipped for every good work." Obviously, the first verse is an imperative, both for the last chapter and this one. It establishes the Bible as being inspired and able to be accepted as the true Word of Almighty God. However, verse seventeen provides the important point for this discussion by stating "that the man of God may be adequate, equipped for every good work." It is that verse that acknowledges the reason that God moved to inspire His Word. God inspired His Word in order to equip Man to accomplish His work, to live according to His Will.

In that respect, ask yourself, "What should a Christian use in order to be "fully equipped" to accomplish God's Will?" Or, to look at this question from the flipside, the Christian can only accomplish God's Will through an adherence to the Bible as the inspired Word of God. The point here is that at the very heart of the Christian Faith is the acceptance of the Bible as the Word of God and the application of its Truth to the life of the Believer. Without the application, the rest of it becomes meaningless; or, in the words of James noted above, "useless."

Concluding Remarks

At the beginning of this project, even before I typed a single word, I realized two important concepts. The first, and main consideration, rested on the significance of establishing a unifying theological perspective for all of Christianity. Not a small task, some might say; but one that it seems ought to have an obvious focal point. Regardless of the number of different Christian denominations, certainly some unifying aspect of the Christian Faith might represent the foundation for the totality of the Faith. I mean, we can debate the nature of God or the means by which His Atonement is provided to the Believer through Christ's crucifixion. We can also debate how God inspired the Bible as His True Word. However, in the long run, Christianity must agree on the "pillars of the Faith" that confirm the Believer as a Christian, regardless of the many denominational influences that separate us.

It was in that mindset that I entered this project and the conclusion one should draw from the effort is that the whole of Christianity does, indeed, accept certain Truths as the basis of the Faith. Those Truths are: God is the One True and Living God and is the Creator of all that is; Jesus, as a result of His incarnation, lived on Earth as God; He died on the Cross as a sacrifice for Man's Sin; Jesus received a bodily resurrection from the dead as a clear sign of His divine nature and as a verification of resurrection for all Believers; and the Bible represents the True Word of Almighty God. Those are the five tenets of the Christian Faith that should unify the faithful; and, they are Truths for which there should be no reasonable debate.

The second concept is that I came to the project with an interesting denominational background and experience. As explained in the Introduction, I stood in a unique position to tackle this project. As such, I took on the challenge to write this book since I felt I could write it from a distinctively ecumenical perspective that most local church pastors, and even many theologians, could not. The result, I believe, is a book that understands and tries to accommodate the entire scope of denominational perspectives (including Roman Catholicism and Eastern Orthodoxy), while maintaining the premise of the book—that the five Tenets of Faith should

231

be something that unites the Church, rather than dividing it. So, through the entire discussion and the various questions that the different denominations might raise, Christians realize that true Christianity does profess five specific tenets that represent the basis of the Faith. Apart from the clear support provided in the preceding chapters, the establishment of the tenets is quite simple. First, God is God. Every religion professes a faith in a "god" of some type. Certainly, one cannot argue against the fact that Christianity does, as well. The debate regarding the nature and characteristics of God may create some of the denominationalism that exists within Christianity, but the acceptance that God does, indeed, exist as God is a tenet of every faith, which includes Christianity.

The second point, that Jesus was God, also represents a clear tenet of Christianity. John acknowledged that Truth in the first chapter of his Gospel when He noted that the Word was God and that the Word became flesh (John 1:1, 14). John wrote his gospel to bring people to a realization that Jesus was God, the Christ, the Messiah. Of course, beyond the biblical references, one can explain that point logically by simply looking at the word that identifies the Faith: "Christian." Obviously, the first six letters of the word Christian are "C-H-R-I-S-T." It then becomes obvious that to be a Christian one must accept Jesus as the Christ. If one simply follows the teachings of Jesus as a great philosopher or rabbi, rejecting the nature of Jesus as the Christ, they no longer can claim to be a Christ-ian. Instead, a better label for them might be "Jesusian," as one who follows the teachings of Jesus. Jesus as the Christ, as God incarnate, represents a uniqueness about Christianity that does not have an equal in the religions of the world and must be maintained as an essential tenet of the Christian Faith.

That leads to the next two tenets of Christianity. The first is that Christianity proclaims that Jesus, as the Christ, died on the Cross to bring God's redeeming Atonement to a sinful world. Atonement, the complete reconciliation of Man to God through His righteous Grace, could only be achieved through His crucifixion. We might argue some theological aspect of the event, but we cannot argue that the event took place and that Believers receive God's Atonement through His crucifixion. The other part of the couplet is the reality of Christ's resurrection from the dead. Christianity believes in the provision of eternal life and the personal resurrection

232

from the dead.   An acceptance of Christ's resurrection then becomes an essential element, a tenet, of the Christian Faith. The resurrection substantiated Jesus as God and established the availability of resurrection for all who believe in Him. The point here is that without the resurrection of Christ, what possibility remains for us as the result of our faith?

The final tenet proclaims the Bible as the Word of God.   A great deal of discussion and debate circulates throughout the seminaries and in a mountain of scholarly monoliths directed at this point.   The typical parameters focus on the inspiration of the Bible.   At the heart of the discussion is how God inspired the Bible and a critique on the difficult historical record of how the current Canon came into being. It is permissible, even somewhat entertaining, to debate the inspiration theories and the historical perspectives of the Bible.   Regardless of the scholarly debate, the result is that Christianity accepts the Bible, however it came into being, as inspired and the True Word of Almighty God.   As such, it becomes a means by which "the man of God may be adequate, equipped for every good work."   As offered earlier, without the application of God's Truth to our lives, what's the point?

So, let us agree to disagree on the practices of faith that separate us denominationally on Sunday morning.   Let us continue to have our discussions on the nature of God and the means by which God inspired His Holy text.   On the other hand, let us unite ourselves around the Tenets of Faith that represent the basic foundation of Christianity: God as God; Jesus as God, the Christ; Jesus' crucifixion as a remedy for the sinful condition of Man; His bodily resurrection from the dead; and the Bible as the true Word of God.   With those five tenets intact, the Christian church can move forward in unity, rather than highlighting the denominational differences that divide us.

In that respect, may we all understand the Christian Faith as Paul proclaimed it to be when he stated in I Corinthians 12:20 that "now indeed there are many members, yet one body." May we all strive to be that "one body!"

SCRIPTURE INNDEX

BIBLIOGRAPHY

Ackroyd, P. R. and C. F. Evans, eds. *The Cambridge History of the Bible : From Beginning to Jerome,* Cambridge: Cambridge University Press, 1970.

Adams, Robert. "The Theological Ethics of Young Rawls and Its Background." In *A Brief Inquiry into the Meaning of Sin and Faith,* edited by Thomas Nagel. Cambridge: Harvard University Press, 2009.

Baillie, D. M. *God Was in Christ: An Essay on Incarnation and Atonement.* New York: Charles Scribner's Sons, 1948.

Barrett, C. K. *A Commentary on the First Epistle to the Corinthians.* New York: Harper and Row, 1968.

Barrett, C. K. *The Epistle to the Romans.* London: Adams and Charles Black, 1973.

Begbie, Jeremy. "Who Is This God?: Biblical Inspiration Revisited." *Tyndale Bulletin* 43 (1992): 259-282.

Berkin, Carol. *A Brilliant Solution.* Boston: Haughton Mifflin Harcourt Publishing, 2002.

Bershears, Jeffery D. *Bibliology: What Every Christian Should Know about the Origins, Composition, Inspiration, Interpretation, Canonicity, and Transmission of the Bible* Eugene, OR: Wipf and Stock, 2017.

Bokedal, Thomas *The Formation and Significance of the Christian Biblical Canon: A Study in Text, Ritual, & Interpretation.* London: Bloomsbury, 2014.

Brake, Donald L. *A Visual History of the English Bible.* Grand Rapids: Baker Books, 2008.

Carroll, James *Christ Actually: The Son of God for the Secular Age*. New York: Viking, 2014.

Carter, Stephen. *The Culture of Disbelief: How American Law and Politics Trivialized Religious Devotion*. New York: Harper-Collins, 1993.

Clarke, Samuel. "Can God Do Evil?." In *Philosophy of Religion: Selected Readings*, edited by William Rowe and William Wainwright. New York: Harcourt, Brace, Jovanovich, Inc., 1973.

O'Collins, Gerald. *Believing in the Resurrection: The Meaning and Promise of the Risen Jesus*. New York: Paulist Press, 2012.

Crawford, Brandon James. *Johnathan Edwards on Atonement: Understanding the Legacy of America's Greatest Theologian* Eugene, OR: Wipf and Stock, 2017.

Davies, Margaret. "The New Testament." In *The Oxford Illustrated History of the Bible*, edited by John Rogerson. Oxford: Oxford University Press, 2001.

De Hamel, Christopher. *The Book: A History of the Bible*. London: Phaidon, 2001.

DeMoss, Matthew and J. Edward Miller, eds. *Zondervan Dictionary of the Bible*. Grand Rapids: Zondervan, 2002.

Drummelow, J. R. *A Commentary on the Holy Bible*. New York: The MacMillan Company, 1973.

Dunn, James D. G. *Jesus Remembered*. Grand Rapids: Eerdmans, 2001.

Earle, Ralph. "Further Thoughts on Biblical Inspiration." *Bulletin of the Evangelical Theological Society* 6 (1963): 7–17.

Filson, Floyd V. "Exegesis on the Second Letter to the Corinthians" *The Interpreter's Bible*, Vol 7. New York: Abingdon Press, 1953.

Farnworth, Richard F. "The Holy Scriptures from Scandals Are Cleared." (1655).

Finstuen, Andrew S. *Original Sin and Everyday Protestants: The Theology of Reinhold Niebuhr, Billy Graham, and Paul Tillich in the Age of Anxiety*. Chapel Hill: North Carolina University Press, 2009.

Friedman, Richard Elliott and Shawna Dolansky. *The Bible Now* (New York: Oxford University Press, 2011.

Geisler, Norman L. "An Evaluation of McGowen's View on The Inspiration of Scripture." *Bibliotheca Sacra* 167 (2010): 17-39.

Gibson, Alaster. "Meanings and Applications of Compassion in Teaching: A Practical Review of the Bible and Educational Literature." *Christian Education Journal* 12 (2015): 8-25

Gilmore, Alec *A Concise Dictionary of Bible Origins and Interpretation*. London: T. T. Clark, 2006.

Graham, Ronald William "The Inspiration of Scripture." *Lexington Theological Quarterly* 22 (1987): 97-105.

Greenslade, S. L., ed. *The Cambridge History of the Bible: The West from the Reformation to the Present Day*, (Cambridge: Cambridge University Press, 1970.

Hanson, R. P. C. "Biblical Exegesis in the Early Church." In *The Cambridge History of the Bible*, edited by P. R. Ackroyd and C. F. Evans. Cambridge: Cambridge University Press, 1970.

Holmén, Tom and Stanley Porter (ed.). *Handbook for the Study of the Historical Jesus*. Boston: Brill, 2011.

Hellwig, Monika K. "A History of the Concept of Faith." In *Handbook of Faith,* edited by James Michael Lee. Birmingham, AL: Religious Education Press, 1990.

Howard, Wilbert F. "Exegesis for the Gospel of John," *The Interpreter's Bible*, Vol. 8. New York: Abingdon Press, 1952.

Johnson, Sherman E. "Exegesis on the Gospel According to St. Matthew" *The Interpreter's Bible,* Vol 7. New York: Abingdon Press, 1953.

Kariatlis, Philip. "The Mystery of the Holy Trinity: A Paradigm for Christian Living?" *Phronema* 33 (2018): 41-62.

Leithart, Paul J. *Delivered from the Elements of the World: Atonement, Justification, Mission*. Downers Grove, IL: IVP Academic, 2016.

Levering, Matthew. *Jesus and the Demise of Death: Resurrection, Afterlife, and the Fate of the Christian*. Waco: Baylor University Press, 2012.

Lewis, C. S. *Mere Christianity*. New York: MacMillan, 1952.

McDowell, Josh. *Evidence that Demands a Verdict*. Orlando: Campus Crusade for Christ, 1977.

Metzger, Bruce M. and Michael D. Coogan, eds. *The Oxford Companion to the Bible*. New York: Oxford University Press, 1993.

Miller, Stephen M. and Robert V. Huber. *The Bible: A History*. Intercourse, PA: Good Books, 2004.

Moller, Philip. "What Should They Be Saying about Biblical Inspiration?: A Note on the State of the Question," *Theological Studies* 74, no. 3 (September 2013): 605-631.

Mosher, Lucinda and David Marshall. *Sin, Forgiveness, and Reconciliation: Christian and Muslim Perspectives.* Washington, DC: Georgetown University Press, 2016.

Murray, John. "The Inspiration of the Scripture." *The Westminster Theological Journal* 2 (1940): 73-104.

Newman, John Henry. "The Bodily Resurrection of Jesus and Christian Spirituality." In *Jesus Risen in Our Midst*, by Sandra M. Schneider. Collegeville, MN: Liturgical Press, 2013.

Nicholson, Adam. *God's Secretaries: The Making of the King James Bible*. New York: Harper-Collins, 2003.

Oates, Wayne. *The Psychology of Religion*. Waco: Word Books, 1973.

Pink, Arthur. *Divine Inspiration of the Bible*. Swengel, PA: Bible Truth Depot, 1917.

Rogers, Jack B. and John K. McKim, *The Authority and Inspiration of the Bible: An Historical Approach*. New York: Harper and Row, 1979.

Romey, Kristen "The Search for the Real Jesus," *National Geographic* (Dec 2017): 30-69.
Satlow, Michael. *How the Bible Became Holy*. New Haven: Yale University Press, 2014.

Schneider, Sandra M. *Jesus Risen in Our Midst: Essays on the Resurrection of Jesus in the Fourth Gospel*. Collegeville, MN: Liturgical Press, 2013.

Schokel, Luis Alonso. *A Manual of Hermeneutics*.
Sheffield, England: Sheffield Academy Press, 1998.

Schweitzer, Albert. *The Quest for the Historical Jesus: A Critical Study of Its Progress from Reimarus to Wrede*.
New York: MacMillan, 1910.

Sexton, Sterling *A Commentary on First Corinthians*. Stone Mountain, GA; Vista Publications.

Smith, Charles Merrill and James W. Bennett. *How the Bible Was Built*. Grand Rapids: Eerdmann, 2005.

Smith, Stuart C. *Dead to Sin, Alive to God: Discover the Power of Reckoning to Set You Free in Christ*. Eugene: Resource Publications, 2016.

Stanford, Matthew. *The Biology of Sin: Grace Hope and Healing for Those Who Feel Trapped*. Westmont, IL: Intervarsity Press, 2012.

Strobel, Lee. *The Case for a Creator: A Journalist Investigates Scientific Evidence that Points toward God*. Grand Rapids: Zondervan, 2004.

Swineburne, Richard "Evidence for the Resurrection." In *The Resurrection: An interdisciplinary Symposium on the Resurrection of Jesus*, edited by Stephen Davis, Daniel Kendall, and Gerald O'Conner. Oxford: Oxford University Press, 1997.

Thompson, William M. *The Jesus Debate: A Survey and Synthesis*. New York: Paulist Press, 1985.

Trembath, Kern Robert. *Evangelical Theories of Biblical Inspiration*. New York: Oxford University Press, 1987.

Von Rad, Gerhard. *Genesis*. Philadelphia: Westminster Press, 1974.

Webster, John. *Holy Scripture: A Dogmatic Sketch*. Cambridge: Cambridge University Press, 2003.

Wedel, Theodore O. "Exposition on Ephesians" *The Interpreter's Bible*, Vol.10. New York: Abingdon Press, 1953.

Wills, Gary. *What Jesus Said*. New York: Penguin Books, 2006.

Witmer, John A. "Biblical Evidence for the Verbal-Plenary Inspiration of the Bible." *Bibliotheca Sacra* 121 (1964): 243-252.

Woodbridge, John D. "Sola Scriptura: Original Intent, Historical Development, and Import for Christian Living." *Presbyterion* 44 (2018): 4-24.

Wright, G. Ernest. "Exegesis on Deuteronomy," *The Interpreter's Bible*, Vol 2. New York: Abingdon Press, 1953.

Wright, N. T. *Scripture and the Authority of God*. New York: Harper One, 2011.

Made in the USA
Columbia, SC
14 January 2020